Postmodern Postures

Purchased by: _Reeves_

Postmodern Postures

Postmodern Postures

Literature, Science and the Two Cultures Debate

Daniel Cordle

Ashgate

Aldershot • Brookfield USA • Singapore • Sydney

Published by
Ashgate Publishing Limited
Gower House, Croft Road
Aldershot
Hants GU11 3HR
Great Britain

Ashgate Publishing Company
Old Post Road
Brookfield
Vermont 05036–9704
USA

Ashgate website: http//:www.ashgate.com

ISBN 0–7546–0095–9

The author has asserted his right under the Copyright, Designs and Patents Act, 1988, to be identified as the Author of this work.

British Library Cataloguing-in-Publication Data
Cordle, Daniel
  Postmodern Postures: Literature, Science and the Two Cultures Debate
  1. Literature and Science. 2. Postmodernism. I. Title.
  809.9'3356

US Library of Congress Cataloging-in-Publication Data
Cordle, Daniel
  Postmodern Postures: Literature, Science and the Two Cultures Debate / Daniel Cordle.
      p. cm. Includes bibliographical references and index.
  1. Literature and Science. 2. Postmodernism (Literature). 3. Science and the Humanities. I. Title.
  PN55.C67 2000
  809'.93356–dc21   99–052631

This volume is printed on acid-free paper.

Printed and bound by Athenaeum Press, Ltd.,
Gateshead, Tyne & Wear.

Contents

Acknowledgements

There are numerous people who deserve thanks for their support and help on this project, and any acknowledgement here will inevitably omit more who deserve mention than it can include. Colleagues at various universities and conferences have been unfailingly interesting and stimulating in their ideas, but a few institutions and individuals deserve special thanks.

The British Academy provided initial funding for this project without which it would not have been possible, and the departments of English at Leciester University, American Studies at Keele University, and English and Media Studies at Nottingham Trent University have all, over the past few years, provided the support that has enabled its completion. Deborah Madsen, Nick Everett, Mark Rawlinson and Steven Earnshaw provided astute and productive criticism at various points, and the forebearance of my family – Derek, Celia, Elizabeth and David Cordle – and of Gillian Greyson, have been invaluable.

Introduction:
Patterns and Postures

[W]anting connections, we found connections – always, everywhere, and between everything. The world exploded into a whirling network of kinships, where everything pointed to everything else, everything explained everything else.

Umberto Eco, *Foucault's Pendulum*

Similarities come in many forms: some are guides to genealogical inferences; others are pitfalls and dangers. As a basic distinction, we must rigidly separate similarities due to simple inheritance of features present in common ancestors, from similarities arising by separate evolution for the same function. The first kind of similarity, called homology, is the proper guide to descent ... The second kind of similarity, called analogy, is the most treacherous obstacle to the search for genealogy ...

Stephen Jay Gould, *Wonderful Life*

At the heart of intellectual activity lies the ability to discern a pattern. A pattern suggests a relationship between separate phenomena or pieces of information, and allows us to draw general conclusions that have widespread applicability. When we classify literature – when we label it as Romantic, Modernist, or postmodernist; thriller, science fiction, or travel writing – we suggest that these different types of literature behave in different ways, and that a conclusion drawn from a few examples may apply to the whole category.

This book seeks to find new kinds of pattern. It argues that an established way of dividing up human knowledge and intellectual activity, the distinction between the arts and the sciences, discussed later on as the 'two cultures model', is limited in fundamental ways, even though it is useful in others.[1] When some of the limitations and presumptions of this traditional pattern are exposed, new ways of perceiving the arts–sciences relationship

---

[1]   The phrase 'the two cultures' comes from C.P. Snow's Rede Lecture of May 1959, in which he claimed a gulf of mutual misunderstanding had arisen between the arts and the sciences. Snow's contention led to a furious debate, principally between Snow and F.R. Leavis, about the relative merits and roles of science and literature in our culture.

emerge, enabling us to tease out conclusions that would otherwise remain hidden.

Yet, although the thesis of the book is that that there are fruitful ways of linking literature and science, and that the two cultures model is too simplistic to do justice to the complexity of our intellectual and cultural lives, a number of potential pitfalls do present themselves when we engage in this sort of interdisciplinary project, and it is as well to be apprised of these from the start. The epigraphs which stand at the head of this introduction signpost these pitfalls in a useful way, drawing our attention to the very real dangers that pattern-forming can pose, and allowing us to neutralise them.

Stephen Jay Gould's *Wonderful Life*, from which the longer of the two epigraphs comes,[2] will be discussed in detail in a later chapter. However, his concern in this quotation with the difficulties of classification draws our attention to a trap which awaits the unwary literature–science critic, and that is worth discussing now. One of the preoccupations of *Wonderful Life* is the classification of fossils and organisms, in order to deduce the lines of inheritance and evolution that have led to the array of species which populate our planet today. This is a process of pattern-forming: when a similarity is shared by two organisms (or fossils) that are in other respects distinct, it can be used to provide a link between them, and allows us to see them as part of the wider interrelation of species.

However, as Gould very clearly indicates here, this similarity is not in itself sufficient. Finding a similarity does not prove the existence of a link; it can only establish the possibility of a link, the potential for a meaningful connection. Gould's description gives us terminology that provides a useful distinction: 'analogy' is a similarity not produced by a genuine connection; 'homology' is a similarity which is the product of a genuine connection. By way of illustration, he goes on to point out that though a bat's wings may tempt us to class it as a bird, this is merely a seductive analogy, distracting us from the features that are indicative of true homology and should lead us to the correct classification of it as a mammal.

Likewise, when we approach literature and science, we need to think carefully about the status of the links that we propose between the two realms. It is never difficult to find something in literature that reminds us of science, or something in science that reminds us of literature, but we need to be aware that this is only the first stage in a process of investigation and does not, of itself, demonstrate a concrete link between the two realms. To push the investigation further we either need to establish a direct series of links that connect the two phenomena; or, at least, we need to propose a model that both plausibly

---

[2]   Stephen Jay Gould, *Wonderful Life: The Burgess Shale and the Nature of History* (1989; London: Hutchinson Radius-Century Hutchinson, 1990), p. 213.

explains how the two phenomena could be linked, and is stated explicitly enough to be open to critical investigation, adjustment or refutation by other scholars.

These observations – that we should look for patterns which tell us something that is true, rather than something which is false – would not rise above the status of an extended series of truisms were it not for the existence of a body of criticism of science, from the perspective of the humanities, which has been the source of much contention in recent years. Literary scholars, researchers working on the philosophy and history of science, and others, have attempted to picture science within a cultural context. The way in which this work has been carried out, and indeed the very presumptions upon which it is built, have been the subject of criticism from a number of quarters, and the dubbing of these arguments as 'science wars' suggests just how fraught is the issue of the relationship between literature and science.[3] Most dramatically, the physicist Alan Sokal infiltrated 'enemy lines' to publish a hoax article in *Social Text* in 1996. Drenched in references to cultural theorists of science, and peppered with the popular buzz words of contemporary literary theory, 'Transgressing the Boundaries: Toward a Transformative Hermeneutics of Quantum Gravity' is a clever parody of contemporary theoretical jargon, and an object lesson in the seductiveness of dense allusion and analogy. Sokal's article, though deliberately false and self-contradictory, appears as if it should be insightful because of the web of 'evidence' from which it draws, and the panache with which the hoax is perpetrated.

Whether the acceptance of the article at face value by *Social Text*'s editors is illustrative of serious intellectual shortcomings in a disturbingly broad section of the humanities, or the unfortunate consequence of an attempt to give space to the (often ignored) voice of scientists in the literature–science debate, or whether it is no more than a pointless prank, has been the subject of heated dispute, and many angry letters, since the article's publication. The debate has not been allowed to smoulder and was reignited in 1998 by Sokal, with a book jointly authored with Jean Bricmont, *Intellectual Impostures: Postmodern Philosophers' Abuse of Science*.[4] Although this text includes in its appendices a copy of Sokal's original article, and some comments on the initial controversy,

---

[3]   The key text in establishing the popularity of the term 'science wars' is the special edition of *Social Text* devoted to this subject, which also took the phrase as its title. *Social Text* 46–7 (1996). This issue of the journal achieved notoriety, and generated much press coverage, because it contained a hoax article by Alan Sokal, discussed below.

[4]   Alan Sokal and Jean Bricmont, *Intellectual Impostures: Postmodern Philosophers' Abuse of Science* (London: Profile, 1998). The book originally appeared a year earlier in a French edition. Another key, and slightly earlier, salvo in the science wars is Gross and Levitt's *Higher Superstition*, originally published in 1994 and now available in an updated edition. Paul R. Gross and Norman Levitt, *Higher Superstition: The Academic Left and its Quarrels with Science* (Baltimore: Johns Hopkins University Press, 1998).

its criticism of what it sees as the abuses of science perpetrated in the humanities is far more substantial than those apparent in the original hoax. Indeed, it is a book which is clearly pivotal in the contemporary incarnation of the two cultures debate, and for this reason a discussion of it is central to this book's presentation of the relationship between literature and science.

I will discuss in detail Sokal's objections to the (mis)uses of science in the humanities in chapter two, but for our current purposes we need merely note that integral intellectual assumptions, from which much literature–science criticism proceeds, have been called into question; the validity of the very types of pattern for which literature–science critics seek has been challenged. To revert to Gould's terminology, the patterns found by literature–science scholarship have been derided as indicative merely of analogy rather than homology. Because the very basis of the field of study is under question, it is crucial to address the issue of pattern-forming, establishing the credentials for a mature literature–science criticism by delineating very carefully the boundaries for such a criticism, and being clear about what it can and cannot say.

Certainly the current fashion for contesting the old arts–sciences divide produces an atmosphere in which it is tempting to leap upon any similarity between the two realms as evidence of a connection between them. It is this seductiveness of connectivity which is one subject of Umberto Eco's *Foucault's Pendulum*, the source of the shorter of the two epigraphs.[5] Near the beginning of the novel, the author of an absurd book about a secret plan for world domination by the Knights of the Temple, dies in mysterious circumstances. Following this, the narrator, Casaubon, gets involved in a game with his colleagues in which they construct ever more bizarre theories about the manipulation of history by the Templars. True believers in the plan, thinking Casaubon and the others have access to a real secret, begin to pursue them, and Casaubon is left, at the end, awaiting his death at the hands of these mysterious individuals.

The overriding concern in the novel is the allure of the ingenious theories Casaubon and his colleagues construct. Casaubon is 'lulled by feelings of resemblance: the notion that everything might be mysteriously related to everything else'.[6] Yet the patterns they form have no meaning, except to themselves and, ominously, to those who believe in a hidden order to disconnected historical events, and are willing to kill Casaubon for the secret.

Whilst lives may not be at stake in the search for links between literature and science, veracity and integrity very clearly are. If we desire too much to establish the interconnection of the two realms, and to refute the two cultures model, it will be all too easy to find resemblances and patterns in literature and

---

[5]   Umberto Eco, *Foucault's Pendulum* (1988; London: Picador, 1990), pp. 463–4.
[6]   Eco, p. 164.

science that are the products not of genuine affinities, but of our mental capacity to make connections. We must beware of the automatic assumption that the existence of a resemblance is proof of a connection. Like Casaubon, in searching for connections we may find that the world explodes 'into a whirling network of kinships' but, unlike Casaubon, we must also distinguish as clearly as possible between that which provides evidence of genuine links, and that which does not. This involves a rigorous self-criticism, as willing to disprove as to assert, and agreeable to a clear statement of assumptions and methodology that enables models and conclusions that are proposed to be critically analysed and adjusted by others.

One of the contentions in this book is that this openness to critique has sometimes been lacking in literature–science criticism, for the recent sudden growth in the subject, along with other developments in critical theory, has created an atmosphere in which connections between the arts and the sciences have sometimes been asserted, with the status neither of those connections, nor of the conclusions that follow from them, being addressed. This may be an excusable excess – indeed, perhaps a period of innovation and experimentation in a new field of study is necessary to test its limits – but it is now important to begin to formulate where those limits lie. Such a formulation does not of course curtail literature–science criticism, and there is no reason why the boundaries established should not be challenged or pushed back, but if we resist setting boundaries at all then the subject is impossible to defend, the goals of the criticism become hard to define, and it is difficult to hone and refine our methodology as we strive to achieve those goals and push beyond them to new ones.

One of the primary intentions in this book, therefore, is to conceptualise what a developed literature–science criticism might look like, and to identify the paths that are open to exploration by the literary critic. This is what part 1 does. It begins, in chapter 1, with a discussion of key two cultures debates between Mathew Arnold and T.H. Huxley in the nineteenth century, and F.R. Leavis and C.P. Snow in the late 1950s and early 1960s (when the phrase 'the two cultures' was coined by Snow). The discussion establishes how literature and science are conceptualised in these debates, with a central contention being that they are defined precisely in terms of their opposition to one another. Despite the time lag of approximately three-quarters of a century between the Huxley–Arnold and Snow–Leavis debates, they are almost entirely consistent with one another in terms of their definitions of literature and science, and for this reason the discussion moves frequently from one debate to the other.

It is not the purpose of the first chapter to give a detailed history of these controversies, but instead to produce an analysis of the terms on which they are constructed. This allows for the production of a 'two cultures model', conceptualised in the diagrams on page 21, and including an explicit statement of how literature and science are defined in this model, and what is at stake in these definitions. Once this is established, it is then possible to go on to discuss alternatives to the two cultures model, and ways in which we might think about the relationship between literature and science.

Chapter 2 does this through a discussion of the contemporary incarnation of the debate. Increasingly, through the 1980s and the 1990s, the relationship between literature and science has been explored by scholars working in the humanities. The debates that have resulted from these investigations are distinct from those between Arnold and Huxley, and Snow and Leavis, because they engage much more directly with the possibilities and dangers offered by linking literature to science. Whereas the earlier debates were dominated by attempts to formulate the differences between the two realms – literature *versus* science – the contemporary discussion has been focused on what they might have in common – literature *and* science. The terms of the debate have moved, then, from discussing the different roles and features of literature and science to an opposition between two camps, one broadly claiming that the insights of science are culturally specific, and one largely opposed to this view, and seeking to extract science from culture in order to emphasise the transcendent nature of scientific knowledge.

Sokal and Bricmont's *Intellectual Impostures* is firmly located in the latter camp. The book's clear statement of the dangers of reducing science to just another cultural discourse provides a useful focus for an assessment of literature–science criticism. As with the discussion of Huxley, Arnold, Snow and Leavis in chapter 1, the purpose of discussing the contemporary debate about literature and science is not to chart the minutiae of every contribution to that debate – to produce a history of it – but instead to produce a conceptual analysis of the terms on which it is based. In chapter 1 this focus allows for the production of the two cultures model; in chapter 2 it enables an identification of the points where the border between literature and science may be crossed. Seven bridges between the two realms are identified, and these correspond to seven possible foci for literature–science criticism. The chapter is, then, about methodology, and makes conspicuous the critical approaches we might legitimately use in interdisciplinary projects focused on literature and science.

The following three chapters – in part 2 of the book – then build on these, essentially theoretical, discussions with three case studies linking literature and science and employing, in various combinations, the methodologies identified at the end of chapter 2. In many ways these case studies are conventional pieces of literature–science criticism, but in the context of the theoretical framework explicitly expounded in part 1, they will hopefully facilitate a much clearer sense of what is being claimed by linking literature and science than is often apparent in interdisciplinary studies of this type.

The primary project of the book, therefore, is to produce a theory of literature–science criticism, and then to see how that theory might operate in practice. However, there is a second concern which, given the context of the current science wars, is impossible to ignore: the issue of postmodernism. Rightly or wrongly, postmodernism has been strongly associated with contemporary attempts to relate literature to science and, indeed, postmodernism frequently becomes the chief target for those objecting to the misuses of science in the humanities. This is apparent, for instance, in the subtitle to Sokal and Bricmont's *Intellectual Impostures*: '*Postmodern Philosophers' Abuse of Science'*.

In contrast to Sokal and Bricmont, this book argues that when postmodernism is seen in these ways, it is wrongly simplified to mean extreme relativism. Instead, it is argued, the term is viable because it does allow us to identify something distinctive about late twentieth-century culture. This issue is approached directly in chapter 2 and in more detail in chapter 6, where it is claimed that postmodern culture can be defined as those aspects of late twentieth-century culture that are positioned in opposition to central tenets of the Enlightenment. Although these often entail an antifoundational impulse, it is argued that they do not necessitate the adoption of a position of extreme relativism about notions of the truth. The texts examined in the three case studies, in chapters 3, 4 and 5, are selected partly because they relate to this issue of postmodernism, and the sense in which they are postmodern is elaborated in more detail in chapter 6. More than anything else, postmodernism is a posture, an attitude toward the past that defines the stance adopted in the present, and it is for this reason that the title *Postmodern Postures* has been chosen for this book.

Nevertheless, it should be noted that the argument that the case studies provide examples of intriguing links between literature and science is no way dependent on the acceptance of the idea that they are postmodern. The claims made about the interdisciplinary study of literature and science, and about postmodernism, though related, are also distinct from one another, and it is not necessary to accept one of these arguments in order to accept the other. For instance, the seven methodologies available to the literature–science critic, identified in chapter 2, stand or fall as critical approaches regardless of the view of postmodernism held by the reader.

The second meaning of the title is tied to its deliberate play on Sokal and Bricmont's *Intellectual Impostures*, and it is hoped that it enters into a more considered dialogue with the arguments about science and postmodernism in their work than some of the more extreme reactions to it. This does not mean that the book is entirely uncritical of their position (whilst accepting their main point about the abuses of science, it disputes their association of this abuse with postmodernism), but it does try to go beyond the current arts versus sciences posturing which is not really so very different from some of the more ludicrous catcalls of the two cultures dispute between Snow and Leavis. Perhaps, rather than a war, the contemporary dispute is more like a posturing; a 'shaping up' across the arts–sciences divide that mitigates against fruitful dialogue.

To return to the concerns of the epigraphs at the head of this introduction, the case studies in this book are linked by two kinds of pattern: a pattern of postmodern gestures, apparent in the postures they adopt toward the past; and a pattern of links between literature and science. The success, or otherwise, of this book is measured by the extent to which the reader is convinced that these patterns are indicative of homology, rather than analogy.

PART ONE

Theory

Chapter 1

The Two Cultures: Literature versus Science

When, on a lecture tour of America in the 1880s, Mathew Arnold took issue with T.H. Huxley's views on literature and science, he referred to his antagonist as 'an excellent writer and the very prince of debaters'.[1] Yet, despite the courteous tone, even this relatively early debate on the topic of the two cultures was characterised by an underlying sense of conflict. Indeed, an atmosphere of profound disharmony is a notable aspect of almost all discussions about the relationship between literature and science.

Arnold was responding to assertions Huxley had made in 1880 at the opening of Sir Josiah Mason's Science College in Birmingham. Near the beginning of his speech, Huxley had used the image of warfare to explain the relationship between scientific and literary education, arguing that whereas in the eighteenth century the battle over education was about the relative merits of ancient versus modern literature, in the mid-nineteenth century 'the contest became complicated by the appearance of a third army, ranged round the banner of Physical Science'.[2] Huxley presented himself as a 'full private' in this new guerrilla force, fighting to place science at the centre of education.

Although metaphors of warfare were apparent in this nineteenth-century debate, it was with the most famous two cultures dispute, between C.P. Snow and F.R. Leavis in the 1950s and 1960s, that the tone of personal respect epitomised by Arnold's description of Huxley was sacrificed for a more belligerent manner. When Snow coined the phrase 'the two cultures' in his 1959 Rede Lecture, he established his authority to speak for both camps by referring to his scientific training and his vocation as a novelist. It was this authority that Leavis sought to undermine with an extraordinary piece of invective:

> Snow is of course, a – no, I can't say that; he isn't: Snow thinks of himself as a novelist ... The seriousness with which he takes himself as a novelist is complete – if seriousness can be so ineffably blank, so

---

[1] Mathew Arnold, 'Literature and Science', *Poetry and Prose*, ed. John Bryson (London: Rupert Hart-Davis, 1954), p. 643.

[2] T.H. Huxley, 'Science and Culture', *Collected Essays*, vol. 3 (1893; London: Macmillan, 1905), p. 136.

unaware ... He can't be said to know what a novel is. The nonentity is apparent on every page of his fictions – consistently manifested, whatever aspect of a novel one looks for.[3]

With the resurfacing of the dispute about literature and science in the 1990s, predominantly as a result of humanities scholars' determination to view science as a social construction, the discourse has again been dominated by images of conflict. The phrase 'science wars' has been bandied about, and the first British edition of Alan Sokal and Jean Bricmont's book, *Intellectual Impostures: Postmodern Philosophers' Abuse of Science* (which protests about the inappropriate use of scientific ideas, and the misconceptions about science, in the humanities) carries on the cover a number of provocative, antagonistic responses to the 1997 French edition of the book, including 'C'est la guerre' from *Le Figaro*.[4]

Despite the warlike nature of the debate, it is not the intention in this chapter to provide a military history of the conflict over the last century and a half, charting with painstaking detail the ebb and flow of sorties, skirmishes and campaigns. Instead, the chapter produces an analysis that scrutinises the terms on which the two cultures debate has been constructed. These have remained remarkably stable over the period, although the last decade has seen a slight shift as researchers – mainly, though not exclusively, in the humanities – have sought to abolish the two cultures model. Because there has been this shift in the terms of the debate in recent years, this chapter will limit itself to the first two manifestations of the conflict, leaving a discussion of the latest battle to chapter 2. The prize for which the war has been, and continues to be, fought is the territory of education, culture and (linking these two) civilisation; and many of the disputes have been for possession of these concepts.

The analysis will begin by looking at the question of why it is that literature and science, in particular, should so frequently be seen to be at odds with one another. I will go on to describe the two cultures model in detail, offering an example, in the work of I.A. Richards, of some of the consequences it has for literary criticism, and suggesting some of the drawbacks of the model.

---

[3]   F.R. Leavis and Michael Yudkin, *Two Cultures? The Significance of C.P. Snow with an Essay on Sir Charles Snow's Rede Lectures* (London: Chatto and Windus, 1962), pp. 12–13.

[4]   Alan Sokal and Jean Bricmont, *Intellectual Impostures: Postmodern Philosophers' Abuse of Science* (London: Profile, 1998). It should be noted that the conflict had, at this stage, broadened in scope. Sokal, for instance, was accused of being anti-French in his targeting of French intellectuals like Julia Kristeva and Jacques Lacan. See note 3 of the Introduction for more information on the phrase 'science wars'.

Why Literature and Science?

There is clearly an imbalance between the terms 'literature' and 'science'. Science denotes a whole range of disciplines and subdisciplines, across the range of chemistry, biology and physics. It is a term which, on its own, is applied in universities to faculties rather than individual departments. Indeed, one of the points of contention that sometimes arises in the two cultures debate is that science is described in the humanities as a single, unified thing, with examples from, say, biology wrongly taken as paradigmatic for the whole of science.[5]

Literature, on the other hand, is a concept of a fundamentally different type. It is only one of the arts, on a similar level to music and history, for example. In an academic context there might be literature or English departments (and these might divide up their study according to different periods or types of literature, or varying theoretical approaches to it), but it does not exist on a faculty level. It is only one aspect of study in arts or humanities faculties.

Why, then, has the vocabulary of the two cultures debate so frequently laid stress upon literature and science, and less frequently the arts and the sciences? One answer is that, for its proponents, literature has been used (perhaps rather self-importantly from the point of view of other subjects) as a champion of the arts. It has, in this sense, been constructed within the literature–science debate as a paradigmatic humanities subject.

For example, when Snow coined the phrase the 'two cultures' he made clear that the distinction he was aiming to enunciate was one between scientists and 'literary' intellectuals; and the person who rose to meet his challenge most readily was F.R. Leavis, whose association with the promotion of English studies as a serious discipline is inescapable.[6] Similarly, in calling for a reassessment of the role of science in education, eighty years before, Huxley had protested science's lack of status in relation to the study of literature (and, more specifically, the classics).

---

[5]   A pertinent contemporary example, given the subject of chapter 3, is the prevalence of discussions of chaos theory in literature–science criticism. Books that were influential in publicising chaos theory, like James Gleick's *Chaos: Making a New Science*, often stressed both the trans-disciplinary nature of chaos theory, and its revision of certain ideas in science. These were seized upon by some (but certainly not all) discussions of chaos theory in the humanities as evidence of a fundamental revision in scientific thought, and even for the existence of a post-Enlightenment science which formed a fundamental break from scientific method of the last 300 years. Chaos theory became, in some minds, paradigmatic of all science, and this has been a key point of controversy.

[6]   One might think, for instance, of Leavis's famous attempt to define a canon of work for literary study in *The Great Tradition* (1948; London: Chatto and Windus, 1962).

This, perhaps, gives us a clue as to the origins of literature's status as the wider champion of arts subjects in the two cultures debate. Education was, before the advent of the systematic study of nature called for by science, essentially text-based. There might have been disputes about the type of literature it was appropriate to study – whether classical or modern literature was the best way to a cultured personality – but texts, of one kind or another, were the repository of knowledge. Indeed, as the insights of other approaches to knowledge – including science – tended (and tend) to get stored and passed on through texts of various kinds, it is perhaps not surprising that the study of texts should itself be seen, by some, to lie at the heart of education.

Another possible source for the importance of literature in two cultures debates lies in the early Enlightenment, with the shift in balance in theology that was occasioned by the success of science. In *Science and the Enlightenment* Thomas L. Hankins draws our attention to three main routes to knowledge about God available before the Enlightenment: the revelation of scripture, the application of pure reason, and natural theology. With the dawn of the modern scientific age, the last of these three – which involved searching for laws and regularities in nature so as to reveal the divine order underwriting it – became more important. 'As the achievements of science grew in the seventeenth century', Hankins argues, 'the argument from design [a key aspect of natural theology] began to replace a priori rational arguments and often even the Revelation of Scripture as the principal evidence for religion'.[7] In other words, the success of science demonstrated the promise of a path to knowledge that rejected literary criticism (analysis of the Bible and other sacred texts) and replaced it with natural philosophy (what we would term science): 'If God could be known from his creation, the Bible was not necessary to prove the existence of God'.[8] If one of the origins of the institutional split between the arts and the sciences is a split between the study of texts and the study of nature, then it is conceivable that these characteristics should persist into the present as a way of characterising the differences between the arts and the sciences.

When the relationship between literature and science is debated, then, although the comments made are specific to literature (or to literary study – another important distinction), they also often have a more general applicability to the arts. So, despite the discrepancy between the two terms, with science a concept which normally operates on a higher level than literature, spanning many disciplines, the effect of the two cultures debate is to promote literature from the level of an individual discipline to a broad umbrella

---

[7]   Thomas L. Hankins, *Science and Enlightenment*, Cambridge History of Science (Cambridge University Press, 1985), p. 3.
[8]   Hankins, p. 3.

term. It comes to function as equivalent to the arts, on the same conceptual level as the sciences. Using the context of the university to understand this transition, we might think of literature as a 'discipline-level' concept which, in two cultures debates, is transfigured into a 'faculty-level' concept so as to make it equivalent to science.

Although literature generally functions in this way in two cultures debates, it is important to note that there is another term which is frequently placed in opposition to science: religion. The religion–science debate opens up a vista of other questions; for instance about whether religious and scientific world-views are mutually exclusive or complementary, and about the nature and purpose of quests for knowledge. These questions, and this debate about the relations between science and religion, clearly intersect with the literature–science debate. For instance, in cruder versions of the debate, literature is sometimes imbued with a moral force and opposed to a stereotypical and simplistic perception of science as the statement of cold facts. However, although the two debates are related, they are conceptually distinct, and in order to maintain a coherent focus, this book only touches upon aspects of the religion–science debate as they pertain to the literature–science debate. For instance, the use of machine metaphors to understand what it is to be human and what it is to be alive, discussed in chapter 4, often relate to a demystifying of the human essence, and a challenge to the idea of human life as divinely ordained.

In order to explore further the relationship between literature and science, and develop an understanding of the parameters of the two cultures debate, it is now necessary to scrutinise exactly what is at stake in the battles between some of the key combatants, from the polite spat between Huxley and Arnold, to the aggressive duel between Snow and Leavis.

The Territory for Conflict: Education and Culture

Although education was the primary subject of T.H. Huxley's speech at Sir Josiah Mason's college, and although culture was the primary subject of C.P. Snow's Rede Lecture, the two terms are closely intertwined. When Huxley called for science to become more central to education, one of the arguments he made supporting this point of view was that 'for the purpose of attaining real culture, an exclusively scientific education is at least as effectual as an exclusively literary education'.[9] Education is important here precisely because it offers a route to the cultured personality. The divergence between him and Arnold lay not so much in the actual definition of what culture entailed,

---

[9]   T.H. Huxley, p. 141.

however, as in the method by which it could be attained, and this explains the focus on education in their debate. Huxley claimed to agree with Arnold that 'real' culture is 'the possession of an ideal, and the habit of critically estimating the value of things by comparison with a theoretic standard. Perfect culture should supply a complete theory of life, based upon a clear knowledge alike of its possibilities and of its limitations'.[10] However, he diverged from Arnold in his belief that literature does not lay a 'sufficiently broad and deep foundation for that criticism of life, which constitutes culture'.[11] By implication, Huxley's argument was that science's broadening of our understanding of the world meant that an appreciation of it was essential to the cultured personality; in a scientific age, scientific education is the means to the acquisition of culture.

Snow's project, eighty years later, was similar. As well as drawing attention to the gulf between the sciences and the arts, his lecture was clearly aimed at highlighting the failure of those on the literary side of the divide to perceive science as cultural. His famous assertion, that not knowing the second law of thermodynamics is equivalent to ignorance of the works of Shakespeare, was a rhetorically effective way of making this point.[12] Just as culture and education are linked by Huxley's attempt to promote the place of science in education by stressing its importance to culture, so also are they joined by Snow's suggestion that the specialisation encouraged by the British education system leads to a failure to perceive science's cultural value.

While both Huxley and Snow identified failures in the British education system with the refusal to see science as cultural, their antagonists, Arnold and Leavis, refused to see science as cultural, and by this refusal implied that it was inferior to literature. For example, although Arnold admitted the need to know science, he denied it the same value as literature. On its own, Arnold claimed, science was just information, devoid of interest and humanity: 'it will be *knowledge* only which they [scientists] give us; knowledge not put for us into relation with our sense for conduct, our sense for beauty, and touched with emotion by being so put; not thus put for us, and therefore, to the majority of mankind, after a certain while, unsatisfying, wearying'.[13]

This is a commonly-used weapon in the armoury of literary contributors to the two cultures debate. By emphasising the failure of science to connect with what it is to be human, and simultaneously stressing the ability of literature to make this connection, their arguments serve to construct science not so much as a culture separate from literature, but as the complete opposite of culture, even an anti-culture. This is apparent further on in Arnold's speech

---

[10]   T.H. Huxley, p. 143.
[11]   T.H. Huxley, pp. 143–4.
[12]   C.P. Snow, *The Two Cultures and the Scientific Revolution* (Cambridge University Press, 1959), p. 14.
[13]   Arnold, p. 650.

where he states that he is 'sure' that 'poetry and eloquence' will be the means through which modern scientific knowledge is related to 'man's instinct for conduct, his instinct for beauty'.[14] Literature, here, is a catalytic agent, the presence of which is essential for the transformation of science into culture.

Indeed, not only is science presented as the antithesis of culture, it is also presented as an unnatural, inhuman form of knowledge. At the end of his speech, Arnold reaffirms the centrality of literary study to education, by accentuating its status as a 'natural', 'human' way of making sense of the world: 'I cannot really think that humane letters are in much danger of being thrust out from their leading place in education ... So long as human nature is what it is, their attractions will remain irresistible'.[15] Note that the rather unsubtle subtext here, as elsewhere on both sides of the two cultures debate, is a power struggle about the centrality of different modes of knowledge in education. Arnold tries to dismiss the threat to the 'leading place' of humane letters in literary study, but one wonders why, if the threat was so insignificant, he felt the need to defend it so vigorously.

Like Arnold, Leavis denies that science is truly cultural. Significantly, the vitriolic attack upon Snow, cited near the beginning of this chapter, undermines Snow's authority by denouncing the quality of his novels. Exactly how much the passage succeeds in extending our understanding of the relationship between literature and science might well be questioned. What it does do is deny Snow's right to talk about literature – and culture 'properly' understood – at all. The implication is almost that, *of course Snow's novels are dreadful – he's a scientist. How can he be expected to understand what it is to be human?* Perhaps this parody is a little unfair on Leavis, but there is certainly a repeat of the sharp distinction between good literature as essentially cultural, and science as the antithesis of that culture, that we found in Arnold. Like Arnold, too, Leavis ends with a strong affirmation of the primacy of the study of literature in education, claiming that a vibrant English school must stand at the centre of a university if it is to be more than just a collection of specialist departments.[16]

At the heart of the two cultures debate, then, stand a pair of fundamental, related contests. The first is about the proper mode of education, and what type of education – literary or scientific – should predominate, and the second is a struggle over the admission of science to the culture. Yet although these contests take place, neither side really denies the basic, essential difference between literature and science. Huxley and Snow both want science to be considered as part of the culture, but they do not investigate in detail how science might operate within the culture, nor interrogate assumptions about the

---

14 Arnold, p. 652.
15 Arnold, p. 656.
16 Leavis, p. 29.

essential differences between science and literature. The definition of each term is almost left alone, and – beyond disputing whether science is or is not cultural – there is a general assumption that we all know exactly what 'literature' and 'science' mean.

However, this focus on the two debates – of Huxley with Arnold, and of Snow with Leavis – must not lead us to assume that there were no mediating voices in these two cultures disputes. But even these mediating voices – operating, if we push the metaphor of conflict almost to the point of absurdity, as diplomats to the warring parties – leave literature and science in positions of entrenched indifference to each other. Two examples of diplomatic essays, seeking to reconcile the opposing armies (one published not long after the Huxley–Arnold debate, and one in direct response to the Snow–Leavis dispute) are provided by John Burroughs's 'Science and Literature' (1889) and Aldous Huxley's *Literature and Science* (1963).[17] These broaden our understanding of the literature–science debate usefully by seeking to define the terms 'literature' and 'science', and thus making explicit that which is often implicit in the disputes between T.H. Huxley and Mathew Arnold, and C.P. Snow and F.R. Leavis.

Both writers move, in their work, toward an ending which offers a rousing affirmation of the compatibility of literature and science: Burroughs claims that the 'true poet and the true scientist are not estranged. They go forth into nature like two friends'; and Aldous Huxley calls for us to 'advance together, men of letters and men of science, farther and further into the ever expanding regions of the unknown'.[18] The peace that they broker is based upon a strict division of intellectual labour between literature and science, and their essays are dominated by the attempt to define clearly the difference between the two areas.

The threat that the success of science might be seen to pose to the educational and cultural status quo is defused by fixing the borders between the two subjects. The next section of this chapter, which extracts a model from the two cultures debate, describes in detail the location of these borders. However, it is appropriate to give a brief description of them now. For Burroughs, the border lies very much where it lies for Arnold and Leavis – science is cold, lifeless and unnatural, and only the catalytic action of literature can give it any worth, and make it human: 'Until science is mixed with emotion, and appeals to the heart and imagination, it is like dead inorganic matter; and when it

---

[17]   Aldous is, of course, T.H. Huxley's grandson, and so might be said to have a familial as well as a professional interest in the debate.

[18]   John Burroughs, 'Science and Literature', *'The Sacred Beetle' and Other Great Essays in Science*, rev. edn, ed. Martin Gardner (Oxford University Press, 1985), p. 166. Aldous Huxley, *Literature and Science* (London: Chatto and Windus, 1963), p. 99.

becomes so mixed and so transformed it is literature'.[19] It is also worth pointing out that although, as already noted, Burroughs ends his essay with a description of the poet and the scientist going out into nature like two friends, these friends are clearly unequal. The distinction lies in the age he ascribes to them. The scientist is younger and less experienced, focusing on particularities without seeing the wider context: 'he is ever and anon stepping aside to examine some object more minutely, plucking a flower, treasuring a shell, pursuing a bird ... and everywhere seems intent on some special and particular knowledge of the things about him'.[20]

The poet, on the other hand, is more interested in the broad context than specifics:

> The elder man has more an air of leisurely contemplation and enjoyment, – is less curious about special objects and features, and more desirous of putting himself in harmony with the spirit of the whole. But when his younger companion has any fresh and characteristic bit of information to impart to him, how attentively he listens, how sure and discriminating is his appreciation![21]

There is a conspicuous power relationship here: to the younger friend, the scientist, is attributed a boyish enthusiasm and, whereas he finds 'information', it is the older man, the poet, who perceives the 'spirit' of the whole. Literature's role is, in a broad sense, religious here, giving a holistic meaning to scraps of information.[22] Although Burroughs describes the poet and the scientist as friends, the older man, to whom is accredited an instinctive wisdom, seems more like a grandfatherly figure, dominant over, not the equal of, his companion.

Aldous Huxley's essay seems more innovative and sophisticated to a modern reader (or at least to one trained in literary analysis). He focuses on issues of language use which are much more in tune with developments in the humanities (for example, the contemporary interest in the analysis of discourses) than any of the contributors to the two cultures debate discussed in detail so far in this chapter. For example, although Huxley's image of men of letters and science advancing together into the unknown, cited above, echoes Burroughs's picture of the two friends, it is immediately preceded by an acknowledgement of the inadequacy of language wholly to render the world which strikes a chord with late twentieth-century theories of language: 'That

---

[19]   Burroughs, p. 153.
[20]   Burroughs, p. 166.
[21]   Burroughs, p. 166.
[22]   It is in this sense that the two terms most frequently contrasted with science – literature and religion – are united by their association with value, with science being defined, in opposition to these two, as fact based and value free.

the purified language of science, or even the richer purified language of literature should ever be adequate to the givenness of the world and of our experience is, in the very nature of things, impossible'.[23] Nevertheless, he strives to distinguish science from literature, commenting, for example, that science focuses predominantly on public experiences, and literature on private ones.[24] As with Burroughs there is an attempt to silence the guns by fixing the borders between the two subjects.

Therefore, although John Burroughs and Aldous Huxley seek to make peace in the two cultures dispute, they also reiterate the sense of a gulf between literature and science that is taken for granted by T.H. Huxley, Mathew Arnold, C.P. Snow and F.R. Leavis. These four fired salvos across the divide between literature and science; John Burroughs and Aldous Huxley tried to broker a ceasefire; none really sought a path across the gulf. Having established the broad lines of disagreement between literature and science, we can now produce a two cultures model which specifies exactly how the debate assumes our intellectual and cultural life to be divided. Although the current incarnation of this debate, that of the 'science wars' of the 1990s, has (as has already been noted) moved on in certain key ways from the earlier disputes discussed above, it is worth bearing in mind that it has not necessarily eclipsed the terms of the earlier debate, but exists alongside and overlapping with it.

Qualities Ascribed to Literature and Science in the Two Cultures Debate

The paired list on page 21 extracts various qualities ascribed to literature and science from the texts by T.H. Huxley, Mathew Arnold, F.R. Leavis, C.P. Snow, John Burroughs and Aldous Huxley discussed above. Below it appears a diagram of the 'two cultures model' distilled from both this list and the discussion in the chapter thus far. These visual aids are, of course, syntheses of a number of not always completely compatible viewpoints. However, they draw together some of the main elements of the relationship between literature and science implicit in the two cultures debate, allowing for a comparison with the alternative model discussed in chapter 2, and an assessment of the efficacy of the two.

This section of the chapter runs through the two cultures literature–science list, justifying the inclusion of each item by detailing the source from which it comes, and discussing some of the issues that it raises. The list and the

---

[23]   Aldous Huxley, p. 99.
[24]   Aldous Huxley, pp. 7–8.

Qualities Ascribed to Literature and Science in the Two Cultures Debate

	Literature	Science
Object of contemplation/ area of concern	Words	Things
	Human nature	Knowledge of nature
	Private	Public
	Qualities	Quantities
	Sublime	Communicable
Method of study	Subjective	Objective
	Inspiration	Logic
	From authority	From experiment
Language	Ends	Means
	Surfeit	Economy
Essence	Emotional, passionate, personal	Cool, rational, impersonal
	Aristocratic	Democratic
	Culture	Anti-culture
	Holistic	Specific
	Natural	Unnatural
	Timeless	Time specific
Outcome of study	Original insight	Cumulative knowledge
	Value	Fact
	Spiritual development	Material progress
	General	Specific

The Two Cultures Model

	Science	
Object	Knowledge	Material progress
From Standpoint of	Objectivity	→
Method	Rationalism / Empiricism	Intellectual progress

	Literature	
Object	Value (spiritual / moral)	Higher civilisation
From Standpoint of	Subjectivity	→
Method	Inspiration	

diagram are intended as starting points for discussion, and provide a way of conceptualising how the literature–science relationship has been presented in the two cultures debate. There are, of course, arbitrary elements in any list of this type, and a number of issues should be borne in mind when using it.[25]

Firstly, it is not comprehensive. Like the above discussion it does not aim to identify every way in which literature has been thought of in relation to science but, by focusing on a few well-known texts it seeks to identify the broad parameters of the debate. Secondly, sorting the list into five categories ('object of contemplation', 'method of study', 'language', 'essence', and 'outcome of study') allows us to think about different aspects of literature and science, but the categories are not mutually exclusive (some items on the list could appear in more than one category), and there are different sets of categorisations that could be used to split up the list. Thirdly, the list identifies tendencies in the debate (bracketing stereotypes and misconceptions along with valuable insights), rather than essences intrinsic to literature and science – so, as should in any case be apparent, it is not an attempt to identify the ways in which science differs from literature, but the ways in which it is seen to differ from literature. Fourthly, it conflates literature and literary criticism, partly because these are frequently discussed as though they are one and the same in the two cultures debate; the precise place of literary criticism in the model is discussed in the analysis of the model below. Finally, because it synthesises the views of a number of people with contradictory opinions, there are some elements which could be swapped from one column to the other.

Although these disclaimers should be borne in mind, the list does give us a valuable way of thinking about and constructively critiquing the assumptions of the two cultures debate. By deliberately eschewing absolute specificity (which might have been achieved by producing a separate list for each contributor to the debate, or including a number of additional columns so as to indicate the degree to which different things are more literary, more scientific, or part way in between) it enables us to push toward some general conclusions about the two cultures paradigm. Most of the examples given to back up the list come from John Burroughs's and Aldous Huxley's essays. This is because, concerned as they are to make a peace and draw the boundaries between the two cultures, they spend much of their time stating what they think science and literature to be, making explicit that which, in the other essays, tends to be implicit.

---

[25] Such lists are rather chic in the world of literary criticism – one thinks, for instance, of Ihab Hassan's distinction between modern and postmodern, and Hélène Cixous's list identifying the social constructions of masculinity and femininity. Ihab Hassan, *The Dismemberment of Orpheus: Toward a Postmodern Literature* (New York: Oxford University Press, 1982), pp. 267–8. Hélène Cixous, 'Sorties', in David Lodge, *Modern Criticism and Theory: A Reader* (London: Longman, 1987), p. 287.

Object of Contemplation / Area of Concern

This heading refers to the different subjects with which literature and science are presumed to deal. In other words, the distinction between literature and science encapsulated in this section of the list is not so much to do with alternative approaches to the world, as to do with the different types of things with which they are concerned.

The source for the first items, words–things (in the interests of consistency and clarity, when the items on the list are presented in this way, the 'literary' ones will always appear first), is Arnold's paraphrase of the opinions of the 'friends of physical science' to whom he is opposed. He says that they contrast science as 'a knowledge of things' with humanist knowledge as a 'knowledge of words'.[26] Arnold does not actually contest this definition, but instead goes on to say that he disagrees that scientific training should predominate in education. This is a good example of the power struggle that takes place even when the borders between literature and science are clearly fixed – there is no disagreement here about the nature of the difference between the two, just the relative importance of them. What is actually being expressed in the words–things binary is a difference between literary *study* and science; literature itself, of course, might be more than a study of words.

However, the second pair, human nature–knowledge of nature, can embrace both literature and literary study in a contrast with science. It again derives from Arnold, who claims that scientists ignore human nature. He argues that human nature is composed of four powers (conduct, intellect and knowledge, beauty, and social life and manners), and that these powers are related to one another.[27] Science might increase our knowledge, but only literature can put that knowledge into a wider framework, relating these powers to one another (as such, it is reminiscent of Burroughs's description, discussed above, of the two 'friends', the poet and the scientist, in which the poet gives 'spirit' to the 'information' provided by the scientist). These observations indicate some of the ways in which notions of human identity are caught up in the two cultures debate – mystical and moral qualities are often ascribed to

---

[26] Arnold, p. 646.

[27] Arnold, pp. 647–8. It is this sort of characterisation of science that T.H. Huxley complains about when he protests against the view that science 'touches none of the higher problems of life ... How frequently one has reason to observe that no reply to a troublesome argument tells so well as calling its author a "mere scientific specialist"'. T.H. Huxley, pp. 140–41. Richard Dawkins provides a contemporary version of Huxley's protest, writing in his latest book that to 'accuse science of robbing life of the warmth that makes it worth living is so preposterously mistaken, so diametrically opposite to my own feelings and those of most working scientists, I am almost driven to the despair of which I am wrongly suspected'. Richard Dawkins, *Unweaving the Rainbow: Science, Delusion and the Appetite for Wonder* (London: Penguin, 1998), p. x.

literature, which is seen to minister to human needs and allow us to understand ourselves in a way which is not possible through scientific investigation. This is, of course, simplistic, not only in its view of science (unnatural, inhuman), but also in its view of literature, and a number of branches of literary theory have contested this simplistic, humanistic conception of literature.

Another objection might be that the Romantics – and, in America, the Transcendentalists – practised a literature which was very much concerned with the knowledge of nature, although their approach emphasised inspiration as a means to insight rather than systematic study. Conversely, the suggestion that human nature is truly a literary concern might well be contested in the sciences. A good contemporary example from popular science writing is provided by Stephen Pinker's *How the Mind Works* which seeks, among other things, to demystify our notion of the mind and explain it in terms of evolutionary adaptations.[28]

Private–public opens up these concerns into a slightly different dimension. Aldous Huxley suggests that science is predominantly concerned with public experiences (by which he means insights reproducible and verifiable by rational interrogation of sense impressions), whereas literature deals to a greater extent with private experiences (emotions and so forth) and their relations to public ones.[29] This also relates to the distinction between objectivity and subjectivity discussed below.

Qualities–quantities, also identified by Aldous Huxley, develops these ideas, implying that whereas the public concerns of science are value neutral, literature is value specific.[30] This is consistent with Arnold's suggestion, discussed above, that literature places our knowledge in a context which relates to our sense of beauty and conduct.

The final pairing is that of sublime–communicable. For example, Aldous Huxley claims that it is only great literature that can push beyond ordinary language to convey the subtleties of human emotions that transcend words: the 'ambition of the literary artist is to speak about the ineffable',[31] whereas the 'aim of the scientist is to say only one thing at a time, and to say it unambiguously'.[32] This distinction repeats the implication, identified earlier, that literature is concerned with the human in a way that science is not, and it assumes that there is something mystical about the human that cannot be touched by rationalism. It is worth noting that this binary opposition can be used not only to define literature by virtue of its difference from science, but also by virtue of its difference from ordinary uses of language. It is, of course,

---

[28]   Stephen Pinker, *How the Mind Works* (1997; London: Penguin, 1998).
[29]   Aldous Huxley, pp. 7–8.
[30]   Aldous Huxley, pp. 9–10.
[31]   Aldous Huxley, p. 12.
[32]   Aldous Huxley, pp. 13–14.

impossible to pin down exactly how literary uses of language differ from other uses (a prime example of this difficulty is provided by the inadequacies of the Russian Formalists' definition of literary language as that which has a defamiliarising function).[33] Whilst contemporary criticism takes pleasure in demystifying these sorts of conceptions of the literary, it could well be argued that the poststructuralist claim that a stable meaning cannot be located in texts, is merely a modern-day example of literary studies' reliance on the sublime, in the absence of a watertight definition of the object of study.

Method of Study

While it may be clear what 'method of study' means in relation to science (how science approaches nature) it may be less clear in regard to literature. In this context it does not predominantly mean the approach of literary criticism to literature (although it can be extended to mean that too), but rather how literature approaches the world – the relationship between literature and the experience it seeks to communicate.

The subjective–objective opposition is a commonplace way of distinguishing literature from science, and is clearly related to the division, cited above, that sees the subject matter of science to be solid, material things, and that of literature to be more intangible, and therefore more open to divergent opinions. Although this perception is fairly common, perhaps Aldous Huxley states it most openly.[34]

These differences find slightly different expression in the next pair, inspiration–logic. This describes alternative routes to knowledge of the world, the former being essentially private and subjective, and the latter giving expression to a method which is independent of the individual practising scientist. The literary side of this divide draws from Romanticist perceptions of artistic endeavour and would be less stressed by naturalist writers, for example – one thinks of Upton Sinclair describing his research for the writing of *The Jungle* as a process of collecting 'data'.[35] Interestingly, though, many naturalist writers who rejected Romanticism in this way would have seen their enterprise as more akin to scientific endeavour in any case.

'Logic' in this case does not just mean the exercise of reason, but more specifically the exercise of reason in relation to empirical observations. The inspiration–logic divide is found most interestingly in Burroughs's essay,

---

[33] See discussion in note 73.

[34] 'Objective and subjective. The world of concepts and the multitudinous abyss of immediate experience. The simplified, jargonized purity of scientific discourse and the magical, many-meaninged purity of literature'. Aldous Huxley, p. 36.

[35] Upton Sinclair, *The Autobiography of Upton Sinclair* (1962; London: W.H. Allen, 1963), p. 119.

where he uses Goethe as an example of someone whose work contains both scientific and literary elements:

> some of the leading ideas of modern science were distinctly foreshadowed by him [Goethe]; yet they took the form and texture of literature ... They were the reachings forth of his spirit; his grasping for the ideal clews to nature, rather than logical steps of his understanding; and his whole interest in physics was a search for a truth above physics.[36]

Science is presented here as 'logical', a series of 'steps' leading inevitably from one to the other, but it is the literary 'spirit' which somehow transcends (is a 'truth above') the possibilities offered by this logical approach. Yet again, literature is presented as dealing with the intangible, and is invested with mystical associations.

The final pairing, from authority–from experiment, relates to the words–things division at the head of the list and, similarly, is predominantly focused on literary criticism (rather than literature) and science. If the object of study is words, then research and conclusions are going to be drawn from words, whereas the regulating authority for scientific endeavour is nature (though social studies of science might contest that this is not the only regulating authority, and even suggest that we have a socially constructed sense of what nature is).

More contentiously, when experiment and authority come into conflict there is sometimes scope in the two cultures debate for complaints from the literary side that science is overreaching itself. Consider, for instance, this from Arnold: 'we come to propositions of such reach and magnitude [in science] as those which Professor Huxley delivers, when he says that the notions of our forefathers about the beginning and the end of the world were all wrong, and that nature is the expression of a definite order with which nothing interferes'.[37] This complaint is essentially similar to that expressed in certain readings of Mary Shelley's *Frankenstein*, which highlight Frankenstein's Promethean failings, and present science as a dangerous form of knowledge because it overreaches itself.[38]

---

[36]   Burroughs, p. 161.
[37]   Arnold, pp. 650–51.
[38]   Lewis Wolpert provides a contemporary example of a protest against this perception of science, drawing our attention to the 'image of scientists as so many Dr Frankensteins'. Lewis Wolpert, *The Unnatural Nature of Science* (London: Faber, 1992), p. 151. Chapter 8 of his book, 'Moral and Immoral Science' (pp. 151–71), discusses this perception in detail, arguing that ethical objections to science often fail to distinguish between knowledge (the responsibility of scientists), and the application of that knowledge (frequently the responsibility of non-scientists).

Language

The words–things binary finds yet another echo in the ends–means distinction, which is another one most clearly expressed by Aldous Huxley.[39] For science, in the two cultures debate, language of whatever kind (for instance, mathematical) is normally presented merely as the medium for the expression of something else, and not the main focus of attention. For literature, however, whilst it may be the means to an end, it is also an end in itself, and this is emphasised by literary criticism's interest in the mode of expression.

This perception is also apparent in the surfeit–economy distinction. Aldous Huxley's concentration upon language in his essay again makes him a useful source for this viewpoint:

> In the scientist, verbal caution ranks among the highest of virtues. His words must have a one-to-one relationship with some specified class of data or sequence of ideas ... There are occasions, obviously, when it is right for them [poets] to be verbally prudent; but there are other occasions when verbal imprudence ... becomes an artistic duty, a kind of categorical imperative.[40]

The distinction between 'verbal caution' and 'verbal imprudence' is indicative of a difference between the need to communicate a meaning already established by the scientist, and the generation of multiple meanings by the artist (and perhaps by the reader). It implies a difference between science's association with certainty, and literature's preoccupation with the intangible. It also suggests that meanings are already settled and closed before the scientist expresses them, whereas in literature meanings might not be prescribed, and may remain open until fixed by the reader.

Essence

This is the hardest category to define, and refers to some of the more general qualities associated with literature and science in the two cultures debate. The first, emotional, passionate, personal–cool, rational, impersonal, echoes the distinction between private and public mentioned above. Aldous Huxley, for instance, suggests that science is rarely incorporated into drama because drama is about high emotion, even irrationality, and so science would be out of place.[41] He also, in an attitude that finds frequent expression in definitions of science, sees the scientific method as working almost independently of those by whom

---

[39] Aldous Huxley, pp. 34–5.
[40] Aldous Huxley, p. 33.
[41] Aldous Huxley, pp. 56–60.

it is operated.[42] This contrasts with the Romantic perception of the writer as a genius capable of insights denied to ordinary people (although when scientists, rather than science, are talked about, they are often imbued with these qualities of insight).

Aristocratic–democratic is perhaps a little more controversial and would be shared by fewer contributors to the two cultures debate. Burroughs makes the distinction (and ascribes it to others) when he says, 'Science is said to be democratic ... while literature is alleged to be aristocratic in its spirit and tendencies. Literature is for the few; science is for the many'.[43]

This clearly differentiates between high and low literature, and may be part of the next pairing, the extremely important culture–anti-culture binary, which equates literature with value and sees science as value free. This is the site of the most important series of battles in the two cultures debate, with contributors from the sciences frequently striving to win recognition for science's centrality within the culture. We have already seen how Leavis tried to deny Snow's right to speak on the issue of culture by attacking his abilities as a writer. T.H. Huxley parodies this perception of science as the antithesis of culture (a perception which was already apparent in the nineteenth century): 'How often have we not been told that the study of physical science is incompetent to confer culture; that it touches none of the higher problems of life; and, what is worse, that the continual devotion to scientific studies tends to generate a narrow and bigoted belief in the applicability of scientific methods to the search after truth of all kinds?'[44]

This is also part of the holistic–specific divide. Science is seen (at least by those on the literary side) to be excellent for acquiring factual knowledge, but a true, rounded perception of the meaning of that knowledge in relation to human life is equated with literature. This is apparent in Burroughs's closing image of the two friends, poet and scientist, walking into nature, with the poet as the wise person who assimilates scientific information; also in Arnold's suggestion that poetry and eloquence will relate scientific knowledge to other aspects of human nature; and in Leavis's claim that a vital English school is at the heart of the true university.[45]

The natural–unnatural division may seem peculiar, given science's devotion to the study of nature, but there is no doubt that scientific knowledge is presented as artificial in a number of ways, and this is inevitably exacerbated by the tendency to associate science with technology. Burroughs perhaps states it more strongly than others: 'In art, in literature, in life, we are drawn by that which seems nearest to, and most in accord with, her [Nature]. Keep me

---

42   Aldous Huxley, pp. 60–64.
43   Burroughs, p. 151.
44   T.H. Huxley, p. 141.
45   See notes 16 and 27.

close to nature, is the constant demand of literature ... I cannot breath the cosmic ether of the abstruse inquirer, nor thrive on the gases of the scientist in his laboratory; the air of hill and field alone suffices'.[46]

By the timeless–time specific distinction is meant the association with science of progress and development, whereas each work of literature, as the product of individual inspiration, is sometimes seen to be less dependent on those which precede it. Burroughs makes this perception apparent by using the metaphor of finance to describe science, and that of nature to describe literature: 'Every man of science has all the science before him to go upon, to set himself up in business with ... Not so in literature; to every poet, to every artist, it is still the first day of creation, so far as the essentials of his task are concerned. Literature is not so much a fund to be reinvested as it is a crop to be ever new-grown'.[47] This is somewhat simplistic, and not a universally-held view of literature during the period of the two cultures debate – one thinks, for instance, of T.S. Eliot's notion, of the reliance of individual writers on those who precede them, in 'Tradition and the Individual Talent' (1919).[48]

Nevertheless, there is often a strong affiliation of science with progress which is not apparent in literature. Snow drew upon this early on in his Rede Lecture when he distinguished between scientists, as part of a culture looking to the future, and literary intellectuals, whom he saw as forming a reactionary, anti-scientific culture.[49] It is also a sentiment which finds frequent expression when science is configured as a threat: by marching us into the future, it is implied, it is taking us away from our natural state.[50] When literature and science are contrasted in this way, the values associated with literature become evocative of a vision of a paradise in the past (an Eden from which we have fallen, and to which we should try to return; this is of course incredibly Romantic and should by no means be taken to apply to all literature), while those values associated with science are tied to a vision of a paradise in the future (as we build our own Eden through greater knowledge and control of our environment).

Outcome of Study

By 'outcome' is meant the result of the scientific and literary investigations of the world. Again, there is a strong divide between the sorts of outcomes we can expect. Building on the association between science and progress just

---

[46]   Burroughs, p. 165.
[47]   Burroughs, pp. 156–7.
[48]   Frank Kermode, ed., *Selected Prose of T.S. Eliot* (London: Faber, 1975), pp. 37–44.
[49]   Snow, pp. 9–11.
[50]   See the discussion of I.A. Richards below for an example of this.

discussed, literature is often coupled with wholly original insight (or the original statement of eternal truths), whereas scientific knowledge is seen as cumulative. This gives us the first binary: original insight–cumulative knowledge. This is apparent in the passage just cited from Burroughs where literature is a crop, renewing itself, but also starting out fresh each year. Science, on the other hand, is depicted as a monetary fund which is reinvested for greater returns. Science is also associated with eternal truths – in the form of laws of nature – but their discovery is presented as dependent upon developing past knowledge, and the laws discovered are assumed to be value free, whereas literary insight is assumed to be value rich.

The next binary, value–fact, stresses the status of knowledge produced by literature and science. Scientific knowledge is assumed to be factual, whereas literary knowledge is presented as invested with value. Arnold's comment, cited above, that scientists give us '*knowledge* only', whereas literature puts that knowledge into the context of other aspects that make us human, is the clearest statement of this perception.

This leads to the next binary, spiritual development–material progress, in which science is assumed to have purely material benefits, whereas literature is invested with moral attributes. For example, this is apparent in Leavis's complaint that Snow sees all progress in material terms, and cannot look beyond 'jam tomorrow'.[51]

The final binary reiterates this sense (and that expressed in the qualities–quantities aspect of the 'object of contemplation' category) of scientific outcomes being strictly quantifiable, whereas literary outcomes are presented as qualitative: general–specific.

The Two Cultures Model

All of these ideas can be distilled into a model which gives expression to the roles of literature and science, produced on page 21 under the title of 'The Two Cultures Model'. As with the discussion of the list carried out in the section above, it is important to bear in mind that this model is a schematic representation, and therefore carries both the benefits and the dangers of such a broad distillation of ideas.

The principal benefit lies in the opportunity it gives us to focus on the essential roles played by literature and science in the two cultures debate. By concentrating on general differences encapsulated in the two cultures model, discarding temporarily the specific details of the disputes between all those who have contributed to the debate, we can arrive at general conclusions about

---

[51]   Leavis, pp. 24–5.

the ways in which literature and science are related to one another by the two cultures perspective.

The danger lies in forgetting that this is just a model, and though a useful way of conceiving of the relationship between literature and science, not one which can cover every manifestation of the two cultures debate. Two key issues should therefore be borne in mind. Firstly, the presentation of literature in the diagram is one which draws most heavily upon Romanticism, particularly in terms of the method, 'inspiration'. A Romantic perspective has been used because when literature and science are placed in opposition to one another, there is a tendency to stress the transcendent and mystical in literature, and thus to invest it with powers of literary discourse akin to those stressed by the Romantics. However, as has already been pointed out, a strict naturalist literature may abandon some of these aspects in favour of a more 'scientific' approach, to both the craft of writing, and the knowledge conveyed by that writing.

The second issue relates to the absence of literary criticism from the model. This is explained by the tendency in two cultures debates to limit discussion to the differences between literature and science, and indeed the study of literature is often conflated with literature itself in these debates. However, the actual place of literary study in the model produced on page 21 can vary quite dramatically. It can, indeed, be seen to exist somewhere in the literary box, particularly if literary criticism is seen as no more than a series of ultimately unprovable assertions about literature. However, there are also currents of criticism – one thinks particularly of structuralism and psychoanalytic approaches to literature – which at least aspire to inclusion in the scientific box. In these accounts literature itself may be separated from science, but literary criticism becomes a 'science' of literature, studying literary artefacts much as scientists study nature (although really these accounts are closer, in their conceptions of themselves, to the social sciences, whose scientific status is also open to dispute).

Given these dangers, what is the value of the diagram used to represent the two cultures model? What does it tell us about the ways in which literature and science are assumed to function by the two cultures debate? One primary aspect of the relationship between literature and science that it attempts to capture is that, despite the metaphors of conflict and the bad-tempered exchanges that are so characteristic of the debate, there is actually a degree of agreement about what literature and science are. Moreover, it is frequently agreed by two cultures protagonists that the culture as a whole functions best when these two constituent elements of it – literature and science – function in harmony.

By this is not meant that they work together, in the sense of joint engagement on the same projects, but rather that they work in parallel, each pulling in the same direction. The furthering of civilisation, in this view, is achieved by a division of labour, with science and literature each keeping strictly to their own territories. The conflict so characteristic of two cultures debates arises when the boundaries between the two are transgressed, or when there is a perception that the culture is becoming unbalanced toward either the scientific or the literary side, with developments in one (usually science) outstripping the other. Of course, part of the problem is that there are divergent opinions about the relative importance that should be ascribed in the culture as a whole, and in education, to each of these territories. Mathew Arnold was quite happy to accept that science was important, but was less happy with T.H. Huxley's suggestion that it should supplant so much of traditional, classical education; and was downright outraged by the implication that it was of equal cultural value to literary study. Similarly, while Snow concentrated predominantly on the ignorance of science displayed by literary intellectuals, Leavis proudly asserted the importance of the study of English at the centre of the modern university, implying that science was merely a peripheral mode of knowledge.

As will have been apparent from the discussion of John Burroughs's and Aldous Huxley's attempts to broker a truce between the warring parties, what the proposed peace actually entailed was a stronger definition of the boundaries between literature and science. This is why so many of their contributions are taken up with the simple statement of what science and literature are, and it is instructive that once they have established these boundaries they end with stirring statements of the march into the future to be undertaken by artists and scientists together. They establish the territories to which each should limit themselves, and then invoke the aim of parallel progression toward a common goal encapsulated in the diagram.

This common goal is, it will be noticed, rather vague, but this is entirely in keeping with the spirit of the two cultures debate. The goals toward which society is seen to move when the culture functions correctly lack clarity because they are in the future and therefore cannot easily be seen; there is a (reasonable) presumption that knowing more is better than knowing less, and that while there may not be a definite point at which the project of scientific and literary knowledge will be complete (particularly for literature, which is not seen to be cumulative in the same way as science), the general target of better understanding is a viable one at which to aim.

The next chapter will seek to develop an alternative model of culture. To some extent this will draw upon developments in literary studies, and particularly on the large body of literature–science criticism that has begun to appear in the last decade. However, it will not wholly accept some of the assertions on which this body of criticism relies, and it will use some of Sokal and Bricmont's objections to the misuses of science in the humanities to formulate the boundaries of a literature–science criticism.

Before moving on to this, however, it may be useful to look briefly at one example illustrating how the two cultures model described in this chapter affects literary study. By turning to the work of a critic such as I.A. Richards (whose contribution to New Criticism, and endorsement of a practical criticism which is still influential today, must make him one of the most significant critics of the century) it is possible to see how a two cultures model determines the purpose and the practice of literary criticism. Despite his influence, his methodologies have been overtaken by other critical practices, particularly in the last quarter of the twentieth century. The sharp divide between 'high' and 'low' culture that is apparent in his work, and the almost mystical qualities with which he imbues the influence of literature and literary study, are particularly alien to the contemporary critic.

It is, in fact, this slightly old-fashioned feel to his work that makes it such an interesting example for studying the impact of the two cultures model on the practice of literary criticism. The developments which have led his style of criticism to be challenged are the same developments which have led to the challenge to the two cultures model which has taken place in recent years within the humanities. For example, the interrogation of the assumption that 'great' and 'popular' literature can easily be distinguished from one another, and the consequent opening up of literary study to fields of popular culture that had previously been ignored, are also surely at the root of the willingness of literature–science critics to look for the ways in which the discourses of scientific writing might be analysed as literature. Our definition of literature has broadened immensely, moving beyond the traditional canon (a capitalised Literature) to embrace a wide range of popular genres, and now scientific writing.

Because Richards contributed to the study of literature before this radical revision in the subject, his writing provides a prime example of the way in which the old two cultures model, although not explicitly stated, provided an important framework for literary criticism, and therefore our whole conception of what literature is. It should be noted that, as in the rest of this chapter, 'two cultures' is being used as a convenient shorthand for a model which was influential at least as far back as the nineteenth century, even though C.P. Snow did not coin the phrase until the 1950s.

A Case Study of Two Cultures Assumptions in Literary Criticism: I.A. Richards

The focus for this analysis of Richards's criticism is provided by three books that he published in the 1920s: *Principles of Literary Criticism* (1924), *Science and Poetry* (1926), and *Practical Criticism* (1929).[52] Concerned as they are with the explicit statement of the purpose of literary criticism, as Richards saw it, and the methodology to be employed in appreciating literature, these books are interesting for the way in which they lay bare some of the assumptions underpinning his literary studies. The analysis which follows concentrates upon these assumptions as they pertain to the issue of the relationship between literature and science.

Quite often, the role of science in Richards's definitions of literature and of literary study is buried deep within his work, and this section will strive to unearth this aspect. However, it actually breaks the surface at a number of points, and one of the most notable of these, being concerned with the tremendous success of science relative to literary study, provides Richards with a justification for the study of literature in universities:

> As the finer parts of our emotional tradition relax in the expansion and dissolution of our communities, and as we discover how far out of our intellectual depth the flood-tide of science is carrying us ... we shall increasingly need every strengthening discipline that can be devised ... The critical reading of poetry is an arduous discipline; few exercises reveal to us more clearly the limitations under which, from moment to moment, we suffer. But, equally, the immense extension of our capacities that follows a summoning of our resources is made plain.[53]

There are a number of noteworthy aspects to this passage. Most importantly, it configures science as a threat, and once it has established this danger it then offers the study of literature as a means of ameliorating the situation. There is a very strong sense here of the need, discussed in the previous section, for literary study and science to pull in the same direction. What Richards finds threatening here is not so much science itself, but the exponential growth of science, unbalanced by similar developments and advances in literary culture.

By describing the critical reading of poetry as 'arduous' he also elevates literary criticism to the same intellectual level as science, implicitly addressing

---

[52] I.A. Richards, *Principles of Literary Criticism*, 2nd edn (1924; London: Routledge, 1967); *Poetries and Sciences: A Reissue of 'Science and Poetry' (1926, 1935) with Commentary*, rev. edn (1926; London: Routledge, 1970); *Practical Criticism: A Study of Literary Judgment* (1929; London: Routledge, 1964).

[53] Richards, *Practical Criticism*, pp. 350–51.

the common perceptions of science as difficult, and the study of literature as an easy option. This passage suggests that literary study is as intellectually demanding, and as important for the progress of civilisation, as science. We have a sense here, as in the debates between Huxley and Arnold, and Snow and Leavis, of a poorly-hidden agenda concerning the relative importance of the arts and sciences in educational institutions, and in the culture as a whole.

We also have a conventional sense of a split between the 'emotional' associations of literature, and those of science as being rational and 'intellectual' in an entirely different way. This split finds expression elsewhere in Richards's work and it is of particular importance where it is used to characterise two halves of the human mind. The following passage provides a prime example:

> It may seem odd that we do not more definitely make the thoughts the rulers and causes of the rest of the response ... Man prefers to stress the features which distinguish him from monkey, and chief among these are his intellectual capacities ... [But] though his intellect is what is distinctive in man, he is not primarily an intelligence; he is a system of interests. Intelligence helps man but does not run him.[54]

There are two aspects to the mind here: 'thoughts' and a 'system of interests'. The former refers to the capacity for rational thought. It is this which is traditionally associated with scientific study, particularly when applied to empirical observations of the world. However, although these 'intellectual capacities' are what distinguish people from animals ('monkey') most obviously, they do not comprise all of what it is to be human for Richards.[55] The 'system of interests' – broadly equivalent to emotional needs – is prioritised over the rational side of the mind by this passage.

This has a very important effect. We need to remember that, as was acknowledged in the description of the 'flood-tide' of science, Richards was writing at a time of considerable scientific success, and growing cultural and educational influence for science. The implication of all this was that for literary criticism to survive, it had to establish its own territory (in terms of subject matter) away from the broadening influence of science. This is where Richards's reminder of the traditional distinction between intellectual and emotional sides of the mind comes in. If science is configured as belonging to the intellect, but the mind is redefined so that there is a split between this intellect and a system of interests (and, indeed, the system of interests is

---

[54]   Richards, *Principles*, p. 30.
[55]   An interesting example of someone else who uses rational capacities to define the human is René Descartes, who is discussed in chapter 4 (see particularly pages 107–8), which deals with contemporary challenges to definitions of the human.

described as being dominant), then the result is to define a province that is beyond the reach of science.

At least, rather conveniently, Richards suggests that for the foreseeable future science will be unable to deal with this side of the mind: 'If we knew enough it might be possible that all necessary attitudes [of the mind] could be obtained through scientific references alone. Since we do not know very much yet, we can leave this remote possibility, once recognized, alone'.[56] This leaves the way clear for attention to literature as a means of understanding and developing the system of interests. Notice also that talking about the mind being split in this way has the effect of naturalising the distinction between the arts and the sciences. If the difference between them is seen to correspond to a natural split in the mind then the effect is to justify a two cultures model as corresponding to an essential truth. A similar effect is produced at other points in Richards's work where binary differences correlate to a science–literature split.

For instance, these splits are apparent when he writes about two streams of experience that the reader receives from reading poetry, and when he writes about two categories of belief. The former occurs in *Science and Poetry* when a minor, intellectual experience (basically, the verifiable truths and certainties about what the words in a poem mean) is contrasted with a more active, emotional stream from which 'all the energy of the whole agitation [in the mind] comes'.[57] Here, the intellectual stream corresponds to scientific certainty, whereas the more vital emotional stream is the essence of the poetry.

The latter, his writing on two categories of belief, occurs in *Practical Criticism*. A 'scientific' aspect is again apparent, in the form of a highly ordered system of beliefs that corresponds here to something very similar to the goal of scientific enquiry, with knowledge slotted together in a cumulative and rational way: 'The whole use of intellectual belief is to bring *all* our ideas into as perfect an ordered system as possible'.[58] This is contrasted with the 'emotional' belief which underpins literature and the reading experience, and is about satisfying our demands as human beings: 'an emotional belief is not justified through any logical relations between its ideas and other ideas. Its only justification is its success in meeting our needs'.[59] There is, once again, a buried agenda here about the relative importance of literature and science in the culture, with the suggestion that emotional belief can meet our needs as humans in a way that intellectual belief cannot.

As in his division of the mind into intellectual capacities and a system of interests, Richards again implicates, in connection with these different

---

[56]   Richards, *Principles*, p. 211.
[57]   Richards, *Poetries*, p. 25.
[58]   Richards, *Practical Criticism*, p. 274.
[59]   Richards, *Practical Criticism*, p. 277.

categories of belief, a *natural* division of the mind between scientific and literary aspects: 'Behind the intellectual assumption stands the desire for logical consistency and order in the receptive side of the mind. But behind the emotional assumption stands the desire or need for order of the whole outgoing emotional side of the personality, the side that is turned towards action'.[60] The two categories of belief are here shown to correspond to a natural division between rational (scientific) and emotional (artistic) sides of the mind. By presenting this split as natural he also presents it as unquestionable.

The recurrence of these distinctions between the literary and the scientific has the effect, then, of clearing a space for literary study: it defines a set of concerns that cannot be reached by science, despite its contemporary success; and literary study is able to come in to fill this gap. It is interesting to see exactly how this is effected.

Firstly, the importance of literature has to be established, and this is done by presenting it as an extremely potent force, which helps or inhibits the development of the reader's mind: 'The raising of the standard of response is as immediate a problem as any, and the arts are the chief instrument by which it may be raised *or lowered*'.[61] This also enables the second logical step, which is to ground the necessity for literary criticism. Not only, in this quotation, is literature seen merely to affect the reader's 'standard of response' in some vague way: it also, crucially, is made clear that it can have both positive and negative effects. This is where, for Richards, literary criticism comes in: it is a means of identifying that literature which is beneficial for the reader (equivalent to the canon of 'great' literature), and distinguishing it from that which may have a negative effect upon the reader. Once this primary role has been fulfilled, secondary tasks can follow from it, including the refinement of students' responses to literature, and the imparting of knowledge that will enable students to identify for themselves the distinctions between high and low culture.[62]

In order to make these points convincing, Richards also needs to be able to back up his assertion that literature has the dramatic impact upon individuals and society that he suggests. These justifications are attempted with the suggestion – which appears at a number of points in his work – that the ordered mind is the best mind, and that fine literature enhances this ordering of the mind, while poor literature has the reverse effect. For instance, he claims

---

[60]   Richards, *Practical Criticism*, p. 274.

[61]   Richards, *Principles*, p. 184.

[62]   The majority of *Practical Criticism*, which is taken up with a discussion of students' responses to unannotated poetry, can be seen to make precisely this last point. Richards is horrified to discover that students at Cambridge are unable, when lacking a poet's name as a clue, to distinguish great from poor literature. The implication is that the teaching of literary criticism is absolutely essential to rectify this state of affairs.

that 'the fine conduct of life springs only from fine ordering of responses far too subtle to be touched by any general ethical maxims'.[63] Literature has, it is suggested, the subtlety to produce this fine ordering. There is clearly a moral dimension to this presentation of literature – it somehow enables one to transcend the vulgarity of 'general ethical maxims', putting one in touch with something that goes beyond explicit statement. Elements of the two cultures model, and the stereotypical associations of literature and science which it reproduces, are readily apparent here: what makes literature different to science is its ability to touch the sublime.

The literary artist is therefore seen here in a guise not far removed from a Romanticist notion of genius. Good artists and poets are better than the rest of us because they are 'further developments of organizations'[64] which our minds already have, and as a result 'give order and coherence, and so freedom, to a body of experience'.[65] Their literature therefore disseminates their superior principles of mental organisation amongst their readers:

> We pass as a rule from a chaotic to a better organized state by ways which we know nothing about. Typically through the influence of other minds. Literature and the arts are the chief means by which these influences are diffused. It should be unnecessary to insist upon the degree to which high civilization, in other words, free, varied and unwasteful life, depends upon them in a numerous society.[66]

Again, there is a suggestion that literature is essential to the well-developed personality, offering something which is, by implication, unobtainable through science – if we accept Richards's belief that it is one of the 'chief' means for the spread of these influences, then we also have to accept the necessity for literary study. This prioritising of literature over science is even more conspicuous in the following passage:

> It is never what a poem says which matters, but what it *is*. The poet is not writing as a scientist. He uses these words because the interests whose movement is the growth of the poem combine to bring them, just in this form, into his consciousness *as a means of ordering, controlling and consolidating* the uttered experience of which they are themselves a main part.[67]

---

[63]   Richards, *Principles*, p. 47.
[64]   Richards, *Principles*, p. 153.
[65]   Richards, *Poetries*, p. 57. There is an interesting contrast here to contemporary discussions of order and chaos which frequently suggest that order is actually restrictive of freedom.
[66]   Richards, *Principles*, p. 43.
[67]   Richards, *Poetries*, p. 33.

Conversely, whilst high culture has a positive effect, popular culture is configured as a dangerous influence, promoting disorder: 'No one can intensely and wholeheartedly enjoy and enter into experiences whose fabric is as crude as that of the average super-film without a disorganization which has its effects in everyday life'.[68] So the value of art is seen to reside in its effect upon the mind, that which is positive ordering the mind further, whilst that which is negative increases disorder. This amounts to powerful rhetoric for an accepted body of 'good' literature to stand at the centre of culture, the study of it neutralising the dangerous chaotic experiences of poor literature, and bringing us into touch with the beneficial ordering of our minds that great literature can produce.[69]

Richards suggests that the way for the reader to access the ordering of the mind achieved by the poet lies not in a direct focus on biography and the writer's state of mind ('far too happy a hunting-ground for uncontrollable conjecture'),[70] but in a concentration on the text itself, where the ordering of experience is made manifest: 'often the critic ... affirms that the effect in his mind is due to some special particular features of the object. In this case he is pointing out something about the object in addition to its effect upon him, and this fuller kind of criticism is what we desire'.[71]

Yet for all that Richards expounds the means by which literature is supposed to affect the mind of the individual reader, and by implication society as a whole, there is still something inherently mystical about the whole process. The better sort of reader, we are told, needs to be 'sensitive',[72] and the literary critic in Richards's criticism seems to act like a priest or vicar, interpreting the word of the divine author.

Perhaps this sense of the sublime, with which both literature and literary studies are associated (and which is far from absent in literary studies today), is tied in with the way in which high culture is defined by Richards. The definition at which he arrives seems to reside less in an essential nature or quality held by that literature or culture, than in a negative definition: a sense of what it is not. This negative definition takes the form of three binary oppositions.

The first binary opposition, which is loudly stated by Richards's work, is that between high and low culture. However, committed though he is to the distinction between the truly literary and the abysmally popular, Richards is

---

[68]   Richards, *Principles*, p. 182. Cinema appears a number of times in Richards's work as an example of the most pernicious effects of popular culture.

[69]   Very different notions of order and disorder are explored in the case study in chapter 3, which investigates the presentation of rigid order as sterile in contemporary culture, whilst a third region, between order and disorder, is opened up as a fertile middle ground.

[70]   Richards, *Principles*, p. 20.

[71]   Richards, *Principles*, p. 15.

[72]   Richards, *Principles*, p. 76, p. 119. Richards, *Practical Criticism*, p. 224.

unable to say exactly what it is that separates one from the other, and is forced back upon what are ultimately rather vague comments about the promotion of order or disorder in the mind.[73] Literature is almost defined by being that which does not appeal to the masses (in other words, that which is not popular): if it is difficult, it can then be claimed that in order to appreciate it training is required to develop the appropriate sensitivity.

The second binary opposition, proclaimed in a forthright way along with the first, is the distinction between order and disorder. Great writers are those who order their experiences more fully than the rest of us, and communicate this through their work. Conversely, the threat that Richards perceives in popular culture is in its promotion of a shallow response to the world which ultimately leads to chaos.

The third binary opposition, voiced much more softly than the other two, but just as important, is between literature and science. Just as great literature is, for Richards, distinguished by virtue of its difference from popular culture, so is it also defined by virtue of an approach to the world which is distinct from the scientific. It appeals to that side of the mind which science is unable to reach, and although Richards is unable to say exactly what it involves (its rarefaction is, after all, that which justifies degree-level study of it), it is clearly opposed to scientific study. Science, it is implied, lacks the nobility, moral dimension and transcendent qualities of great literature.

It is apparent, then, that the rather stereotypical assumptions identified in the two cultures model contribute significantly to the criticism Richards produces. They furnish elements of the definition of literature with which he works (distinguishing it from the scientific object of study); they dictate aspects of the methodology of literary criticism (the 'sensitive' response to the work of literature which is so much more mysterious than the clear statement of findings associated, rightly or wrongly, with science); and they inform the purpose of literary study (which carries a moral dimension – the idea of value is central to Richards's work – supposedly lacking in other subjects).

Yet despite the importance to Richards's work of a framework of knowledge like that encapsulated in the two cultures model, there are also two key senses in which his work is apparently bound to science. Firstly, he draws on psychology to confer a degree of scientific authenticity to his comments

---

[73] Richards is not, of course, alone in being unable to define the difference between Literature and literature. The most famous and rigorous attempt was probably produced by the Russian Formalists' definition of the literary as that which 'defamiliarizes' us from ordinary experience, and yet even this definition is inadequate in, for example, its inability to distinguish between advertising and literature, and its inability to account for the literary success of the sparse prose style of writers like Ernest Hemingway. For an account of defamiliarization see Victor Shklovsky, 'Art as Technique', *Russian Formalist Criticism: Four Essays*, trans. Lee T. Lemon and Marion J. Reis, Regents Critics Series, (Lincoln: University of Nebraska Press, 1965), pp. 3–24.

about the human mind, as in this instance: 'enough is known [of the mind] for an analysis of the mental events which make up the reading of a poem to be attempted. And such an analysis is a primary necessity for criticism'.[74] Secondly, by stressing the need for the critic to concentrate on the apparent stability and reality of the text itself, rather than being distracted into details of autobiography and other contexts, he seeks to attain an objectivity equivalent to that aspired to by science. So in striving to wrestle back from science a position at the centre of the university and of the culture for literary study, he also transforms literary study, investing it with some of the aspects of the scientific approach to nature that will enable it to affirm its findings more readily.

None of these comments about the two cultures framework, from which Richards's criticism speaks, necessarily invalidate his work. However, they do make clear its origin in a specific intellectual context, and might therefore make us question whether the comments he produces about literary study are really as self-evident as he implies. Certainly, the two cultures model is responsible for the course upon which he tries to set literary study. As this model has been rejected by a number of critics in recent years, and as the next chapter will formulate an alternative model, it may be useful to outline the main objections to this splitting of the culture between literature and science.

Problems with the Two Cultures Model

Some of the objections that might be made to the two cultures model will be apparent from the discussion above – for instance, the tendency to draw on stereotypical notions of what literature and science are, without recourse to an interrogation of the assumptions upon which such ideas are based. However, it may still be claimed that whatever the deficiencies of the particular version of the model presented on page 21, it is still, in its general conception, truthful to the essential difference between literary and scientific modes of knowledge.

It is certainly not the intention in this book to argue that literature and science are one and the same thing, and to make the hubristic claim that by exposing a few deficiencies in an established way of thinking about literature and science, one has somehow bridged the chasm and proven the equivalence of the two. In taking on the two cultures model, the aim is to arrive at a revision that addresses some of its conceptual inadequacies, whilst doing justice to the different locations at which literature and science are based within our culture.

The primary problem with the two cultures model, and the debate based upon it, is that it fails to address the vibrant role that science plays in our

---

[74] Richards, *Principles*, p. 62.

culture. Science itself is a culturally highly-charged term, conveying all sorts of meanings, and the various ideas with which science is associated clearly resonate throughout our culture and into literature. One has only to think about the passions and prejudices aroused by the current debate concerning genetics to see how this is the case.

Of course, many of the meanings ascribed to the various sciences are apocryphal, and the term 'science' may itself convey very different things to different people, not least to practising scientists and the general public. However, without wishing to address at too great a length this issue of the gap between professional and public conceptions of science (which is explored in the next chapter), what the two cultures model singularly fails to do is to allow us to see how ideas move from science into the public domain (or even, though this is more contentious, from the public domain into science).

Science very much *is* a part of our lives. Even if we do not have direct access to science (whether defined as a series of insights, or as a mode of knowledge), there are routes by which we come into contact with it. These routes include the explicit popularisation of scientific ideas in the media and in books, and the less direct appearance of scientific ideas as they become accepted as a general background of shared information (even on the wildly simplistic level of, say, agreement that the earth goes around the sun; though the blank acceptance of this sort of idea, merely from authority, is of course itself profoundly unscientific). The impact of technologies upon our lives is also important (even though science and technology are distinct, and many technologies are not dependent on science, there are technologies that would not exist without the scientific revolution), as are the ways in which scientific insights contribute to our investigation of those notions also strongly associated with literature and, indeed, religion (who we are, where we come from, and so forth).

It is not that the protagonists in the two cultures debate would necessarily have denied any of this, but the understanding of literature and science with which they worked discouraged any serious contemplation of science as a participant in the culture, by emphasising distinction and separation. Much more fruitful is the understanding of the culture described in chapter 2.

A second problem with the older conception of the two cultures is that it suggests that there is an essential, natural difference between scientific and literary modes of knowledge, and that the divide between different approaches to the world cannot be reconciled. Yet they approach the same world; though the focus of their study differs, they do not deal with entirely separate territories, and there is an overlap where they bear upon the same problems. Even accepting that our notion of reality is not entirely given, and that prevailing discourses construct, to a degree, our notion of what the world is, and what is real, the idea that literature and science are utterly irreconcilable and antagonistic toward one another does not bear rigorous examination. This is a fashionable enough insight in the humanities, and much literature–science criticism makes the claim – explicitly or implicitly – that scientific discourse is amenable to literary analysis (though it will be argued, in the next chapter, that such claims need to be very carefully supported by evidence, and must be made with an awareness of their limits).

It is perhaps less fashionable to consider how scientific insights might have a bearing on the study of literature (perhaps because, for all the talk of 'one culture', literature–science criticism tends to be located in the humanities, and tends to export its ideas rather imperialistically, without embracing the benefit of imported notions from the sciences). However, if areas of science do make claims about the functioning of the human mind, and about the operations of language, then they are relevant to the study of literature and their consequences need to be critically interrogated and, if found to be correct, integrated into our understanding of the operations of literature.

Finally, the conceptions of literature and science embedded in the two cultures model are, very frequently, stereotypical. As a result two cultures debates frequently do little to advance our understanding of the places of literature and science in our culture, but much to promote a mutual hostility through educational power struggles. It is not always that the stereotypes are wrong (sometimes they have become stereotypes precisely because they capture something useful about the difference between literature and science), but that by constantly opposing the literary to the scientific they fail to encourage a critical awareness of what each term entails.

There are, then, a triumvirate of objections to the two cultures model: science is a part of our culture, and our knowledge of the culture is incomplete if we fail to bear this in mind; there are overlaps between literary and scientific modes of knowing; and the two cultures debate encourages the unthinking acceptance of stereotypical definitions of literature and science. The approach described in chapter 2 attempts to address these deficiencies without collapsing the distinction between literature and science.

However, even if we renounce the two cultures framework as a cultural construct, it is unlikely that we will be able to restart our approach to literature from an entirely objective perspective. What we can do, however, is to make explicit to as great a degree as possible the new framework of assumptions from which we begin. No doubt there are blind spots in our knowledge of this framework, but one thing that has been lacking in the intriguing body of literature–science criticism that has been produced over the last fifteen years is a direct attempt to interrogate the starting point for this new branch of literary criticism. However limited first attempts at such an interrogation might be, it is essential for the intellectual credentials of any branch of knowledge that it be willing to examine the precepts on which it is based. The following chapter seeks to contribute to this process of self-examination, stating the principles of literature–science criticism on which the case studies in chapters 3, 4 and 5 are built. It therefore offers an alternative to the two cultures model, although it is an alternative that is more moderate than that implicit in many examples of literature–science criticism. The reasons for this moderation will be made clear in the description of the new model.

Chapter 2

Literature–Science Methodology and the Science Wars

The ceasefire has been broken. In recent years the two cultures dispute has erupted into conflict again, although this time the terms of the dispute have shifted significantly from those discussed in the last chapter.

Previous incarnations of the dispute, like those between Huxley and Arnold, and Snow and Leavis, assumed a basic, unproblematic distinction between the Arts and the Sciences, although there was an awareness that the two cultures characterisation was a simplification.[1] There might have been disagreements about the relative importance of literature and science – for instance, about which is the more essential to the cultured personality – but the debate was not significantly dominated by attempts to cross the basic gulf assumed by the two cultures model.

The current dispute has been precipitated by the popularity in the humanities of sociological approaches to science, of one kind or another. These approaches – by, for instance, influential figures like Thomas S. Kuhn, Paul Feyerabend, and Jean-François Lyotard[2] – have concentrated on scientific discourse as a social construction. Inspired by figures like these, literature–science criticism has taken as its starting point the idea that science is a discourse and, as such, is as amenable to analysis as the more conventionally-studied narratives of literature. One effect of seeing science in this way is the perception of scientific knowledge as specific to its historical and social contexts. In other words, the implication in much of the literary criticism that has followed from these sociological approaches is that science does not

---

[1] Snow himself, for instance, showed an awareness that it was possible to identify more than two cultures. C.P. Snow, *The Two Cultures and the Scientific Revolution* (Cambridge University Press, 1959), pp. 8–9.

[2] See, for example, the following texts: Thomas S. Kuhn, *The Structure of Scientific Revolutions*, 2nd edn, International Encyclopedia of Unified Science 2.2 (1962; University of Chicago Press, 1970); Paul Feyerabend, *Against Method*, 3rd edn (1975; London: Verso, 1993); Jean-François Lyotard, *The Postmodern Condition: A Report on Knowledge*, trans. Geoff Bennington and Brian Massumi, Theory and History of Literature 10 (1979; Manchester University Press, 1986).

discover universal truths, but is revealing of the dominant social and cultural concerns of the societies in which it is produced.[3]

A strong subtext of this sort of approach is a recapitulation of the power struggles over education and culture discussed in the last chapter. By using tools of cultural analysis to present science as culturally bounded, one significant effect has been to undermine (or, at least, to attempt to undermine) science's power to reveal the truth and, by thus undercutting its authority, to challenge its strong position in the educational establishment.

Alan Sokal's spoof article in *Social Text*, and his book *Intellectual Impostures*, co-written with Jean Bricmont, are the most famous defences against these perceptions of science. *Intellectual Impostures* argues, broadly, that there has been a failure to understand science in the humanities, and that it is insufficient to allege that science's claim to speak the truth can no more be legitimated than the discourses of alternative models of reality (for instance, those provided by folk myths). Furthermore Sokal and Bricmont suggest that these challenges to science come from an extreme relativist position, equivalent to a postmodernist stance.

This chapter explores both the alleged attack on science and the defence mounted against this attack. It then goes on to propose a new model of culture, and a means of linking literature and science based on this model, that inform the three case studies that follow in chapters 3, 4 and 5. This methodology takes issue with both the attacks on science, arguing that it is insufficient to describe science as just discourse (though it has a cultural aspect which it is reasonable to approach as a discourse), and the defences of it, arguing that the reduction of postmodernism to extreme relativism is insufficiently simplistic. Chapter 6 develops this discussion of postmodernism by exploring the ways in which the texts discussed in the three case studies in the preceding chapters display postmodernist characteristics.

The position which the book arrives at is, therefore, one which is in some sense midway between the two sides of the contemporary literature–science argument. It should be stressed that this is not a position that is reached because I am attempting to find a compromise, but because it is my belief that it is the position which is logically most consistent with what we currently know. Indeed, to set out with the intention of finding a midpoint would be foolhardy in the extreme as it would, firstly, suggest that conclusions precede evidence, and secondly, given the intense emotions aroused by the debate, be more likely to alienate both sides than to find favour with either.

---

[3]   These two points of view of science are often presented as mutually exclusive, and this has had the effect of polarising debate in the science wars. In fact they need not be mutually exclusive – it is possible to accept the broad truth of science, whilst maintaining that it usually has effects, or may be deployed in ways, that vary between cultures.

One thing that has been almost entirely absent in the contemporary incarnation of the two cultures dispute is a clearly-stated model of how science is seen to operate within the culture. Enunciating such a model therefore offers the hope of significant progress because it allows for the development (by refutation or – hopefully – refinement) of the model.

Literature and Science: The Contemporary Debate

One of the ironies of the contemporary argument about literature and science is that the winning of one of the objectives for which T.H. Huxley and C.P. Snow were fighting – the admission of science to the culture – has led to a whole new series of battles in which combatants on the 'scientific' side have sought to extricate science from the culture, while their 'literary' opponents have desperately tried to hang on to it. Of course, all this talk of sides is not necessarily helpful, particularly if our common aim is to understand accurately the extent to which, and the way in which, science and literature are related. Nevertheless, it remains true that there has been a move forwards (or, some might argue, a regression back) from the terms of the original two cultures debate, and that the current disputes centre around the way in which science is, or is not, cultural. Broadly speaking, two sides have emerged from these disputes and, with some notable exceptions, there has been a tendency in the humanities to regard science as culturally bounded (though the extent to which it is thus bounded is a matter of controversy), while there has been a tendency in the sciences to dispute this perception of science.

Evidence for the perception in the humanities that science is a product of culture and can therefore be treated as a discourse, can be found in the immense body of literary criticism that has followed on from sociological approaches to the sciences. For example, this perspective is stated explicitly by a number of critics: L.J. Jordanova claims that 'our primary object of study is language – that which mediates all thought, action and experience. We focus largely on the discourses common to science and literature';[4] Robert J. Scholnick introduces a book on American literature and science with the suggestion that 'Historians have learned to approach science as only one among other social constructs, and so the subject has been opened to the sort of critical analysis directed at any other form of cultural expression';[5] Stuart Peterfreund's introduction to a collection of essays on literature and science synthesises the work of the

---

[4]   L.J. Jordanova, introduction, *Languages of Nature: Critical Essays on Science and Literature*, ed. Jordanova (London: Free Association Books, 1986), p. 17.

[5]   Robert J. Scholnick, 'Permeable Boundaries: Literature and Science in America', *American Literature and Science*, ed. Scholnick (University of Kentucky Press, 1992), pp. 1–2.

various contributors by claiming that all 'make a start out of the assumption
that, typically, the discourse of literature and science, like any other discourse
of a given culture, is language-bound ... and that language itself is the
repository of ideological values and critical and methodological praxis';[6] and in
the same book James J. Bono reiterates the point in his essay when he
proposes that central to an enterprise to challenge the assumption that language
operates as a transparent medium for science is 'an adequate understanding of
the textuality of scientific discourse and of the metaphoricity of the languages
of science'.[7]

This is a crucial point of contention in the current debate about literature
and science. For instance, the reading of science as discourse is identified as one
of the key abuses of science, perpetrated by some sections of the humanities,
in Alan Sokal and Jean Bricmont's *Intellectual Impostures*.[8] The opening
paragraph of the introduction states this clearly when it identifies, as one of the
trends that have 'surprised and distressed' the authors, 'a cognitive and cultural
relativism that regards science as nothing more than a "narration", a "myth" or
a social construction among many others'.[9] It is science as a cultural product –
and the reduction in its authority when it is viewed as such – that is at issue
here. Sokal and Bricmont go on, in their book, to detail misconceptions about
science apparent in the work of, among others, Jacques Lacan, Julia Kristeva,
Bruno Latour, and Gilles Deleuze and Félix Guattari. Arguing carefully from
examples they show how the science cited in works by these critics has been
misunderstood. Given the ire that Sokal and Bricmont have provoked, it is as
well to be aware that their targets are very clearly defined, and they do not
claim that the examples they use are symptomatic of work in the humanities as
a whole, nor that other work by the writers they discuss is necessarily flawed
because of the mistakes exposed by *Intellectual Impostures*. Because of this
cautious and considered approach, any renunciation of Sokal and Bricmont's
objection to the deployment of science needs, itself, to be scientifically
informed. If it is not then it cannot demonstrate that they are wrong and the
critics they expose are right – it is insufficient to offer a vague denunciation of

---

    [6]   Stuart Peterfreund, introduction, *Literature and Science: Theory and Practice*
(Boston: Northeastern University Press, 1990), pp. 5–6.

    [7]   James J. Bono, 'Science, Discourse, and Literature: The Role/Rule of Metaphor in
Science', *Literature and Science: Theory and Practice*, ed. Stuart Peterfreund (Boston:
Northeastern University Press, 1990), p. 60.

    [8]   Alan Sokal and Jean Bricmont, *Intellectual Impostures: Postmodern Philosophers'
Abuse of Science* (London: Profile, 1998). Although there have been a number of objections to
the misuses of science, Sokal and Bricmont's combines the qualities of clarity and notoriety,
and for this reason I concentrate upon their work. (As with the last chapter on earlier two
cultures debates, the intention is not to provide a comprehensive history of the debate, but a
clear, conceptual analysis of the opposing points of view).

    [9]   Sokal and Bricmont, p. 1.

Sokal and Bricmont, claiming that they do not 'get' their own cultural situatedness, or that their work is merely another example of scientists' hostility toward the humanities; nor is it sufficient to claim that they are part of a reactionary backlash against leftward-leaning and progressive elements in the academy. Such critiques – while possibly motivated by a justified sense of the generally embattled state of the left in contemporary society – fail if they do not address the central issue in Sokal and Bricmont's work, which is that the science has, in the samples used, been misunderstood and inappropriately deployed.[10]

It is certainly not the intention of this book to attempt such a criticism. For any scholar trained only in the humanities to attempt to speak about the truth value of science, or to make claims about the significance of certain scientific developments, is to speak beyond their expertise.[11] Any argument about science thus formed would be an argument based solely upon authority, and such an argument is immediately handicapped by the inability to judge whom we should invest with authority. Which scientists – and which popularisers of science – are right about, say, the significance of chaos theory? With no way to judge, based on a scientifically sophisticated appreciation of the evidence, it would be wrong to pass comment (which does not mean that it is wrong to talk about the *literary* aspects of popularisations of chaos theory, nor that the *presentation* of the significance of chaos theory cannot be discussed).

Admittedly, it is neither possible nor desirable for everyone to limit themselves solely to carefully-defined pockets of expertise, when it is apparent that our carving of knowledge into disciplines and subdisciplines, though convenient, is but an artificial way of dividing up our experience and knowledge

---

[10]   One objection that has been made to Sokal and Bricmont is that they imply a paucity of intellectual rigour in the humanities, without ever actually stating it. This sort of conjecture is not particularly helpful and, given that they explicitly state the limits of their project, it is hardly fair to pull them up for an implication that they explicitly and repeatedly deny making in their book. By lumping them in with reactionary opinion, such a reading blithely sidesteps the real questions they raise and itself levels the (false) accusation at their readers, that being for Sokal and Bricmont is to be against a leftist critique, as in this excerpt from a review of *Intellectual Impostures* by John Sturrock: 'they know they don't need to [move to a broad critique of Lacan after attacking his use of topology], so ready will those of like mind with themselves be to leap to the conclusion that they smugly withhold, and those who are already of like mind will be the only obvious beneficiaries of this book'. John Sturrock, 'Le pauvre Sokal', *London Review of Books* 20.14 (16 Jul. 1998), p. 8.

[11]   This does not mean that science cannot be discussed at all. Further on in this chapter it is made clear that such a discussion can take place as long as it identifies exactly how science is being understood, and the boundaries within which such a discussion takes place. One way of doing this, which dominates this book, is to talk about how science has been presented in the culture.

of the world. One thing is clearly connected to another, and so some sort of overall picture is desirable.

However, we must use some self-awareness of our limitations in painting this picture. It is reasonable for a non-expert to come to a personal opinion about a scientific controversy by reading the work of those involved, and descriptions of the work of those involved. For example, in debates about evolution it is surely not wrong to compare competing claims about the primary unit of selection (such as Richard Dawkins's belief that it is the gene, with Stephen Jay Gould's proposal that it is the individual organism)[12] and come to a personal opinion, as long as one does not then go on to publish papers about the issue that claim the authority to speak about it.

This is the problem that Sokal and Bricmont identify. By treating science as a discourse, the critics they attack also make, by implication, sweeping claims about what science is and is not. This would not be such a problem if there was a significant body of opinion within the sciences themselves that supported the claims that are made. To take an extreme example, were there to be a significant body of mathematicians who supported the link made by Jacques Lacan between the square root of minus one and an erection (gleefully discussed by Sokal and Bricmont), then the conclusions that follow could legitimately be made with the proviso that they hold if such mathematicians are right.[13] However, in the absence of such a body of thought, it is hard to defend the use of science in this case and others like it.

A similar point applies to the treatment of science as discourse. It is not sufficient to justify the cultural analysis of science merely by stating that it is a discourse, and then going on to treat it exactly the same as any other use of language (especially as the use of language discussed is more likely to be a popularisation – and hence a translation – of the science, rather than the technical and mathematical incarnation of the science itself, used by expert practitioners in the field). We need to be aware of exactly *how* it is (and is not) a discourse, how this discourse is shaped by the context of the natural world it describes, and how it relates to the culture in which it finds expression.

---

[12] See note 14 in chapter 4 and note 7 in chapter 5. The other major area of disagreement between Dawkins and Gould is the pace of evolutionary change (see notes 10 and 11, chapter 5).

[13] Sokal and Bricmont, p. 25. Lacan can also be defended by saying that the use of the square root of minus one is metaphorical, as long as one can also, as Sokal and Bricmont point out elsewhere in the chapter, demonstrate that such a metaphor is an enlightening way of understanding what it is meant to describe.

Literature and Science: A Way Forward

Having stressed these limits upon literature–science criticism, and the ways in which we should rightly be chastened by Sokal and Bricmont's comments, it is also vital to stress that not all criticism (and this includes that quoted above, which talked about science as discourse) falls into the traps identified thus far. The crucial step to take, which enables us to talk about literature and science without overreaching ourselves, is to distinguish between what, for ease of reference, I shall call 'professional science' and 'cultural science'.

Professional science refers to the set of practices and expertise that make up the life of the working scientist, and in order to participate in which he or she must be trained. This will obviously vary between different scientists, according to their interests, but the crucial point is that it is the aspect of science to which the general public – and literary scholars – do not have direct access.

Cultural science, on the other hand, is all about the relationship between science and the public, being anything that contributes to the general perception – the cultural 'value' – of science. The boundaries between this and professional science are obviously permeable, with cultural science being shaped partly by activities that take place within the sphere of professional science (for instance, the reporting of developments in professional science, technological developments that stem from scientific work, and the popularisation of scientific ideas by scientists themselves). It also, though, includes literary and other representations of science – anything which serves to define it in the popular imagination – and so it may well consist of misrepresentations of professional science.

This conceptual distinction between two different uses of the word 'science' is liberating in terms of our discussion of the relationship between literature and science. One very important consequence is that it allows us to extricate ourselves from the debate over the relationship between the language of science and reality. It puts to one side the status of professional scientific discourse, leaving this to those scientists and philosophers of science with the expertise (the basic literacy in the language) to discuss the question.

If we work with a model of culture as discourse, it allows us to talk about science as discourse, without reducing science to just discourse. This might limit the scope of what we say about science, but it is hard to see how an alternative position can be logically justified. The starting point for our investigations of literature therefore cedes territory (a question such as, what is chaos theory? is a question for a scientist, not a literary critic), in order to legitimise our hold upon more modest boundaries (questions such as, how is chaos theory represented? – an investigation of the literary techniques deployed in popularisations of chaos theory might tell us something about the importance, or otherwise, with which it is invested in our culture). This distinction must be borne in mind when reading the case studies which appear in the following chapters – although they will discuss certain aspects of science, these deliberations should always be read with the proviso in mind that they are not attempting to ask essentialist questions about science (what is science?), but questions about the role of science in our culture (how is science represented?).

Although the division between cultural and professional science offers some new (if rather unimaginatively coined) terminology, the distinction on which it is based is hardly original. Much other literature–science criticism displays an awareness of the limits of speaking about science from the perspective of the humanities. Sometimes this is implicit in the work, but at other times the subject of the difference between literary and scientific discourses is openly broached. For instance, a slightly more sophisticated version of one of Sokal's put-downs – 'anyone who believes that the laws of physics are mere social conventions is invited to try transgressing those conventions from the windows of my apartment. I live on the twenty-first floor'[14] – is used by G.S. Rousseau to illustrate the difficulties facing literature–science criticism:

> [Literature–science critics] try to entice all potential audiences in the name of common assumptions ... especially the common assumption that scientific models are just another set of models to describe nature's laws: ultimately neither more nor less accurate than competing models, rarely free of value or ideology when set into discursive narratives, and certainly no 'truer' than any other fictions. And yet the two aspirins that relieved my headache on the airplane yesterday are not rhetorical, ideological, value-laden or polemical aspirins until I start *talking about them*.[15]

These preliminary comments provide, then, the justification and the starting point for the type of investigation of literature and science advocated by this book. The claim being made is that despite the implication in much of the two cultures debate that science is not cultural, science is, and has for a long time been, an integral part of our culture. Although there are certain aspects of science which are not amenable to analysis by those without a specialist

---

[14]   Sokal and Bricmont, p. 249. This comes from a footnote to 'Transgressing the Boundaries: An Afterword' by Alan Sokal, first published in 1996, and reprinted in Sokal and Bricmont (1998) as appendix C.

[15]   G.S. Rousseau, 'Discourses of the Nerve', *Literature and Science as Modes of Expression*, ed. Frederick Amrine, Boston Studies in the Philosophy of Science 115 (Dordrecht: Kluwer Academic Publishers, 1989), p. 40.

training, the significance and range of meanings ascribed to science in our culture can be analysed with literary theoretical techniques because they take place on the level of discourse. For example, popularisations of science (such as those of genetics and evolution) are integral to the stories that we tell about who we are and where we come from.

In order to develop further the way in which this perspective can launch an investigation of literature and science, it is now necessary to offer further details of the alternative to the two cultures model described in the last chapter, defining key terms such as 'culture' and 'discourse', and establishing the rationale behind the case studies that appear later in the book.

A New Model of Literature and Science

There are a number of terms that are used frequently in literature–science criticism, and that are also at the heart of this volume. A definition of them as they will be used here will help to explain how the proposed model of culture works.

'Culture' itself is used in a way that draws on two sources. The first is cultural anthropology, providing us with an explicit statement of what is perhaps self-evident given our current familiarity with using the term in this way: culture is *'that complex whole which includes knowledge, belief, art, morals, laws, customs, and any other capabilities and habits acquired by man as a member of society'*.[16] This is significantly different from the use of the term in the two cultures debate discussed in the last chapter. When Leavis, Snow, Arnold, and T.H. Huxley used the term it often carried judgemental overtones, indicating something of value (though Snow's use of it was often close to that cited above). It implicitly denoted 'high' culture; so for Leavis, and perhaps Arnold, science is not cultural in much the same way as popular literature is not really 'cultural'. Snow and Huxley were fighting to get science accepted as something of equal value to literature, and by deriding Snow's ability as a novelist Leavis was denying him the authority to judge what really constituted high culture.

The second source which informs the definition of culture used here is the body of criticism – some of which was cited above[17] – that sees culture as being comprised of various discourses. This view of culture therefore leads us to see literature and science acting as streams of discourse feeding into, and fed by, the rest of the culture. Hence the interactions between literature and science

---

[16]   Edward B. Tyler, quoted in John Friedl, *Cultural Anthropology* (New York: Harper's College Press, 1976), p. 41. Friedl's italics.

[17]   See notes 4–7, and the texts to which they refer.

take place on a general cultural level. This is self-evident in the case of literature which must always, by definition, be cultural. It is not so self-evident for science, however, because science carries with it a strong association with truth and objectivity that makes the truths which it reveals appear universal, unbounded by temporal and geographical boundaries.

While the debate about the extent to which science can speak transcendent truths is important, as indicated earlier it is also a debate in which the contributions of literary critics can hardly carry authority, and so by necessity it is one from which this study must withhold. However, what can be said with certainty is that science has a very definite cultural side to it, whether or not it also exists on another ethereal plane, apart from the influence of more local cultural trends. There are a whole series of cultural meanings attached to the term 'science', and to related terms, and these meanings inevitably get entangled with non-scientific discourses, like literature and art, in webs of mutual influence.

This 'cultural science', to use the terminology cited earlier, can be thought of as a series of discourses flowing through the culture, and so it is with these that the following case studies engage. Although 'discourse' is a commonly-used term, it is sometimes deployed rather vaguely, so a definition of what is meant by its use in this study, where it has three main interwoven characteristics, and an explanation of how it differs from 'narrative', may be useful here.[18]

Firstly, discourse implies a manifestation of power as a consequence of its deployment (perhaps, for instance, as a result of a claim to truth within a particular discourse). Secondly, it operates as a sort of unspoken narrative, a story which is taken to be so fundamental as generally to pass unchallenged when it is invoked by a specific narrative. Thirdly, and importantly, it makes other narratives possible (this is perhaps where its power lies) because it embodies all those assumptions which are fundamental for the working of those narratives.

The difference between narrative and discourse might be defined as the difference between a specific text and the assumptions which it is necessary to make in order for that text to have meaning. We might go further and suggest that narrative is what is spoken, and discourse is what remains largely unspoken. Although this distinction is not absolute – there is certainly a sense in which discourses can be spoken – it is useful, because it gives us a way of thinking about how the meaning we ascribe to texts is produced by the cultural concerns which underlie them.

---

[18]   Jeremy Hawthorne gives an overview of the many different ways in which 'discourse' has been employed. Jeremy Hawthorne, *A Concise Glossary of Contemporary Literary Theory* (London: Edward Arnold, 1992), pp. 46–9.

Another way of conceiving of the difference between narrative and discourse in a book is to imagine the narrative as a horizontal line which represents the sequence of words the reader encounters in reading the book. The various discourses which underpin that book can then be thought of as a series of vertical lines that intersect the narrative at numerous points, informing the meaning the reader extracts from the book. This meaning will, of course, vary from reader to reader, but it is reasonable to identify certain discourses as culturally favoured, and therefore more likely to be shared by most readers.[19]

So science is described as a discourse in this book, because it is a potent part of our culture, giving meaning to a large number of narratives. Of course, there is a danger of reifying the notion of discourse when we start to speak of it in these terms. It is therefore important to make the obvious point that discourse is not anything which exists 'out there' in any physical sense – it is, instead, a model which gives us a useful way of schematising the influence of various cultural trends. A discourse, as far as we can define it, is a story which is crucial to the systems of meaning to which our culture subscribes. It is not pre-existent, and although it makes individual narratives understandable, and is therefore key in making them possible, it is also constituted by those narratives. Discourses are, as a result of this property, open to change – a narrative might draw upon a discourse but it will also, as soon as it is read, become one of those narratives which make up the discourse, and may contribute to how that discourse is understood in the future.

The model of culture that is being proposed, then, is one that is radically different to that discussed in earlier incarnations of the two cultures debate. Rather than seeing literature and science as separate territories, it is assumed that there are numerous links between them. Although these links might not be direct (there may be no single, simple connection between a scientific idea and literature), a series of discourses flow through the culture, connecting different sites, albeit often by long and winding routes. Moreover, at different sites, discourses may appear in slightly different forms.

Rather than imagining a simple division of the culture into two halves, then, as depicted on page 21, the new perception of culture entails the construction of a much more complicated image. This image needs to acknowledge multiple connections between various sites in webs of mutual influence (each site representing an idea, or an incarnation of knowledge or of cultural values in a book or some other media). One way of thinking of it might be as a series of islands, connected by the various currents that flow between them, but the image must also give a sense of dynamic change. We must,

---

[19]   This conception of the reading experience is similar to that invoked by Roland Barthes in *S/Z*. Roland Barthes, *S/Z*, trans. Richard Miller (1970; London: Jonathan Cape, 1975).

therefore, also think of these islands as constantly shape-shifting as they are both eroded by the currents that connect them, and built up by the sediment that is carried between them. Moreover, the currents must be imagined as criss-crossing each other in a latticework of influences between the various islands.[20]

While this image is, of course, highly artificial, it does provide a useful contrast with the relative simplicity of the two cultures model described in the last chapter, and lets us think of the relationship between literature and cultural science in a way that acknowledges the existence of numerous currents connecting them. Professional science stands, in this model, as an archipelago of islands slightly apart from the rest (though not completely disconnected as it is in the two cultures model). The connection between this archipelago and the broad culture will vary according to how the truth value of professional science is seen. Three main variations can be identified.

The first possibility is that the development of science is entirely separate from the rest of the culture, speaking the truth and fed only by the internal logic of the development of ideas, each building on those which came before it. The currents that connect it to the rest of the culture flow in only one direction, manifesting themselves in the islands to which they are connected as cultural science, in terms of the popularisation of scientific ideas and in various other cultural effects, precipitated by, for instance, technological developments that are dependent on scientific understanding, and literary responses to scientific ideas. Nature, in this view, is a separate archipelago of islands, knowledge of which feeds the professional science archipelago, which in turn pumps ideas into the rest of the culture.

The second possibility is that currents flow in both directions between professional science and the rest of the culture, but that most still flow from science to other islands, rather than vice versa. This would be a way of conceiving of science as speaking the truth, whilst acknowledging that the particular truths it is able to speak at any one time are limited by (in addition to the restrictions of disciplinary development at that time) cultural factors like the vagaries of government and private funding and the broader cultural climate. So, for instance, funding might prioritise scientific research that has potential spin-offs in terms of weapons technology in time of war; or a culture which is dominated by a certain ideology may produce scientific research which works within the parameters of that ideology. A range of cultural influences would shape the sort of science that we have at any given time, but that science would still be articulating the truth. As with the first possibility, nature still directs

---

[20]   This is a more fluid version of the 'archipelago of chaos', an image invoked by N. Katherine Hayles to explain the development of similar ideas about chaos at different cultural sites. N. Katherine Hayles, *Chaos Bound: Orderly Disorder in Contemporary Literature and Science* (Ithaca: Cornell University Press, 1990), p. 3.

professional scientific understanding, but those aspects of it to which we have access are partially determined by cultural factors.

The third possibility is that currents flow freely in both directions, and that the archipelago that constitutes professional science is as dependent as everything else on the sediment from other cultural sites. This is a view of science as just discourse, and in extreme versions nature almost disappears entirely as a shaping influence upon professional science (indeed, the distinction between professional and cultural science is erased in this view – all science is entirely cultural). Science is not an archipelago of knowledge that is discovered, in this perspective, so much as invented. It is this view of science to which Sokal and Bricmont object in *Intellectual Impostures*.

It has already been indicated that choosing between these different versions of professional science is not appropriate for anyone who does not have a scientific training, with the consequence that it is more appropriate to concentrate on cultural science. As long as there are ways in which science does act as a cultural discourse, it is not necessary to broach the question of whether it acts in other ways as well.

It would, however, be disingenuous to duck entirely the question of science's truth status. Given the current climate, any discussion of science as discourse is liable to be taken as an attack on the integrity of scientific claims to speak the truth. As this book is distanced from such a position (though it acknowledges that the deployment of truth claims may never be an innocent enterprise), it is therefore appropriate to declare an opinion. It should be noted, however, that the methodology described in this chapter, and the case studies that follow in subsequent chapters, are not dependent on the acceptance or otherwise of this opinion. The analysis of science as a part of the culture holds true as long as one accepts that ideas from science enter into and participate in the wider culture; obviously, if you believe that science is just discourse, then the ramifications of the studies are greatly increased, but this is an addition to – not a refutation of – the more cautious position adopted by this book.

The concept of 'truth' evokes highly emotive responses in the humanities, and nowhere more so than in discussions that seek to link the arts and the sciences. Claims to speak the truth are often linked – and frequently with good reason – to discourses of mastery, and it is often pointed out that one person's self-evident truth is actually highly provisional, and dependent upon the social and historical position from which they speak. For instance, postcolonial theory reminds us that a dominant culture may imperialistically situate itself at the centre, marginalising other cultures and denying them a voice.[21]

---

[21]   Steven Connor summarises the postcolonial perspective usefully: 'In terms of the imperialism of representation, this domination of universal narrative may bring about the

However, this immediately raises the problem of legitimation: how, once we accept that we are ourselves socially and historically situated, can we ground what we say? How can we claim to speak the truth? Moreover, how can we even ground our statement that we are all socially and historically situated?

One of Sokal and Bricmont's key objections to 'postmodern philosophers' abuse of science', as they put it in the subtitle of their book, is that science gets dragged into these sorts of debates by the way in which it is approached in the humanities. It is discussed as a discourse, and because it is unfashionable to treat discourse as speaking the truth, science is approached with no regard for its differences to other discourses. It is seen as just one more opinion about the world, neither more nor less verifiable than any other. Sokal and Bricmont argue that the sort of radical relativism that this leads to is characteristic of postmodern philosophy.

A detailed response to these issues will be made in chapter 6, which concentrates upon the issue of postmodernism, focusing a definition of it through the case studies of chapters 3, 4 and 5. However, it will be useful to outline now some of the points that will be there made in more detail.

One of the key contentions in this book is that Sokal and Bricmont's characterisation of postmodernism is insufficiently simplistic, even though their exposure of the misconstrual and inappropriate use of science is chastening and productive. Postmodernism, as far as it can be described as a philosophical position, is indeed, as they claim, antifoundationalist. One of the things postmodernist approaches seek to do is interrogate the assumptions on which our understanding of the world rests. However, using this radical questioning of the foundations of our knowledge to identify and think about some of the leaps of faith our knowledge requires, and using it to construct a viable approach to the world, are two entirely different things.

The former outcome, the identification of the leaps of faith our knowledge entails, is a product of many discourses of postmodernism, as chapter 6 argues; however, fewer of these discourses necessarily provoke the latter position by claiming that radical antifoundationalism offers a practical way in which to live our lives. Rather than adopting an extreme relativism, the lesson postmodernism surely should teach is 'provisionalism'. This neologism is a useful way of balancing self-awareness with practicality. If nothing can ever be absolutely proven, there is a danger of lapsing into inaction and, more

---

projection from the 'civilizing' imperial centres of fetishized images of Africa, the 'Orient', Latin America, etc. as civilization's Other, in ways that simultaneously bring these regions into being for Europe, fulfil its need for psychological and political centring, and silence any attempts at self-representation by these people and their post-colonial descendants'. Steven Connor, *Postmodernist Culture: An Introduction to Theories of the Contemporary* (Oxford: Basil Blackwell, 1989), p. 232.

ominously, giving equal credence to every point of view in a relativistic free-for-all – fine if one wants to demonstrate the socially provisional nature of patriarchal or racist philosophies, but of less use when one wishes to assert non-patriarchal or non-racist positions. It is an obvious – perhaps even a clichéd – example, but it is important to point out that if one believes the evidence points toward the existence of the Holocaust in the Second World War, it is insufficient merely to say that all history is fabrication, and dependent on eyewitness accounts, documentary evidence, and various means of telling stories that are not ultimately verifiable.

Pushed to an extreme this is true – there is an insane and chilling logic to revisionist accounts of history in their rejection of overwhelming evidence as being either fabricated or misinterpreted. However, to say that something is untrue because it cannot be proven, is to become a victim of a dangerous logical misconception: saying something is *not* true is as much a positive assertion about the nature of reality as saying something *is* true. Given the evidence, the most economical explanation of numerous eye-witness accounts and personal testimonies is not that there was a conspiracy of fabrication, but that a National Socialist regime attempted to enact a genocide.

A similar point might be made in relation to science. Jean-François Lyotard is right to argue that a justification of science often rests on 'grand narratives' of knowledge and emancipation, and that these narrative knowledges (more scientific knowledge is better; more scientific knowledge leads to freedom) cannot themselves be absolutely legitimated by scientific discourse. However, this sort of perspective on science does not in any sense 'disprove' science, although it might make us aware of the rather vague way in which we try to justify its value, and allow us to identify the narrative strategies that surround the deployment of scientific knowledge. (This deployment may, of course, be far from innocent).

Moreover, to show that science cannot justify the assertions it makes beyond any level of doubt at all, is not necessarily a dramatic insight which undermines our trust in scientific knowledge. Our senses are liable to deceive us, and therefore all knowledge is open to doubt. An appropriate response to this is not to say that nothing is true, but to work with a provisional notion of knowledge. Rather than encouraging us to stick unflinchingly to our view of the world as absolute truth, such a position asks instead that we construct a model of the world which is consistent with occurrences thus far (or, in areas of doubt, that we hold in mind a few alternative explanations), and that we be prepared to change it should future events contradict the basis of that model.

This sort of approach is hardly at odds with scientific methods, which have allowed previous ideas to be overturned in the interests of better explanations. Indeed, this sort of perspective even allies quite neatly with

Thomas S. Kuhn's famous argument that science proceeds through a series of paradigm shifts, altering its world view in a revolutionary way when data ceases to fit established outlooks. However, it does not fit with an extremist version of the Kuhnian view of development via paradigm shift, which makes no distinction between the truth value of different paradigms. By definition, one paradigm is ditched because it does not explain things as well as subsequent paradigms and, though there may be reversions to old, discarded ideas, it will almost always be because they are found to explain things better or more fully – the general direction will, therefore, be toward more and more accurate views of the world. One does not, of course, have to believe that everything will ultimately be explained at some point in the future – that a paradigm will be found which exactly matches reality – and nor does one have to believe that every paradigm shift is always an advance on the preceding world view, nor that cultural factors are unable to influence the preference for different paradigms.

This brings us back to the vexed issue of truth. The suspicion of truth, where it does occur, in the humanities, is a suspicion of truth in a transcendent sense; a wariness that claims to truth might also be claims to a capitalised Truth. To assert the true does not, however, mean that one believes one's view of the world to be divinely preordained and therefore beyond question; it might, and should, merely mean that it is probably right, but is also open to refutation and revision. Nor does asserting the true preclude other points of view; defending and arguing the case for competing truths is a means of establishing which carries the greater probability, or – perhaps more frequently in the humanities – establishing the assumptions that are necessary for each truth to be accepted. Of course, one can go into infinite regress – how, after all, can the probability of competing views of history be quantified, and how can we ground the very concept of probability? – but it is a mistake to think that this is a profound insight. It is, perhaps, important to accept the validity of this foundational question – this assumption we make in order to speak – and periodically to return to it, but should one arrive at the belief that it undermines the validity of the whole concept of knowledge, then on grounds of integrity one really ought also to question rigorously the whole concept of education, and the role one plays in the perpetuation of that system.

This refusal to acquiesce to relativism is one aspect of Sokal and Bricmont's project; however, as will be made clear in chapter 6, postmodernist discourses are not necessarily relativist in an extreme way. This book argues that they are, rather, provisionalist.

What all this means for literature–science criticism is that it is reasonable, even necessary, if one's subject is culture, to consider science's role in that culture. This does not, though, mean that one sees science as a discourse that is indistinguishable from others; merely that one is suspending judgement on particular claims to truth within the sciences (unless one has the credentials to speak of them), or making an argument that is provisional upon certain declared authorities within the sciences (if one declares the authority cited, then one is acknowledging that one's argument is provisional upon that particular point of view).

This is all rather abstract at the moment, so a sensible next move is to identify the different subjects with which literature–science critics might reasonably engage, and the methods they might use. This identification is therefore a statement of both the possibilities and the limits of literature–science criticism. It is a starting point that is also open to interrogation and extension.

Literature–Science Criticism: Avenues for Research (Methods and Topics)

i) The Two Cultures Debate

All those texts, lectures and other contributions to the debate about literature and science – just a few of which were discussed above – themselves constitute a viable and fruitful topic of study. They are important because they explicitly address definitions of literature and science, the purposes and methodologies of the two subjects, and our sense of how the culture, as a whole, is constituted.

The issue of definition is important because when, as so frequently, literature and science are placed in opposition to one another, they may be defined not in terms of their intrinsic essences, but by the way in which they differ from one another (although this is not usually the sole source of definition). For instance, as the discussion of I.A. Richards in chapter 1 showed, when his work is read carefully it becomes apparent that his definition of literary study is to some extent dependent on the role he sees it to fulfil in contrast to science. This definition itself dictates method, and a sense of culture being split in two between the arts and the sciences.

Although this particular area of study hardly offers a radical bridging of the divide between the arts and the sciences, it is an important context for literature–science criticism. The extent to which the two cultures model is accepted or rejected dictates aims, methods and outcomes for the literature–science critic. For instance, George Levine's book, *One Culture*, begs, with its very title, that it be distanced from the Snow–Leavis debate, while the considered introduction makes clear that a rejection of two cultures does not mean an erasure of all differences between literature and science.[22] There is, as this example testifies, much to be gained by trying to formulate exactly how we see literature and science to be related, and how we see them to be distinguished from one another. This sort of approach allows for the formulation of models of the culture which can then be tested against experience.

ii) The Influence of Science and Technology on Writers

This is the most obvious area of interest for the literature–science critic, and involves perhaps the simplest form of connection between the two areas: a direct influence from science to literature. Technology is also included as a possible influence, because although it is conceptually distinct from science (one is about artefacts; the other is about a mode of thought and investigation), the two are linked in the popular imagination, and as there is a case for seeing certain developments in recent technology to be dependent upon scientific advance, writers may themselves make a link between the two.

The writer may or may not be conscious of this influence. For instance, a work of literature may well result partially from a writer's deliberate investigation or exploration of a scientific idea that interests him or her. That idea may be presented for its own sake, or deployed as a metaphor for a broader purpose. Some branches of science fiction – but by no means all – are conspicuously dependent on such influences (and they often include extrapolations from them), but this sort of influence is by no means limited to science fiction.

Conversely, a writer may be the product of a background which makes certain assumptions about the world that are the result of scientific or technological influences of which the writer is only partially aware, or even completely unaware. Nevertheless, this 'background' knowledge is an important determining factor upon the eventual shape of the work of literature.

These sorts of influences do not have to be 'pure'. The ideas from science and technology may be mixed with other contemporary currents (Social Darwinism would be an example of a mix – in this case a rather unhealthy one – between science and other factors). Neither is there any reason why the science should, in its passage to a literary incarnation, stay true to its source: science may be distorted as it is popularised or otherwise disseminated, and the writer may in any case misunderstand the science. It is unlikely to be the task of the literature–science critic to sort out any such misapprehension, because a list of ticks and crosses against the writer's scientific references is unlikely to be of

---

[22]   George Levine, ed., *One Culture: Essays in Science and Literature* (University of Wisconsin Press, 1987).

much interest, and a critic with a literary background may in any case be unqualified for such a task. Certainly, though, the form in which the science is presented is of interest, and a particular 'take' on a scientific idea may well be significant. The case study in chapter 5 provides such an example, where Kurt Vonnegut's view of evolution is central to the presentation of the meaning of human life in *Galapagos*.

iii) The Representation of Science, Scientists and Technology in Literature

This is closely allied to the last category, and there is a manifest overlap between the two. It is distinguished from the previous one, however, in encapsulating a more general presentation of science within literature. There may be no traceable influence from a specific scientific site to the work of literature, but science is present in a general sense. To use the terminology coined earlier in this chapter, whereas some sort of movement of an idea from professional science to cultural science is involved in category (ii), category (iii) is almost entirely associated with cultural science. It is to do with the general cultural perception of science, to which the work of literature responds and contributes.

So, for instance, there may be a general feeling about science (a stereotypical one would be an association between it and technological mastery) that finds no specific grounding in scientific developments. A similar effect may be the result of the presentation of a scientist in literature – say as a character – where some of the qualities of that character are transferred, by association, to science itself.

An investigation of this allows a general consideration of the status science holds within the culture. One could imagine, for instance, an interesting monograph on the characteristics attributed to scientists in works of fiction. It would be interesting to see whether such a study would find further evidence of a two cultures split, in terms of a generally hostile presentation of scientists, consistent with Mathew Arnold's and F.R. Leavis's perception of science; or whether scientists actually enjoy a more favourable literary presentation.

iv) Science Writing as a Genre of Literature

This is where literature–science criticism begins to push back the boundaries of criticism and open up new areas to literary analysis. Science writing offers an expansive, generally unexplored, vista for literary and cultural analysis.[23]

---

[23]   This vista is not entirely ignored. See, for instance, Murdo William McRae, *The Literature of Science: Perspectives on Popular Science Writing* (Athens: University of Georgia Press, 1993).

Although the adjective 'popular' frequently qualifies the term, it has been dropped here because it does not really add to our understanding of the genre, and can carry pejorative overtones. An alternative terminology was offered by a panel of contributors to the 1995 meeting of the Society for Literature and Science in Los Angeles, who suggested 'reflective science writing' as a term, defining it as 'writing by scientists for nonspecialists in prose styles that reveal recognizable "literary" qualities, differing in this way from the writing of scientists for other scientists'.[24] The definition is useful, and 'reflective' is an epithet which aims to counter the implication of superficiality in 'popular'. Again, though, the word 'reflective' is redundant when 'science writing' will suffice on its own, and also implies an easy distinction between low and high culture which is disabling in a literary critical climate which favours the study of literatures from beyond the traditional canon.

There is certainly a growing interest in the serious study of science writing. 1995 saw the publication of a major anthology of science writing, the excellent *Faber Book of Science*, edited by John Carey, Merton Professor of English Literature at Oxford University. In his introduction Carey argues that some scientists 'have created a new kind of late twentieth-century literature, which demands to be recognised as a separate genre, distinct from the old literary forms, and conveying pleasures and triumphs quite distinct from theirs'.[25]

Once we accept that this is a burgeoning genre of literature, and that a failure to scrutinise it will leave our knowledge of literary history incomplete, we are faced with a number of exciting and challenging critical choices. Although these choices are similar to those faced by traditional literary study, they are given an unusual accent by the nature of science writing. To list all these decisions would deflect this chapter from its attempt to give an overview of a new model of culture, but two of the most important ones follow.

Firstly, what selection criteria might we use to construct a canon of science writing? Although we may be unhappy with the notion of a canon, we need to narrow our area of study to a manageable size, however provisionally. Do we select writing which reflects the history of science? (but if so, might we just end up trying to give a history of a subject we are not really qualified to talk about?); do we select the best writing? (looking for literary qualities might

---

[24]   Sidney Perkowitz, et al., 'The Art of Reflective Science Writing' (unpublished programme for the 1995 conference of the Society for Literature and Science). Contributors to the panel were Sidney Perkowitz, from the Department of Physics at Emory University, Atlanta, Peter Brown, editor of *The Sciences*, and K.C. Cole, science writer for the *Los Angeles Times*.

[25]   John Carey, introduction, *The Faber Book of Science*, ed. Carey (London: Faber, 1995), p. xiv. It should be noted that Carey also includes some earlier science writing in this new literary genre.

be something we are well qualified to do, but modern criticism is rightly chary of the idea that it is possible to distinguish objectively between great and poor literature). It may be that the most productive critical choice will be to resist the production of a rigid canon, allowing texts to be selected for the purpose of specific research projects. While this sort of *ad hoc* approach runs the risk of neglecting, and ultimately forgetting, texts that deserve inclusion (and also the risk of focusing only on those texts which support particular agendas, whilst ignoring those that contradict them), it carries the benefit of a flexible, interrogative approach to the notion of what it is beneficial to study. At some point a canon would emerge, but it would at least be the product of a multitude of separate research projects undertaken by individual scholars.

Secondly, what are we actually going to 'do' with these texts? What is the purpose of studying them? One very important reason might simply be to appreciate the role that science plays in our culture and understand contemporary developments but, beyond the step of reading science writing, or rather more absurdly, cohorts of us copying Carey to produce our own anthologies of science writing, this purpose is not going to sustain us for very long. Yet to find something to 'do' to science writing, merely because we enjoy reading it and would like an excuse to study it, is hardly a satisfactory outcome. Fortunately, as this book hopes to demonstrate, there is a productive role to be played by the critic.

This role might be descriptive of the incursion of science into the rest of the culture, mapping its influences upon, for instance, works of literature. Alternatively, it might identify and consider the literary techniques employed in science writing, exploring the consequences of their deployment, or it might seek to analyse the language in which certain scientific ideas are caged. This sort of analysis begins to take us toward the next category of literature–science criticism.

v) Shared Metaphors and Discourses

This is the most common and the most interesting form that literature–science criticism currently takes, and it is in this form that there is the truest link between the two cultures. However, it is also the approach which is fraught with the most dangers, including the difficulty of identifying, and quantifying the importance of, discourses; the perils occasioned in separating those aspects of science writing that can be treated as discourse from the rest of science; and the danger of straying into areas beyond the expertise of literary critics and theorists.

It is the area of literature–science criticism in which it is most tempting, having made the decision to study science writing, to treat it as exactly equivalent to other forms of literature. However, this would be a mistake and, here again, the issue of truth comes to the fore. Once one sees that the discourses of science writing in, say, a given period are tantalisingly close to those apparent in other contemporary forms of literature, culture presents itself as a linking and determining factor. However, this link does not necessarily prove that science is entirely culturally determined: it could mean that science itself is merely partially determined by the cultural environment in which it exists; that presentations of science, but not science itself, are culturally determined; or that, while science speaks the truth, those aspects of the truth which it is able to speak are limited by the culture (because of constraints on funding, or the priority given to certain forms of research by dominant cultural concerns). Indeed, if in defiance of this one holds an extreme relativist position, one also needs to show how particular scientific insights – and predictive claims – could be wrong given a different cultural context.

Again, the crucial conceptual leap to make is the distinction between professional and cultural science. Although the issue of truth is extremely important, getting dragged into debates about science's truth value without the requisite expertise to contest the issue from within, can seriously impede a productive literature–science criticism. By limiting ourselves to science's manifest cultural presence, we may lose the right to speak of some aspects of science's relation to the natural world (such a right is, in any case, only gained by a usurpation as fundamentally characteristic of a two cultures disciplinary power struggle as any of Snow's and Leavis's comments), but our energies are productively concentrated on some extremely important fields of study. Science's function within the culture continues to grow, and an understanding of this inevitably enhances our understanding of the culture as a whole.

The model of culture which sees cultural artefacts as the product of (at least partially) a series of discourses, linking different sites, gives us a way of understanding the close integration between cultural science, literature, and other aspects of the culture. It is this model which underpins the studies in chapters 3, 4 and 5. Chapter 3, for instance, provides a case in point of the value of distinguishing professional from cultural science. It is, in many ways, a highly conventional piece of literature–science criticism, taking a trendy science – chaos theory – and linking the disruption of a straightforward order–chaos binary division in journalistic accounts of the science, with a similar disruption in a representative postmodern text, Thomas Pynchon's *Gravity's Rainbow*. In *Intellectual Impostures*, Sokal and Bricmont devote a whole chapter to the popularity of chaos theory with literature–science critics, and their abuse of it.[26]

---

[26] Sokal and Bricmont, 'Intermezzo: Chaos Theory and 'Postmodern Science', *Intellectual Impostures*, pp. 125–36.

However, by distinguishing professional from cultural science most of Sokal and Bricmont's objections can be short-circuited. Particularly important objections to the popular use of chaos theory by literary critics include the following: the reliance on journalistic and popular accounts instead of actual scientific texts; a misapprehension of the importance of chaos theory to contemporary science and a consequent tendency to see it as a revolutionary development that has transformed science as a whole; and the use of terms with a specific technical meaning ('chaos', 'nonlinear', and so on) as though they are equivalent to their popular meanings. However, if one admits that a discussion of chaos theory by literary critics is really a discussion of the way in which chaos theory is represented (cultural science), rather than of chaos theory itself (professional science), then these objections can be met and dealt with.

Firstly, if one is trying to gauge the cultural impact of a particular aspect of science, then the place to look is not within science itself, but in popular representations of that science within the culture (in other words, journalism and science writing). Secondly, however limited the impact of chaos theory upon science as a whole has turned out to be, in one piece of science writing after another it has been represented as revolutionary (the most prominent example being that found in James Gleick's *Chaos: Making a New Science*, which is discussed in chapter 3). Such a presentation does not prove that it is in fact revolutionary for science, but it does demonstrate a desire to see certain aspects of it as revolutionary, and this might well tell us something about our desire for the new (indeed, the more conservative chaos theory really is, the more important its misrepresentation as radical turns out to be, because more is being done to twist it into something it is not). The desire for chaos theory to be truly revolutionary may tell us something very significant about the attempt in contemporary culture to reject the past. Finally, terms like 'chaos', which carry so many meanings, echo into the culture precisely because of the potency they already carry – the significance which is attached to something like 'chaos' theory may then be arbitrary to the extent that it is the product of coincidence or a scientist's flair for creating catchy neologisms, but even so, that aspect of science becomes culturally significant (even if it is not, in the long term, particularly significant for professional science).

In all these instances, reasonable objections to the use of chaos theory can be rendered irrelevant by being clear about exactly what is being discussed: not chaos theory *per se*, but the representation of chaos theory within the culture. Of course, the argument that results might well be objected to on other grounds (for instance, that chaos theory is not even culturally significant), but while such an objection may very reasonably be used to refute a specific argument, it does not in any way constitute a rejection of the conceptual grounds on which this sort of literature–science criticism is based. Again, one cedes ground, resisting the temptation to launch an incursion into territory in which scientists have the local knowledge to provide much better guides, in order to map more completely that territory – culture – with which one is more familiar.

Such an approach may proceed by looking, for example, for evidence of a linking discourse in the metaphors shared by literature and science writing. It may also employ some of those techniques embraced by the categories discussed above, seeking for those scientific ideas which have influenced writers, looking at the representation of science in literature, and looking at the literary techniques employed in science writing to see how these formal characteristics influence the reception of the content. Finally, it may employ the method discussed in the following subsection.

vi) The Responses of Literature and Science to Common Topics

Very closely linked to the above is another avenue for research: those areas, numerous in number, where the concerns of literature and science overlap. These areas might be thought of in a general sense – for instance, questions about who we are and where we come from – or in a more specific way – for example, the roles played by environment and heredity in making us who we are.

These areas again provide a fertile focus for research and, again, to ignore science's role in forming our perception of them is to distort significantly our understanding of the culture. The feeding of scientific ideas – however much they may get distorted – into the culture, and the place of science within that culture, cannot be ignored in an age when so many advances in our understanding have come from science. A well-worn but highly pertinent example is the influence of evolutionary theory, not only on Victorian culture following the publication of Charles Darwin's *The Origin of Species*, but also on our contemporary perceptions of human identity. Chapter 5 discusses one small aspect of these contemporary perceptions, and their relation to ideas of both development over time, and human identity.

vii) Relations Between Literary Theory and Science

This is rather different to the preceding categories, being concerned with literary theory rather than literature itself. It involves a consideration of the different modes of description, and different methodological procedures, within literary and scientific disciplines.

One focus might be the claim to speak scientifically in certain branches of literary theory. This is apparent, for example, in the claim embedded in some structuralist theory that it is a 'science' of literature, and the implication in psychoanalytic criticism that a certain understanding of the human mind gives us a means of appreciating the formative influences upon literature. This focus raises two particular questions: are these things really scientific? (and what do we mean by the term?), and what is the purpose of claiming a scientific foundation? (is it a claim to speak the truth?).

A more interesting focus, however, is to look actively within science for ideas which may be pertinent to our understanding of literature. This could involve a number of areas, but perhaps two of the most important are those which concern the human mind and language. The former, for instance, is surely relevant to our understanding of the creation and reception of literature. Sigmund Freud and Jacques Lacan, among others, have wielded tremendous influence in literary studies, but it is surely a pressing concern to ask whether their ideas are verifiable, whether there are alternative conceptions of the human mind, and whether they might have been superseded.

The latter, where a scientific approach has been brought to bear upon the study of language, might be used to interrogate some of the assumptions we make in literary studies about how language works. For example, although the structuralist conception of language as a system of signs divorced from, and arbitrarily dividing up, that which it signifies, has proven very useful and continues to wield influence in poststructuralist discourse, there are alternative means of understanding language. To give just one example, Stephen Pinker, in *The Language Instinct*, contests the argument which often follows from structuralism, and is dominant in the humanities, that language and culture are entirely responsible for constructing our sense of reality. In summarising the view to which he is opposed, he offers an example that will be familiar to anyone who has taught Ferdinand de Saussure's theory of linguistics to undergraduates:

> physicists tell us that wavelength is a continuous dimension with nothing delineating red, yellow, green, blue, and so on. Languages differ in their inventory of color words: Latin lacks generic 'gray' and 'brown'; Navajo collapses blue and green into one word ... You can fill in the rest of the argument. It is language that puts the frets in the spectrum.[27]

The problem with this argument, Pinker claims, is that it generalises out from an incomplete understanding of the ways in which colour-recognition works.

---

[27] Stephen Pinker, *The Language Instinct: The New Science of Language and Mind* (1994; London: Penguin, 1995), p. 62.

Light might well exist in a continuous wavelength, but this is not how the eyes interpret it – there is a biological imperative that overrides most cultural differences:

> Eyes do not register wavelength the way a thermometer registers temperature. They contain three kinds of cones, each with a different pigment, and the cones are wired to neurons in a way that makes the neurons respond best to red patches against a green background or vice versa ... No matter how influential a language might be, it would seem preposterous to a physiologist that it could reach down into the retina and rewire the ganglion cells.[28]

If Pinker is right then there are some important consequences: we may still be able to maintain that language structures some aspects of thought (and, more broadly, that the languages of different cultures produce different conceptions of reality), but we would have to concede that in other cases language reflects reality, or at least reflects a perception of reality by the human brain which transcends cultural differences.

A literary theoretical perspective on this may, initially, be one of suspicion: is this not just another discourse of mastery, masquerading as the truth to impose a culturally-specific point of view on others? However, two defences might be raised to this objection. Firstly, if Pinker is wrong, then cultures should divide up the world in radically different ways, and we should be able to demonstrate this. Secondly, to make a claim about truth (about how the world is constituted) is not to make a claim about how the world should be (how it ought to be constituted).

Certainly a serious consideration of the potential value of scientific insights could prove to be immensely productive for our understanding of the production and reception of language and literature, and could, at the very least, help us to critique the assumptions with which we start. It may well be that nothing will change as a result of such an interrogation, but the arguments with which we defend our position will be all the more robust for passing such a test.

This sort of approach is probably the least used of the avenues of literature–science criticism, and this may result partly from some of the dangers that lurk (if you will excuse the extended metaphor) in dark alleys adjoining the avenue. One risk is that such a search for scientifically valuable insights involves crossing the boundary, maintained as far as possible in this book, between cultural and professional science. If a particular scientific point of view is going to be taken to inform an area of literary criticism, there is the problem of establishing the veracity of that point of view over another. Such

---

[28]   Pinker, p. 62.

leaps of faith are dangerous, but it might be asked whether it is not just as dangerous to continue to trust in, for instance, older conceptions of the human mind.

Another risk is the misapplication of ideas from science, taking a productive-sounding theory and using it in a situation to which it does not apply. This is, indeed, another of Sokal and Bricmont's objections to the use of chaos theory in the humanities, and it is certainly important to be clear about why a particular scientific idea is appropriate in regard to the study of literature. As a guiding rule, it will be appropriate if it relates to literature in more than metaphorical ways.[29] For instance, if Stephen Pinker's ideas about language, cited above, are right, they are relevant to our study of literature because they tell us something concrete about how language relates to reality and to the mind – they are not just ideas which find a handy reflection in our understanding of literature.

Despite its importance, this category of literature–science criticism is not one which is employed to a great degree in this book, partly because it may involve rethinking literary study itself on a broad scale. Such an approach would, therefore, run the risk of taking the book away from its theoretical orientation, which is firmly grounded in the contemporary literary critical paradigm.

However, the measure of the success of literature–science criticism, and of the genuine commitment of critics to the frequently-expounded doctrine of 'one culture', may well prove to be the extent to which literary criticism is itself transformed by science. If there really is a genuine dialogue between literature and science, then the outcome is unlikely to be limited to the cultural specificity of science (or aspects of the representation of science), and should extend to an acceptance of the relevance of scientific insights both to our view of the world, and to our practice (where appropriate) of literary criticism. It is hardly likely, when the avenues between literature and science are opened up, that it will turn out that everyone on one side of the great divide was wrong, and everyone on the other side was right; and so to insist, from the outset, that science's claim to speak the truth is the result of elaborate self-deception, is a view that is blinkered in the extreme.

Perhaps it is this – an apparently arrogant assumption, by non-scientists, that scientists just do not appreciate the cultural specificity of their work – that has resulted in the current hostility apparent in the science wars. Of course, much (perhaps most) literature–science criticism does not make this assumption at all, but it is as well to be aware that a claim to abolish the two

---

[29]　Note that this insistence on a more than metaphorical connection is specific to this category of literature–science criticism, and would be entirely inappropriate in relation to, for example, category (v) where metaphors are at the heart of the connection between the two realms.

cultures divide should not be used as a Trojan horse to sneak in an argument which is really about proving the inferiority of scientific understanding compared to that of the humanities. It would be a different matter should it prove to be the case that one or the other modes of knowledge turns out to be plain wrong, but this is, on current evidence, a highly unlikely scenario.

These different categories of literature–science criticism offer, then, ways of thinking about the relationship between literature and science that take us beyond the rather simplistic assumption of the two cultures model that the two are entirely distinct. They do not, however, collapse the distinction between literature and science, turning science into just another type of discourse, no different from any other. The value of these sorts of critical approach can only be proven, in the end, by the results they produce. It is hoped that the following case studies will give a taste of some of the literary criticism that might flow from such approaches.

PART TWO

Practice

Chapter 3

Discourses of Knowledge: Chaotic Order

The opening chapters focused directly upon the framework which we use to structure our knowledge, contrasting a two cultures model, discussed in the first chapter, with a newer model, described in chapter 2, which enables us to think in a more sophisticated way about the relationship between literature and science. Although the latter model does not result – indeed, given fundamental differences between the arts and the sciences, could not result – in the absolute abolition of the distinction between literature and science, it does enable us to formulate crucial links between the two realms.

The three case studies, in this and the following two chapters, are designed to do two things. The first is to demonstrate some of the ways in which the methodologies identified in chapter 2 as being available to the literature–science critic, might work in practice. The second is to relate these aspects of contemporary literature and science to the broader postmodern culture. In each case study the identification of the literature and science with postmodernism comes through two main routes: an (explicit or implicit) identification of the present as a revolutionary moment, and – tied to this – a questioning of categories or concepts associated with the Enlightenment (frequently involving an interrogation of established binary oppositions). The issue of postmodernism is then picked up in greater detail in chapter 6, but it should be noted now that the identification of a contemporary postmodern discourse in the case studies does not mean that postmodernism is being championed here – that these case studies aim to be descriptive of postmodern culture does not imply an assertion of the primacy of that culture. Indeed, postmodernism is seen in this book as a posture – a gesture of defiance toward the past – and while this gesture links different facets of postmodern culture, there is no reason why it should have substance (and involve a real and effective revolution) in every instance.

In this chapter the postmodern posture is focused through the issue of knowledge. Certain contemporary discourses contest fundamental binary divisions between chaos and order, and global and local, striving to open up territory not explored by Enlightenment narratives. These contemporary discourses attempt to formulate new sorts of knowledge (though they do not necessarily succeed), opening up a middle ground between the binary distinctions identified above. The texts that are used in this chapter to illustrate this postmodern assault upon the past are Thomas Pynchon's *Gravity's Rainbow*, James Gleick's *Chaos: Making a New Science*, and Ilya Prigogine and Isabelle Stengers's *Order Out of Chaos*. Other presentations of chaos theory are also referred to (although they are not discussed in detail) in order to establish that the presentations of chaos theory under discussion are in many ways typical of the presentation of the science within the culture.

Gravity's Rainbow is a suitable novel for this study because it is overtly concerned with the issue of knowledge, and is also often cited as a key text of the postmodernist era. For instance, Edward Mendelson suggests that it is an 'encyclopedic narrative', one which attempts 'to render the full range of knowledge and beliefs of a national culture, while identifying the ideological perspectives from which that culture shapes and interprets its knowledge'.[1] This makes it a highly relevant novel to focus upon, because it is seen to articulate a new cultural identity.

Although the term 'postmodern' was not a critical commonplace when Mendelson was writing, the key features which he associates with Pynchon's text are those which came to be seen as central to postmodernity. These are a sense of a new international culture, transcending traditional geographical boundaries via innovations in high-speed communication technologies, and a concern with an economy which is grounded upon information, not material goods: 'Pynchon's international scope implies the existence of a new international culture, created by the technologies of instant communication and the economy of world markets ... The distinguishing feature of Pynchon's new internationalism is its substitution of data for goods'.[2]

Admittedly, there are problems with Mendelson's argument, especially in its reification of the notion of culture, and its implication that it throws up one, and only one, encyclopaedic narrative at moments of crisis, in some sort of deterministic fashion. This suggests that the narrative is produced directly by the culture, or by a writer mystically 'chosen' by the culture, rather than that it is something written by an author who is struggling with a sense of his or her culture's identity.

Nevertheless, Mendelson's argument is generally sound, and his contention that these encyclopaedic narratives 'appear near the beginning of a culture's or a nation's sense of its own separate existence',[3] and that they

---

[1]   Edward Mendelson, 'Gravity's Encyclopedia', *Mindful Pleasures: Essays on Thomas Pynchon*, eds George Levine and David Leverenz (Boston: Little, 1976), p. 162.
[2]   Mendelson, pp. 164–5. The importance of these new technologies, and of how they shape the way in which we see the world, will be a central concern of chapter 4.
[3]   Mendelson, p. 164.

originate in 'moments of hierarchical strain and cultural distress',[4] are extremely useful. They suggest that *Gravity's Rainbow* responds to a new cultural climate – which we would now label as postmodernist – and new definitions of knowledge.

Another reason for choosing Pynchon's novel is that it was published before the term 'chaos' was coined to describe corresponding developments in various sciences, and a decade before chaos theory began to penetrate the popular imagination. We therefore avoid the trap of finding analogies to chaos theory in *Gravity's Rainbow*, merely because they are self-consciously alluded to in the novel. Any parallels that we find will be indicative of a genuine shift in perception of the status of knowledge, not just the result of Pynchon self-consciously alluding to a contemporary science which he finds interesting. Therefore the main focus in this case study is (as in the others) on the fifth category of literature–science criticism ('shared metaphors and discourses') identified in the last chapter. This type of critical approach predominates because it is both the most interesting and the most controversial, but it should be noted that the other available methodologies are also used where appropriate.

Chaos theory is a good subject to place alongside *Gravity's Rainbow* because it is often presented with a revolutionary rhetoric that locates it in direct opposition to traditional science, and which carries with it many of the hallmarks of more conventional postmodern discourses. There are, of course, many ways in which chaos theory does not break with traditional science, and the dramatic revolution in scientific thought with which it is frequently associated does not seem to have materialised. This issue of the rather disappointing (or, depending on your point of view, rather relieving) mismatch between postmodernism's revolutionary claims and its actual effect, is central to the idea of postmodernism as a posture which is advocated by this book: postmodernism is an attitude, it is not necessarily a concrete effect.

The particular explanations of chaos theory chosen for this case study demonstrate the advantages of distinguishing carefully between cultural and professional science, and looking to presentations of science which are aimed at a general audience. For one thing, they inevitably reach a wider readership than more technical articles. Thus, while they may not be as important for the actual development of a science as scientific papers which are read by a small but expert community, they can be said to be more influential in terms of forming the public perception of that science. Whilst they are obviously themselves in debt, to a degree, to more technical scientific papers, it is reasonable to suggest that they contribute more directly to the discourse of science which runs through, and influences, our culture.

---

[4]   Mendelson, p. 174.

Gleick's book is one of the best selling and most influential of the presentations of chaos theory which line the popular science sections of book shops. Prigogine and Stengers's work is probably less well known. Nevertheless, it has been translated into twelve languages and, because it deals with a different aspect of chaos theory and employs markedly different rhetorical strategies from Gleick's work, it provides an important illustration of another route down which discussions about chaos theory can travel whilst remaining true to the central features of postmodern culture.

According to Katherine Hayles, the basic difference in the content of the two books is that despite many points of convergence, Gleick's mainly deals with work that finds order within systems which had seemed to be disordered, whereas Prigogine and Stengers's deals with systems which actually are disordered, but which spontaneously organise themselves into an ordered form.[5] The two also differ significantly in terms of style: Gleick's relies on popular cultural references and structures, whereas Prigogine and Stengers's adopts a much more philosophical tone, using chaos theory as a point of departure for musings upon the reconciliation of being with becoming.[6] Indeed, it is reasonable to suggest that much of the difference between the two works is consequent upon the roots of one, Gleick's, lying in American culture, and of the other, Prigogine and Stengers's, lying in the traditions of a European continental philosophy – characterised by references to the eclectic musings of historians of science and culture like Michel Serres, and different in degree from Gleick's work, much as the writing of Julia Kristeva and Hélène Cixous departs from the mainstream of Anglo-American feminist criticism.

Despite these very important differences, both enunciate a history of science that is commensurate with postmodern perspectives. In the process of simplifying and justifying chaos theory for a general and inexpert audience, they have a tendency to lay bare, and state explicitly, the prime assumptions that they make about the position of chaos in relation to previous scientific enterprises. The history they write is by no means proven, and it is certainly controversial, but it is also influential.

It is the idea of history that provides a starting point for this case study, and the first part of the study establishes the ways in which both the literature

---

[5]   For a more detailed explanation of these differences see N. Katherine Hayles, *Chaos Bound: Orderly Disorder in Contemporary Literature and Science* (Ithaca: Cornell University Press, 1990), pp. 9–11.

[6]   For definitions of 'being' and 'becoming' see my discussion of Prigogine and Stengers on page 84. Hayles comments, at the beginning of chapter 4 of *Chaos Bound*, that Prigogine and Stengers's work often extrapolates beyond what many chaos theorists would be willing to grant as legitimate conclusions, drawn from the data. This is ironic, given that popular science books are often condemned for failing to appreciate the limits of the subject when they are written by journalists like Gleick: Ilya Prigogine won the Nobel Prize in 1977 for his work on dissipative structures.

and the science postulate a 'revolutionary moment', when the old ways of knowing were replaced by the new ones. Because this results in a juxtaposition of opposed perspectives on knowledge (the Enlightenment or modern against the postmodern) it is sometimes represented as a point of crisis in our epistemologies. This is discussed through the disruption of binary oppositions of order–disorder and global–local.

The Revolutionary Moment: *Gravity's Rainbow* and Chaos Theory

> Our working hypothesis is that the status of knowledge is altered as societies enter what is known as the postindustrial age and cultures enter what is known as the postmodern age. This transition has been under way since at least the end of the 1950s.[7]

Although Jean-François Lyotard is a controversial figure, and his theories of postmodernity are far from being universally accepted, his influence on perceptions of postmodernism is undeniable. It is for this reason that he is cited here, and his identification of the starting point of postmodernism, apparent in the quotation, is certainly consistent with that apparent in most discussions of the shift from modern to postmodern. It requires two things of a postmodern discourse: that it register a shift in the status of knowledge, and that this shift be shown to take place in the second half of the twentieth century. Similarly, Katherine Hayles's *Chaos Bound*, probably the most comprehensive description of the rise of the importance of chaos theory in literature and science, describes postmodern culture as an evolving denaturing of experience during the twentieth century. A crucial moment comes with the Second World War, when the need to coordinate rapid troop movements across varied theatres of conflict in effect 'made information real'.[8] This, Hayles argues, along with other twentieth-century developments, led to the rise of postmodernity during the last half of the century.

Evidence that chaos theory is often written into a history of science that mirrors the concerns that predominate in postmodern histories – that it is situated in a revolutionary moment, overturning the assumptions of the

---

[7]   Jean-François Lyotard, *The Postmodern Condition: A Report on Knowledge*, trans. Geoff Bennington and Brian Massumi, Theory and History of Literature 10 (1979; Manchester University Press, 1986), p. 3.

[8]   Hayles, *Chaos Bound*, p. 269. Both Lyotard and Hayles are criticised by Sokal and Bricmont in *Intellectual Impostures* for misrepresenting science. Whilst this is of itself an important issue, it is a distraction from the central project in this chapter which is to focus on the representation of chaos theory in cultural – not professional – science. What is being analysed is not the significance or otherwise of chaos theory to science, but the discourse of chaos theory which runs through the culture.

Enlightenment – comes from a number of descriptions of the science. For instance, *The New Scientist Guide to Chaos* reprints a complete series of articles about chaos theory and its implications from the *New Scientist* magazine. In her introduction, the editor, Nina Hall, offers a brief four-page history of science leading up to the development of chaos theory, which equates it with the overturning of Enlightenment assumptions. After two initial paragraphs explaining the appeal of chaos theory, she states that scientists have always searched for the underlying laws which control the universe, offering Isaac Newton as a prime exponent of this, and describing how Pierre Simon de Laplace proposed an entirely deterministic view of the universe, based on Newtonian principles. Key Enlightenment figures are therefore associated with a particular sort of science.

In her next paragraph Hall describes a crisis in this viewpoint, precipitated by the challenge to strict determinism from quantum physics. She makes clear that although this constituted a crisis in the old world view, it did not serve to undermine it completely because it retained some semblance of the old ideas: 'Nevertheless, physicists have used quantum mechanics to construct a reasonably robust theoretical framework for describing the fundamental properties of matter and the forces at work in the Universe'.[9] Quantum physics is therefore characterised as an attack upon Newtonian assumptions, but one which leaves some of those assumptions intact.

Chaos theory is then introduced as a revolutionary moment (or, in the terminology used in this book, a postmodern science), interrogating the assumptions of modern, Newtonian science by completing the revolution begun by quantum physics: 'chaos is revealing fundamental limits to human knowledge in an uncomfortable way'.[10] By stressing the ubiquity of chaos theory in different disciplines, Hall then implies that chaos should not be seen as just another sub-discipline of science, but as a key development that takes science in general into new territory: chaos, she says, 'can be found in virtually every discipline from astronomy to population dynamics'.[11]

The same argument is repeated in Paul Davies's essay, which ends Hall's anthology, and which is partially reprinted in John Carey's *Faber Book of Science*. He, too, cites Newton and Laplace, and situates quantum physics and chaos theory as 'Two major developments of the 20th century' which have 'put paid to the idea of a clockwork universe'.[12] Again, quantum physics does

---

[9]   Nina Hall, Introduction, *The New Scientist Guide to Chaos*, ed. Hall (London: Penguin, 1992), p. 8.
[10]   Hall, p. 10.
[11]   Hall, p. 9.
[12]   Paul Davies, 'Is the Universe a Machine?', *The New Scientist Guide to Chaos*, ed. Hall (London: Penguin), p. 215. It should be noted that other presentations of this history of science sometimes include relativity theory, alongside quantum physics, as another example of

not quite break with Newtonianism, although it challenges it, because 'there remains a sense in which quantum mechanics is still a deterministic theory'.[13] It is chaos theory which, as in Hall's introduction, marks the crucial break – again, therefore, chaos theory is situated in the 'postmodern' moment in the development of science.

We must remind ourselves, at the risk of being repetitive, that what is being discussed here is cultural, not professional, science (although Davies is a professional scientist). This book is not concerned with the question of whether chaos theory actually is revolutionary in the way described above (this is an important question for scientists, not literary critics, to answer); it is interested, however, in the fact that there is a strong discourse of chaos theory which presents it as revolutionary, and does so in a way which ties it very clearly to more conventional postmodern discourses.

We find the pattern identified in Hall's book repeated in Gleick's *Chaos*, which may be responsible for spreading the doctrine of chaos theory more than any other single text. He, too, presents chaos as a completely new way of doing science, subtitling his book, '*Making a New Science*', and calling one chapter 'Revolution', describing chaos theory as a wide-ranging revolution of the kind described by Thomas Kuhn.[14] His prologue makes a similar point: 'With the coming of chaos, younger scientists believed they were seeing the beginnings of a course change for all of physics'.[15] The emphasis is on a break between old and new ways of doing science: 'Where chaos begins, classical science stops'.[16]

Significantly, this emphasis on the revolutionary nature of chaos theory is carried not only in the content of Gleick's book, but also through its style.[17] Three main rhetorical elements can be identified as contributing to the construction of chaos theory as a revolutionary phenomenon in Gleick's work: the presentation of the chaos theorists as Romantics, the presentation of them as frontiersmen, and the structure of the narrative in *Chaos*.

For instance, take the opening of Gleick's book. The first sentence of the prologue introduces an air of mystery, telling us that the police in Los Alamos, New Mexico, were briefly worried about the strange, nocturnal perambulations of a man in 1974. This, it turns out, was one of the pioneers of chaos theory,

---

an early twentieth-century development which began the questioning of Newtonian physics, culminating in chaos theory.

[13]   Davies, p. 215.
[14]   Thomas S. Kuhn, *The Structure of Scientific Revolutions*, 2nd edn, International Encyclopedia of Unified Science 2.2 (1962; University of Chicago Press, 1970).
[15]   James Gleick, *Chaos: Making a New Science* (1987; Middlesex: Penguin, 1988), p. 6.
[16]   Gleick, p. 3.
[17]   It will be noted here that I am switching briefly to the fourth category of literature–science criticism, 'science writing as a genre of literature', identified in chapter 2.

Mitchell Feigenbaum, whose hair was 'a ragged mane, sweeping back from his wide brow in the style of busts of German composers' and whose eyes were 'sudden and passionate'.[18] Gleick's description of two things about Feigenbaum – his habits and his appearance – immediately serve to locate him as distinctive and maverick. He is Romantic (with wild hair and flashing eyes), he is a man alone, facing the world (out confronting nature), and of course this description of him as distinctive and maverick serves to lend the science of chaos these self-same characteristics.[19] Elsewhere, Gleick reiterates this point: 'A few freethinkers working alone, unable to explain where they are heading, afraid even to tell their colleagues what they are doing – that romantic image ... has occurred in real life, time and time again, in the exploration of chaos'.[20]

The structure of *Chaos* also emphasises this revolutionary aspect. In the prologue, Gleick withholds from the reader the importance of Feigenbaum, leaving his contribution to chaos theory a mystery. He is obviously important, but although he is presented as an alluring figure it is not until the central chapter of the book (chapter 6) that we are to find out his significance. The first five chapters present scientists paving the way for chaos in highly disparate fields, working alone, unappreciated by their colleagues, and mostly unaware of similar breakthroughs being made in different disciplines.

In chapter 6, though, we return to Feigenbaum and things come together: he discovers a 'universal theory' which 'made the difference between beautiful and useful'.[21] After this, the first chaos conference takes place in 1977, in Como in Italy, 'a stunningly deep blue catchbasin for the melting snow from the Italian Alps'.[22] The idyllic setting functions as pathetic fallacy in the text, highlighting the new-found confidence and identity of the new science, and we are told that the delegates were 'weepingly grateful'[23] to find others pursuing similar research in different fields.

Feigenbaum figures in lengthy anecdotes at the beginning and the end of this pivotal chapter in Gleick's book, and he is brought in as the figure who draws all the other stories about chaos together. At the end, after the Como conference has been described, he is presented as being at ease, talking to an interviewer (presumably Gleick) as he smokes cigarette after cigarette and muses upon the links between art's approach to the world, and that of chaos. The earlier anecdotes, at the beginning of the chapter, are especially interesting because they suggest that chaos is made possible by a new sort of scientific

---

[18]   Gleick, p. 2.
[19]   Hayles analyses Gleick's drawing of his characters with reference to gender issues in *Chaos Bound*. Hayles, pp. 171–4.
[20]   Gleick, p. 37.
[21]   Gleick, p. 180.
[22]   Gleick, p. 184.
[23]   Joseph Ford, quoted in Gleick, p. 184.

approach, and perhaps even a new sort of scientist. The way in which this new approach breaks from classical science is emphasised by invoking those opponents of modern science, the Romantics.

As we begin the chapter, Feigenbaum is strongly associated with nature. He stands a little upstream from a waterfall, and speculates about the recurring patterns of foam on the water's surface, realising that science has no way of expressing these sorts of phenomena. After a little detail about the problems facing scientists at the time, and how Feigenbaum came to be hired by the Massachusetts Institute of Technology (MIT), we flash back to Feigenbaum's experience as a graduate student at MIT and, in particular, an epiphanic episode by the Lincoln Reservoir in Boston. Visiting the reservoir with some friends, he becomes detached from the group and begins to speculate about the precise distance at which it becomes impossible for him to understand the conversations of neighbouring groups of picnickers. Inspired by his 'Romantic inclinations',[24] this crucial moment leads him to dwell upon the transition from intelligibility to unintelligibility, and other problems of human perception.

These ponderings lead us to Feigenbaum's insights into an early nineteenth-century dispute about the nature of light between Goethe and Isaac Newton's followers. Newton's theory saw each colour as a certain wavelength of light, whereas Goethe argued that 'color is a matter of perception'.[25] Newton's optics eventually proved themselves right, but Feigenbaum nevertheless tracked down a copy of Goethe's relevant treatise and 'persuaded himself that Goethe had been right about color'.[26]

Feigenbaum's eventual contribution is not to alter theories about the behaviour or substance of light. Nevertheless, Gleick uses this episode to demonstrate a different way of looking at problems which eventually produces the key breakthrough in chaos theory: Feigenbaum's universal theory. What is interesting about it is that it shows Feigenbaum going back to the father of modern science, rejecting his view, and exploring a different path, the Romantic path, which was not taken by science and which was regarded as 'pseudoscientific meandering'.[27] Feigenbaum understands that there is 'true science' in Goethe's theory of colour, and thus allies himself with a key Romantic figure.

Gleick does not, by any stretch of the imagination, suggest that Newtonian science, and all that came from it, was wrong. What he does is imply that the chaos theorist has to look at things in a radically different way to the practitioner of classical science. The identity of the scientist has, in some

---

[24]   Gleick, p. 163.
[25]   Gleick, p. 164.
[26]   Gleick, p. 165.
[27]   Gleick, p. 164.

degree, to change. This identity is recast in Romantic terms, by virtue of the references to Goethe in chapter 6 of *Chaos*, and the descriptions of the chaos theorists themselves as men (they are all men in Gleick's book) who work against the grain of traditional science.

What we are presented with in this chapter of Gleick's book, is a moment when the revolution crystallises – the 1977 Como conference – and a figure who represents the revolution, and who was able to produce the key theory which linked its disparate strands together by having the courage to go back to the dawn of modern science, and think things through in a different way. Feigenbaum becomes an icon of the new science, a symbolic figure who renounces the old science and clears the way for the new.

So, in terms of both content and form, Gleick's presentation of chaos theory postulates it as a revolutionary approach to science. The case of Prigogine and Stengers's work, in relation to this need to postulate the move from classical to 'postmodern' science, is rather more complicated. This is because they locate the first challenge to classical science with a nineteenth-century development, the second law of thermodynamics. This, we are told, contradicted the time-reversible principle of classical physics by suggesting that entropy (disorder) always increases – in other words, it made time flow in one direction. This is a key development for Prigogine and Stengers because they situate their insights as a reconciliation between classical notions of reversible time (being), with the sense that time flows in one direction (becoming). In fact, it is this reconciliation of being with becoming which allows us to slot Prigogine and Stengers's work into the same late twentieth-century framework as *Gravity's Rainbow* and *Chaos*, because it is a reconciliation which takes place during the last few decades.

Indeed, Prigogine and Stengers even mirror the narrative pattern identified above which locates relativity theory and quantum mechanics as moments of crisis in classical physics, before invoking chaos theory as the final crisis which undoes, once and for all, the presumptions of traditional science: 'At the end of the twentieth century we have learned to understand better the meaning of the two great revolutions that gave shape to the physics of our time, quantum mechanics and relativity'.[28] This phrase suggests that it is only now, after the work of scientists like Prigogine, that we can appreciate the true role of relativity and quantum mechanics in the history of science, as it developed towards the insights made by chaos theory. Gleick also, it should be noted, reproduces this pattern, citing the physicist Michael F. Shlesinger's claim that 'Relativity eliminated the Newtonian illusion of absolute space and time; quantum theory eliminated the Newtonian dream of a controllable measurement

---

[28]   Ilya Prigogine and Isabelle Stengers, *Order Out of Chaos: Man's New Dialogue with Nature* (1984; London: Flamingo, 1985), p. 9.

process; and chaos eliminates the Laplacian fantasy of deterministic predictability'.[29]

Like these presentations of contemporary science, *Gravity's Rainbow* also registers a shift in the status of knowledge, locating it quite specifically during the Second World War. The actual nature of the new mode of knowledge appears in the novel's form, and more specifically in the style of science practised by Roger Mexico, which is contrasted with that of Ned Pointsman. This is discussed in more detail later on in the chapter. For the moment we need merely establish the way in which the Second World War is situated as a key moment in history.

This appears most dramatically in the form of the Zone, the open, anarchic state of Europe after the defeat of Germany and before the end of the war. This Zone is described as setting the stage for what will follow from the war – a key moment when history could take any one of a number of directions. The origins of the post-war world, and the postmodern world, lie in the Zone. For instance, Mr Information, a highly bizarre personality in a novel of freakish characters, describes the war as a set of railway points in history that will throw the post-war world in one direction or another.[30] Slothrop, the central protagonist, also sees the Zone as crucial, sensing that 'somewhere inside the waste of it [is] a single set of coordinates from which to proceed, without elect, without preterite, without even nationality to fuck it up'.[31]

The Zone is therefore posited as the starting point for the late twentieth-century world, and as such offers not only the hope that Slothrop expresses, but also immense danger. This ambiguity is summed up neatly by the Argentine anarchist, Squallidozzi, who has travelled with his compatriots in the hope that the Zone will allow them to restart history from the right set of coordinates: '"In the openness of the German Zone, our hope is limitless." Then, as if struck on the forehead, a sudden fast glance, not at the door, but *up at the ceiling* – "So is our danger."'[32]

Each of the core texts for this chapter, then, locates a fundamental shift – a revolutionary moment – taking place in the twentieth century. Exactly how these shifts are tied together will be explored through their sabotage of the

---

[29]   Gleick, p. 6.

[30]   Thomas Pynchon, *Gravity's Rainbow* (1973; London: Picador, 1975), pp. 644–5. The image of railway tracks is a dominant motif in the novel. The sense of a dense network of tracks recalls chaos theory's doctrine of sensitivity to initial conditions: the train's course along the tracks is completely determined by the points over which it travels, but if just one set of points is thrown in another direction, the train may end up somewhere completely different.

[31]   Pynchon, *Gravity's Rainbow*, p. 556.

[32]   Pynchon, *Gravity's Rainbow*, p. 265.

strong Enlightenment distinctions between order and disorder, and global and local.

Mining the First Binary Divide (a): From Disorder to Chaos in the Work of Gleick and Prigogine

> Postmodern science – by concerning itself with such things as undecidables, the limits of precise control, conflicts characterized by incomplete information, *'fracta,'* catastrophes, and pragmatic paradoxes – is theorizing its own evolution as discontinuous, catastrophic, nonrectifiable, and paradoxical. It is changing the meaning of the word *knowledge*, while expressing how such a change can take place.[33]

In *Intellectual Impostures* Sokal and Bricmont pull apart this passage from *The Postmodern Condition*, contesting Lyotard's conflation of different aspects of mathematics and physics, and suggesting that the philosophical conclusions at which he arrives are not borne out by the science he cites.[34] As will be apparent from earlier discussions, it is not the place of this book to comment on the status of professional science, and so Sokal and Bricmont's approach to this passage has to stand as a warning against taking Lyotard's description as an accurate representation of trends in contemporary science.

Nevertheless, it certainly does apply – at least in part – to the popular presentation of chaos theory in our culture. What is interesting is that this passage suggests that postmodern science not only does science in a different way, but that in doing so it creates a complex history for itself: it does not just work according to new conceptions of knowledge; it also implies something about the shift to those new conceptions. Old and new ways of knowing are, in some sense, juxtaposed. However limited this might be as a description of the reality of the sciences Lyotard cites, precisely because popular presentations of chaos theory tend to present it as revolutionary – as entirely new – they inevitably do juxtapose old and new, and struggle to find a language to express this transition.

This happens partly for reasons that I have already talked about in relation to the revolutionary moments posited by the three texts that comprise this case study: the two descriptions of chaos theory describe the coming into being of the science, and therefore explicitly describe the movement from old ways of knowing to new ways; and *Gravity's Rainbow*, as an encyclopaedic

---

[33]   Lyotard, p. 60.
[34]   Alan Sokal and Jean Bricmont, *Intellectual Impostures: Postmodern Philosophers' Abuse of Science* (London: Profile, 1998), pp. 127–8.

text, expresses a moment of crisis in the culture as it shifts into a new phase, and as a result brings discordant ways of knowing into close proximity with each other. It also happens because there is a difficulty in expressing new ways of knowing, when our language is so tightly regulated by the old ways. Consequently, we find descriptions of chaos theory struggling for a way to express the new territory between order and disorder, and we find *Gravity's Rainbow*, in its contrast between the old science of Ned Pointsman and the new science of Roger Mexico, tussling with the difficulties of describing a science which has not even come into existence yet. I will start with this struggle as it appears in chaos theory.

It is manifested most obviously in the term 'chaos' itself.[35] What presentations of the theory frequently do is redefine this word, trying to disassociate it from 'disorder', and complete opposition to 'order', and instead place it somewhere between these two terms. Chaos theory is often presented as opening up territory between the two ends of a binary divide that was previously considered to be absolute.

This means that we get a clash between two languages for knowing the world. The first assumes a sharp binary distinction between order and disorder, and the second finds this distinction to be less meaningful, considering it necessary to find new ways of articulating the world. This is made apparent within Gleick's book, and in many other presentations of chaos theory, by the frequent juxtaposition of two words (or sometimes phrases) which have opposite meanings. Because the science deals with phenomena that cannot be accurately described by the binary oppositions which populate our language, two associated rhetorical tactics are deployed: two antonyms are harnessed as adjectives to describe the same noun; or, one word is deployed as an adjective to describe a noun, normally associated with an opposite meaning to that adjective. So, Mitchell Feigenbaum speculates that cloud formations are both 'random' and 'not-random', 'fuzzy and detailed', and 'structured and unpredictable';[36] Edward Lorenz's work on 'deterministic chaos' produces a simulation of the weather which behaves according to a principle of 'orderly disorder', and which can be described by a representation which signals both 'pure disorder' and 'a new kind of order';[37] Philip Marcus's model of the Red Spot on Jupiter's surface denotes a 'stable chaos';[38] James Yorke coins the

---

[35]   Sokal and Bricmont point out that misunderstandings frequently arise in relation to chaos theory because chaos is such an evocative word. Sokal and Bricmont 136. This is an important point and suggests why we should both be concerned with analysing chaos as cultural science, and yet also be careful to hold back from assuming that the comments we make necessarily apply to professional science.

[36]   Gleick, p. 3.

[37]   Gleick, p. 139, p. 15, p. 30.

[38]   Gleick, p. 55.

term 'chaos' to describe systems which operate according to the principle of 'deterministic disorder';[39] and Benoit Mandelbrot makes the insight that the world displays a 'regular irregularity', while, in the Mandelbrot set, which 'commingles complexity and simplicity', the 'irrational fertilized the rational'.[40]

In Gleick's presentation of chaos theory, therefore, we do not get an impression of the new science of chaos as just another extension of scientific knowledge into new territory (though he does acknowledge that some scientists see it in this way). Instead, chaos seems to make problematic our fundamental assumptions about what knowledge is; it even exposes the inadequacy of our everyday language for describing these newly discovered phenomena. The term 'chaos' has itself to be redefined, to mean 'that which is neither ordered nor disordered', if it is to label accurately the new scientific theories as they are presented in contemporary culture.

A similar rhetorical strategy to Gleick's juxtaposition of words with opposite meanings is Prigogine and Stengers's emphasis on the reconciliation of being with becoming. In their book there is certainly an emphasis on the revolutionary status of chaos theory which mirrors that in Gleick's work. For instance, the opening sentence of the preface claims that 'Our vision of nature is undergoing a radical change toward the multiple, the temporal, and the complex', and a page later this process is described as a widespread 'conceptual revolution'.[41] As in *Chaos*, therefore, there is an emphasis upon the distance between chaos theory and previous scientific methods and objects of study. This clash of opposing epistemologies is foregrounded by the devotion of large proportions of the book to the history of science since the seventeenth century. This draws our attention to chaos's position as a reworking of some fundamental ideas in classical science. It is important to point out that the history of science is presented as being much more fragmentary and contradictory than it is in Gleick's work – in general, *Chaos* suggests a radical departure from classical science, whereas *Order Out of Chaos* suggests a philosophical reorganisation of some fundamental ideas.

This is brought out in both the subtitle of Prigogine's book, *Man's New Dialogue with Nature*, and in the original, French title of the book, *La Nouvelle Alliance*. The subtitle suggests a new interaction between humans and nature; the French title suggests a new interaction between the arts and the sciences; both imply that something completely new will follow from chaos theory.

So, although chaos is presented as a 'postmodern' science – as something which contradicts the presumptions of Newtonian science – as I showed earlier on in the chapter, some of the old ways of knowing are caught up in Gleick's

---

[39]   Gleick, p. 69.
[40]   Gleick, p. 98, p. 221, p. 223.
[41]   Prigogine and Stengers, p. xxvii, p. xxviii.

and Prigogine and Stengers's work, and there is not a completely clean break from traditional scientific principles. (It is important to reiterate that there is an alternative history to the one I have described, and that some scientists deny that there is any break between chaos theory and classical science).[42] But in what ways is chaos theory postmodern, and how exactly does it disrupt the distinction between order and disorder?

The 'butterfly effect', a popular term for the slightly more technical 'sensitive dependence on initial conditions', is a cliché of attempts to explain chaos theory to the general public. It is worth focusing on here because it gives an indication of how presentations of chaos theory align with postmodern discourses. The idea itself is fairly simple, and gives expression to the notion that without perfect information (which is itself impossible to get) there are many situations which evade predictability (knowing the approximate state of a system now, and all the laws that govern its development, does not mean that we will know the approximate state of the system in the future). In other words, very small differences now can quickly magnify to produce very large differences later on: the system is completely determined, but evades our predictive power. The butterfly effect expresses this through the assertion that the weather is so sensitive to minor fluctuations that if a butterfly flaps its wings in Tokyo, a hurricane may hit New York which would not otherwise have done so.[43] The place names change as the butterfly analogy gets retold (Appleyard's Tokyo butterfly disrupts Chicago; Gleick's Peking butterfly ruins the New York weather; and, rather more parochially, Davies and Gribbin's Adelaide butterfly has an unstated effect upon Sussex – quite why cabbage whites in Britain or America never ruin southern hemisphere weather remains a mystery), but the effects are almost always deemed to be violent,

---

[42] This alternative perspective on chaos theory is suggested in a review of Gleick's book by John Burrow, who argues that there has 'been no Kuhnian revolution here', and that chaos theories merely extend the scientific enterprise into a new area because they are concerned with 'a *different* class of problems'. John Burrow, 'Making a New Science', *New Scientist* 26 May 1988: p. 73, p. 74.

[43] See, for example, the following passages for references to the butterfly effect: Bryan Appleyard, *Understanding the Present: Science and the Soul of Modern Man*, 2nd edn (1992; London: Picador-Pan, 1993), pp. 161–2; Gleick, p. 8; Paul Davies and John Gribbin, *The Matter Myth: Beyond Chaos and Complexity* (1991; London: Penguin, 1992), pp. 34–5; David Ruelle, *Chance and Chaos* (1991; London: Penguin, 1993), p. 74; Ian Stewart, *Does God Play Dice? The Mathematics of Chance and Chaos* (1989; London: Penguin, 1990), p. 141. An interesting literary forerunner to the butterfly effect, comes in Ray Bradbury's short story, 'A Sound of Thunder', in which time-travelling tourists completely change the course of history when they inadvertently kill a prehistoric butterfly. Ray Bradbury, 'A Sound of Thunder', *Ray Bradbury*, The Pegasus Library (London: Harrap, 1975), pp. 69–84. Harriet Hawkins points out that Edward Lorenz, who first formulated the butterfly effect was reminded of Bradbury's story by colleagues after he had written and presented his paper on the phenomenon. Harriet Hawkins, *Strange Attractors: Literature and Chaos Theory* (New York: Prentice-Harvester Whestsheaf, 1995), p. 2.

perhaps to illustrate the importance of chaotic systems to our lives. Strangely, no one bothers to point out that a butterfly flapping its wings in Tokyo can result in New York suffering a light breeze with scattered showers moving in from the west.

Gleick devotes his first chapter to the butterfly effect, providing a summary of its consequences through the story of the meteorologist, Edward Lorenz. Lorenz, we are told, invented a simple, idealised computer simulation which modelled the world's weather with twelve equations. Importantly, Gleick's language associates Lorenz's expectations of his simulation with expectations of Enlightenment science. Significantly, he is described as a 'god of this machine universe' who put 'into practice the laws of Newton, appropriate tools for a clockmaker deity who could create a world and set it running for eternity'.[44] In other words, Lorenz expects his simulation to behave according to the principles of Newtonian science – he has created a deterministic system, so it should function in a way that is both deterministic and predictable.

Yet what Lorenz finds is that even though his simulation captured the deterministic principles of the universe described by Newtonian science, there was something fundamentally unpredictable about how it would develop. If the starting conditions were varied only ever so slightly – by one part in a thousand – then the simulation would evolve in a radically different fashion, and the weather on his artificial world would quickly depart from its expected course. The insights which are extrapolated from this constitute the main body of Gleick's text and involve a renunciation of three important principles of Newtonian science (again, it must be stressed that this chapter is not arguing that chaos theory actually does renounce Newtonian, Enlightenment, classical or modern science; just that it is often *presented as* renouncing it in ways that inevitably tie these presentations of the history of science to other postmodern postures).

The first of these principles is a firm belief in the power of human reason to unlock the secrets of nature. Because science is used to studying linear systems which behave in a straightforward way, and are amenable to analysis, it takes on board the assumption that the whole universe behaves in a stable, orderly way.[45] The second principle, which follows from this, is that of prediction: if everything can be known about a system, then we can predict how it will behave in the future. This accords directly with the beliefs of two figures, frequently associated with the Enlightenment in 'postmodern'

---

[44] Gleick, p. 12.

[45] Sokal and Bricmont also point out that like 'chaos', 'nonlinear' is a term which is frequently misunderstood by non-scientists. Sokal and Bricmont, pp. 133–4. It is used here because Gleick deploys the term, and because this chapter is about representations of science in culture (including misunderstandings and misrepresentations of that science).

presentations of the history of science: Descartes, who claimed that with the application of reason 'there can be nothing so distant that one does not reach it eventually', and Laplace who asserted that 'nothing would be uncertain' for the intellect which had enough information.[46] The third principle is that of control: if everything can be known about a system, and if we can predict how it will behave, then we can alter the conditions under which it operates and control its future development. This does not mean that modern science knows, predicts and controls everything, but that in principle these things are believed to be possible – they are ideals according to which modern science conducts its investigations.

The implications which follow from Lorenz's computer simulation, as they are presented in Gleick's text, contradict these principles directly. Firstly, very small inaccuracies that we have in our information about a system will always plague our measurements of it. To eliminate these discrepancies in the information we have, we would need to be able to measure it with infinite accuracy – an impossibility, because no matter how accurate our measurements are, there will always be a finer level below them which we do not take into account. This must have been accepted by modern science, but was thought to be unimportant because it was assumed that in most situations, a close understanding of the system now would lead to a close understanding of the system in the future. However, secondly, these minute inaccuracies sabotage any hopes of making long-term predictions because very small-scale causes magnify to have large-scale effects in nonlinear systems (this is part of the disruption of the global–local opposition, which is discussed later on in the chapter). This also obviously subverts our hopes of controlling a system – if we cannot predict how it will behave in the future, we cannot wholly predict what effects our attempts to manipulate the system will have.

So, although Lorenz's simulation operated according to deterministic principles which were known in their entirety – he had designed the twelve equations governing the system himself – it is presented as acting in a way which subverts the ideals according to which modern (classical) science went about its business. Gleick emphasises that although it was known that there were limits to what we could know about the universe in practice, chaos theory demonstrates that nonlinearity is actually predominant, and that there are also theoretical limits upon our knowledge: 'In science as in life, it is well known that a chain of events can have a point of crisis that could magnify small

---

[46]   René Descartes, 'Discourse on Method', *'Discourse on Method' and Other Writings*, trans. F.E. Sutcliffe (Middlesex: Penguin, 1968), p. 41. Pierre Simon Laplace, *A Philosophical Essay on Probabilities*, trans. Frederick Wilson Truscott and Frederick Lincoln Emory, 6th edn (1819; New York: Dover, 1951), p. 4. See discussion on pages 174-5.

changes. But chaos meant that such points were everywhere. They were pervasive'.[47]

In proposing chaos as a new sort of science, which unsettles three key principles of modern science, outlined above, Gleick's book implies a subversion of the strict binary oppositions between order and disorder, and, as will be shown later on, global and local. The subversion of the order–disorder distinction arises because Lorenz's simulation mimicked a world which is simultaneously ordered (the 'laws' – equations – which governed it were well known) and disordered (there was an inevitable unpredictability in the system). Part of the posture of postmodernism is to stress this disruption as being of great significance. For instance Katherine Hayles argues that when 'a dichotomy as central to Western thought as order/disorder is destabilised, it is no exaggeration to say that a major fault line has developed in the episteme'.[48]

This is, perhaps, the central aspect of the change in the status of knowledge claimed by postmodern discourses. Because order and disorder were seen as mutually exclusive states, the order–disorder divide had prioritised one over the other: the option was between accepting absolute chaos (that which could not be understood in any except the most banal terms), or trying to impose order on that chaos (encompassing it within strict, deterministic bounds). With the growing popularity of postmodern discourses of various kinds, a stress was laid on opening up the territory between order and disorder; to see the two states not necessarily as antitheses of one another, but to see chaos as a site with great potential for producing new meanings and new kinds of order. It is this understanding of chaos which is emphasised in Prigogine's book: 'We come to one of our main conclusions: At all levels, be it the level of macroscopic physics, the level of fluctuations, or the microscopic level, *nonequilibrium is the source of order. Nonequilibrium brings "order out of chaos."* But as we already mentioned, the concept of order (or disorder) is more complex than was thought'.[49] An equivalent, though slightly different, emphasis is apparent in Gleick's work, where he describes how chaos theorists in various disciplines have found powerful tools to describe phenomena that otherwise appeared to be random.

Like these presentations of chaos theory, *Gravity's Rainbow* also subverts the order–disorder distinction. Although it makes no reference to chaos theory (it was published two years before James Yorke even coined the term),[50] it imagines a new science which embodies some of the 'postmodern' characteristics of chaos theory.

---

[47]   Gleick, p. 23.
[48]   Hayles, *Chaos Bound*, p. 16.
[49]   Prigogine, pp. 286–7.
[50]   The word 'chaos' was first coined to describe the new science in 'Period Three Implies Chaos', a paper by James Yorke and Tien-Yien Li in 1975, *American Mathematical*

Mining the First Binary Divide (b): From Pointsman to Mexico in *Gravity's Rainbow*

Just as presentations of chaos theory struggle with language to get it to express the new ideas, and eventually solve the problem by effectively redefining 'chaos', so *Gravity's Rainbow* also draws our attention to the limits, and the ideological biases, of our language. This is, in fact, a central theme of the novel. For instance, it suggests that the language used to describe the development of plastics is intricately bound up with the political atmosphere of National Socialist Germany – so, the 'target property most often seemed to be strength – first among Plasticity's virtuous triad of Strength, Stability, Whiteness (*Kraft, Standfestigkeit, WeiBe*: how often these were taken for Nazi graffiti [...])'.[51]

With Ned Pointsman's and Roger Mexico's differing approaches to the problem of explaining why V-2 rockets fall on every part of London in which Slothrop has an erection, what we are presented with is a clash between two languages for knowing the world, as well as two scientific methods. They are set up as complete opposites, for Roger Mexico, we are told, is the 'Antipointsman', and Pointsman the 'Antimexico'.[52]

Pointsman's approach to the problem involves the three principles of modern science which I outlined above, and which I showed Gleick's text to refute: a belief that everything can be known, and that, following from this, prediction and control are possible.[53] Significantly, Pointsman finds a role model in Pavlov, who is specifically associated with the understanding and control of creatures' responses to various stimuli. Pavlov's Book (it is, significantly, capitalised in the text) circulates among Pointsman and six other owners like a mystical text, charged with religious significance. Steven Weisenburger points out that the book had actually appeared in an English translation in 1941, and so the secrecy with which it is rotated by Pointsman,

---

Monthly 82: pp. 985–92. However, the term did not gain wider, popular recognition until the 1980s.

[51] Pynchon, *Gravity's Rainbow*, p. 250. Here, and elsewhere, I use square brackets to distinguish my ellipses from Pynchon's.

[52] Pynchon, *Gravity's Rainbow*, p. 55, p. 89.

[53] Yet again, it must be emphasised what is being claimed here: not that modern science necessarily possesses these characteristics, but that it is associated with them in postmodern discourses. It should also be stressed that the postmodern position does not necessarily entail falling back on a rather dangerous irrationality, claiming that it is better not to know than to know, but rather draws our attention to the ways in which the deployment of knowledge may not be innocent. It is this position which is most consistent with *Gravity's Rainbow*.

Spectro and the others is a 'bit of melodrama' on Pynchon's part.[54] Actually, Weisenburger may have missed the fact that the book's rarity stems, in *Gravity's Rainbow*, not from the unavailability of a translation, but from air-raid damage to existing stocks ('most existing copies had been destroyed in their warehouse early in the Battle of Britain').[55] The origin of the book's scarcity is, however, a minor point; what is interesting is that Pynchon engineers its destruction in order to give it this rarity value, and so to lend this air of mystery to the science practised by Pointsman, Spectro and the other keepers of the book.

Pointsman sees himself as taking up Pavlov's work where it was left unfinished at his death, and has no doubt that there is an answer to the mystery posed by Slothrop: '[Pavlov] died at the very threshold of putting these things on an experimental basis. But I live. I have the funding, and the time, and the will'.[56] This self-justification is important because it shows that, for Pointsman, there is nothing which cannot be known given enough time and funding, just as Laplace thought that all was knowable, given enough information.

He is also certain that the truth, when it becomes apparent, will demonstrate the efficacy of a particular scientific world view, characterised in the text as 'cause-and-effect'. Pointsman follows Pavlov in believing that 'the ideal, the end we all struggle toward in science, is the true mechanical explanation [...] No effect without cause and a clear train of linkages'.[57] This, he is certain, will underpin the mystery posed by Slothrop: 'But if it's [the cause is] in the air, right here, right now, then the rockets follow from it, 100% of the time. No exceptions. When we find it, we'll have shown again the stone determinacy of everything, of every soul'.[58]

Pointsman is only one among many representatives of the 'cause-and-effect' view in the novel. His approach to solving the problem of the link between Slothrop and the rocket is based upon the belief that, given enough information, it will be possible to identify a direct chain of links which tie them together. Prediction is tied in with this notion of cause and effect. Franz Pökler, the 'cause-and-effect man' according to his wife Leni,[59] is part of the team who are obsessed with predicting the flight path of the nascent V-2 rockets on which they work. Similarly, the delightfully named Brigadier Pudding hopes to

---

[54] Steven Weisenburger, *A 'Gravity's Rainbow' Companion: Sources and Contexts for Pynchon's Novel* (Athens: University of Georgia Press, 1988), p. 37. The 'Book' is vol. 2 of Pavlov's *Lectures on Conditioned Reflexes*.

[55] Pynchon, *Gravity's Rainbow*, p. 87.

[56] Pynchon, *Gravity's Rainbow*, p. 90.

[57] Pynchon, *Gravity's Rainbow*, p. 89.

[58] Pynchon, *Gravity's Rainbow*, p. 86.

[59] Pynchon, *Gravity's Rainbow*, p. 159.

write a definitive political treatise entitled *Things That Can Happen in European Politics.*

This, in turn, is linked to the doctrine of control. The actual language of the engineers who work on the rocket reflects this: 'they thought this way, Design Group, in terms of captivity, prohibition'.[60] Pointsman, also, is obsessed with the need to assert various forms of control, holding ultimate responsibility for sending Slothrop off across the Zone on the trail of the rocket, and trying to keep Mexico under his control by sending Jessica to Cuxhaven, where she cannot distract him from his work. Indeed, from the outset, Pointsman is presented as an ominous figure – our first impression of him is as a smell of ether[61] – and his urge to control is linked in with sadistic sexual fantasies: 'And how much of the pretty victim straining against her bonds does Ned Pointsman see in each dog that visits his test stands ... and aren't scalpel and probe as decorative, as fine extensions as whip and cane?'[62] His journal entry on Slothrop – *'We must never lose control'*[63] – perhaps illustrates how his fear of the unknown is the fear of losing control.

Yet this whole doctrine – the association between knowledge, prediction and control – is shown to be false in the novel. The information that Pointsman gets about Slothrop is shown to be beset by inaccuracy and uncertainty. For instance, it is impossible to get perfect data on Slothrop as Harvey Speed and Floyd Perdoo find as they strive to trace the women marked on the map Slothrop kept of his affairs in London. Just as there are limits on the quantity and quality of information attainable by those who attempt to understand Slothrop, so there are also limits on the extent to which predictions can be made and control can be wielded by the proponents of cause-and-effect.

Brigadier Pudding's attempt to predict all possible paths down which European politics might travel, is beset from the outset by the impossibility of processing sufficient data quickly enough to outpace actual events, and he finds himself becoming increasingly uncertain as his predictions are overtaken by the events themselves: 'Begin, of course, with England. "First," he wrote, "Bereshith, as it were: Ramsay MacDonald can die." By the time he went through resulting party alignments and possible permutations of cabinet posts, Ramsay MacDonald had died'.[64] Similarly the perfect rocket, that will land exactly on its target, is never built, although Franz Pökler, waiting at 'Ground Zero' to observe a test flight (on the basis that no rocket is perfect, so it is safest to wait at the exact point at which it is aimed), finds his fears of being

---

[60]   Pynchon, *Gravity's Rainbow*, p. 518.
[61]   Pynchon, *Gravity's Rainbow*, p. 42.
[62]   Pynchon, *Gravity's Rainbow*, p. 88.
[63]   Pynchon, *Gravity's Rainbow*, p. 144.
[64]   Pynchon, *Gravity's Rainbow*, p. 77.

controlled by others feeding a raging paranoia that the perfect rocket will be aimed at him.[65]

Pointsman, too, is finally unable to control Slothrop. What we have in all these attempts to know, predict and control is the conviction that it is possible to find order within the universe. Yet the novel's central mystery – the link between Slothrop and the rocket – is never solved, and part of the reason for this is the inadequacy of the disciplines that are brought to bear upon the problem.

However, an alternative mode of knowing is offered. Although the world with which the characters are faced does not turn out to be ordered in the ways they expect, this does not mean it is wholly disordered. Mexico's science differs from Pointsman's in terms of the sort of explanations it seeks for phenomena. This is, perhaps, epitomised by his use of the Poisson equation, which does not tell exactly where the rockets will strike, or indeed offer a cause-and-effect explanation for why they will hit a particular place. Rather, it 'will tell, for a number of total hits arbitrarily chosen, how many squares will get none, how many one, two, three, and so on'.[66] Of course the Poisson equation is not chaos theory; it comes from standard mathematics, and illustrates Mexico's commitment to statistics as a way of dealing with random phenomena. However, the twist given to Mexico's science in its presentation by Pynchon lends it characteristics which also come out, over a decade later, in Gleick's and Prigogine and Stengers's narratives of chaos theory.

Mexico questions Pointsman's methods, particularly his desire to take everything apart and divide it into its constituent elements in order to get perfect data: 'I wonder if you people aren't a bit too – well, strong, on the virtues of analysis. I mean, once you've taken it all apart, fine, I'll be the first to applaud your industry. But other than a lot of bits and pieces lying about, what have *you* said?'[67] Mexico seems to operate on a level which is between parts and whole, between global and local, and he certainly practises a style of science which is not concerned with binary oppositions, but sees the world in a more complex way: 'Pointsman can only possess the zero and the one. [...] But to Mexico belongs the domain *between* zero and one – the middle Pointsman has excluded from his persuasion – the probabilities'.[68]

Pointsman can only see things in terms of a binary opposition that works in an either–or relationship, whereas Mexico is concerned with uncovering the

---

[65] Pynchon, *Gravity's Rainbow*, pp. 424–6. It is, in fact, reasonable to argue that the novel does imagine the perfect rocket to be built, and that it is this which hangs above the cinema at the end of the book – if so, then it is associated with the imposition of a cause-and-effect viewpoint in the face of the novel's expressed desire for a less rigid philosophy.

[66] Pynchon, *Gravity's Rainbow*, p. 55.

[67] Pynchon, *Gravity's Rainbow*, p. 88.

[68] Pynchon, *Gravity's Rainbow*, p. 55.

ground in between. This reference to the ground in between has its origins in the expression of probabilities in terms of decimal points between zero and one (whereby zero represents something which will never happen, and one represents something which will always happen). Although this is an aspect of 'modern' science, Pynchon gives it a postmodern twist, lending it characteristics not unlike those apparent in popular presentations of chaos theory.

Mexico is described as seeing things in a way which is fundamentally different to that of Pointsman. He also resists the notion of direct prediction, for which Pointsman and the other representatives of cause-and-effect strive. Although he can predict the distribution of rocket strikes, he cannot predict which places are more likely to get hit by the rockets. This is because there is no cause-and-effect link between separate rocket firings, and the likelihood of one area of the city getting hit by the rockets is not in any way altered by previous hits upon that area; as he tells Pointsman, 'Each hit is independent of all the others. Bombs are not dogs. No link. No memory. No conditioning'.[69]

Importantly, Mexico's distance from Pointsman is not presented as just another way of doing science, but as a new methodology which will supersede the cause-and-effect method – an insight which is crucial to my characterisation of Mexico's science as postmodern. Both men perceive the threat which Mexico's approach to phenomena poses to Pointsman's. For instance, Mexico tells Pointsman that 'there's a feeling about that cause-and-effect may have been taken as far as it will go. [...] The next breakthrough may come when we have the courage to junk cause-and-effect entirely, and strike off at some other angle'.[70]

It is interesting that Mexico does not see the new science as a continuation of previous scientific enterprises, in the way that Pointsman sees his work as a continuation of that of Pavlov, but as a 'junking' of them. This ties it in with the revolutionary characteristics which are given to chaos theory by Gleick (particularly through his suggestion that it constitutes a Kuhnian revolution), and Prigogine and Stengers.

Pointsman also sees Mexico's science as a fundamentally new approach to the world but, unlike Mexico, he finds it tremendously threatening rather than liberating:

How can Mexico play, so at his ease, with these symbols of randomness and fright? Innocent as a child, perhaps unaware – perhaps – that in his play he wrecks the elegant rooms of history, threatens the idea of cause and effect itself. What if Mexico's whole *generation* have turned out like this? Will Postwar be nothing but

---

[69]   Pynchon, *Gravity's Rainbow*, p. 56.
[70]   Pynchon, *Gravity's Rainbow*, p. 89.

'events,' newly created one moment to the next? No links? Is it the
end of history?[71]

A number of critical elements in this soliloquy by Pointsman signal that he is
giving expression to a gulf, not only between himself and Mexico, but also
between the age of the Enlightenment and that of the postmodern. Firstly, he
makes an association between a method of rational analysis ('the ideas of cause
and effect') and a way of conceiving of the world ('the elegant rooms of
history'). Secondly, this is under threat from a new way of perceiving history
– Mexico 'wrecks' the elegant rooms of history with his 'symbols of
randomness and fright' (the equations with which he analyses data). Thirdly,
the new methods of perception may well eventually completely overcome the
old ones, for Mexico's whole 'generation' may turn out like this, leaving the
old beliefs behind with the previous generation. Finally, the new generation is
'Postwar', and thus the Second World War is identified as the point at which
the new paradigm began to assert itself over the old – tying in with Lyotard's
contention, referenced earlier, that there was a change in the status of
knowledge at about the middle of this century, and suggesting that the novel is,
as Mendelson suggests, an encyclopaedic narrative, concerned with the origins
of the contemporary world.

It is important to remember that Mexico's science, like Pointsman's, fails
to explain Slothrop. This does not, however, diminish the distinctions that the
text makes between his science and that of Pointsman. *Gravity's Rainbow*
shows Slothrop to be beyond any explanation, but this does not lessen the
impression that the novel gives of Mexico's methods (limited though they are)
replacing those of Pointsman.

So, we get a clear sense of Mexico practising a science which poses a
threat to that of Pointsman, and looking forward to a post-war science which
will supersede the linear, cause-and-effect methodologies and beliefs of
Enlightenment epistemologies. Mexico is shown to be dispensing with
simplistic binary oppositions, to renounce the belief in ultimate knowledge and
prediction, and to shift away from a paradigm which denotes complete control
over nature and people. As I have shown, these characteristics appear, albeit in
a slightly different way, in Gleick's and Prigogine and Stengers's presentations
of chaos theory. Having established the existence of this shared discourse,
overturning the order–disorder binary opposition in presentations of chaos
theory and postmodern literature, we can now go on to see how the same texts
also contest the distinction between global and local.

---

[71]   Pynchon, *Gravity's Rainbow*, p. 56.

Mining the Second Binary Divide: Between Paranoia and Anti-Paranoia

> But as we have seen, the little narrative [*petit récit*] remains the quintessential form of imaginative invention, most particularly in science.[72]

After characterising modernity as the age of grand narratives, or metanarratives, Lyotard offers postmodernity as a renunciation of this emphasis upon all-embracing meaning structures. He claims that the alternative offered by postmodernity is that of the *petit récit*, the 'little narrative' which contests things on a small scale, and has no presumptions to speak for the global picture. In other words, he sees an emphasis upon the local replacing that on the global. This is perhaps equivalent to a relativist philosophy – for Lyotard no point of view can legitimately aspire to speak a truth which transcends the particularities of time and place.

This section argues that the alternative to the grand narrative, offered in the postmodern discourses of knowledge identified here, is in fact somewhat different to that envisioned by Lyotard. This is because although the discourses reject the global (the possibility of an overall picture) they also reject the local (the picture which denies its ability to transcend in any way its position in the culture). To adopt *petit récits* instead of metanarratives is to maintain the binary opposition between global and local, just emphasising one pole instead of the other. What postmodern discourses do is contest the basis of this binary distinction between global and local, emphasising the way in which scaling factors connect the two. As this is perhaps most obvious in certain presentations of chaos theory, we will turn to these first.

One of Gleick's emphases, in his description of chaos theory, is on the way in which it involves reconsidering nature from a point of view which transcends the boundaries between the very small and the very large, seeing them to be linked by a continuum of ever-increasing scale, rather than as being completely separate. This ties in closely with his presentation of chaos as a revolutionary science, because it involves reconceptualizing the world, and draws our attention to the biases that are built into our conceptions of it:

> *How big is it? How long does it last?* These are the most basic questions a scientist can ask about a thing. They are so basic to the way people conceptualize the world that it is not easy to see that they imply a certain bias. They suggest that size and duration, qualities that depend on scale, are qualities with meaning, qualities that can help describe an object or classify it.[73]

---

[72]   Lyotard, p. 60.
[73]   Gleick, p. 107.

As in his disruption of the chaos–order binary opposition, Gleick here draws our attention to two different languages for knowing the world: the commonsensical terms which we are used to employing, and the insights we can achieve when we interrogate these categories. Of course, this sort of consideration of the notion of scale is not identical to that at issue in Lyotard's discussion of the differences between grand narratives and *petit récits*: one is to do with the difference between large and small in the physical world; the other is to do with the difference between transcendent notions of truth and relativist perspectives. Nevertheless, the emphasis on a move between large-scale and small-scale, stressing the interdependence of the two, is characteristic of postmodern perspectives, and although the connection between the disruption of global and local in these two areas is therefore metaphorical, it is also a genuine postmodern link.

Sensitive dependence on initial conditions (the butterfly effect) draws our attention to the importance of scaling – tiny differences at a microscopic level have a huge effect on the macroscopic level because these different scales are connected to each other in a continuum; they are not separate phenomena. This comes out in Gleick's discussion of the weather, in which he links hurricanes to smaller atmospheric phenomena like litter swirling in a gust in the street: '*Hurricane*. By definition, it is a storm of a certain size. But the definition is imposed by people on nature ... Categories mislead. The ends of the continuum are of a piece with the middle'.[74] Gleick suggests that global and local cannot be seen as phenomena that are, to all intents and purposes, separate (as the categories implied by the language we use imply) if we are to understand how complex systems like the weather really work.

Another way in which this idea of multiple scales, linked by continual transitions between them, comes out, is in the visual images with which chaos is associated: fractals. Some of these images, familiar from t-shirts, posters and elsewhere, are reproduced in Gleick's book, and can be said to be some of the most important icons in the canon of chaos.

He introduces us to them in the chapter, 'A Geometry of Nature', which describes the mathematical shapes (the 'fractals') created by Benoit Mandelbrot, as a geometry which departs in a significant way, Gleick claims, from that initiated by Euclid. Euclidean geometry dealt in idealisations – cones, spheres, and so forth – whereas Mandelbrot's concentration on 'fractional dimension' becomes 'a way of measuring qualities that otherwise have no clear definition: the degree of roughness or brokenness or irregularity in an object'.[75] Mandelbrot's most widely known creation was the 'Mandelbrot set' which is one of chaos's most compelling visual icons, and appears on many t-shirts and

---

[74]   Gleick, p. 108.
[75]   Gleick, p. 98.

posters. This is, essentially, a set of instructions to a computer – or, more accurately, an equation which can be explored graphically by a computer. The pattern it produces can be magnified infinitely. As you zoom in you find the same pattern – with slight differences – recurring on every level.

This image – a set of frames from which are reproduced in Gleick's book – illustrates perfectly the disruption of the global–local binary opposition, and how it relates to that of the order–disorder dichotomy. There is no fundamental distinction between global and local, because a similar pattern recurs regardless of the magnification at which the set is viewed: the infinity of scales contained within the image is what lends it its potency. Yet, although there is this resemblance between the images at different scales, the relationship between the separate images is neither ordered nor disordered. They are not disordered, because there are visual echoes which can be easily identified, and recurring twists to the shapes show that the images are related – they have definitely not been randomly assembled. However, neither are they ordered in a conventional sense, because the images are not identical – rather they are 'self-similar'; nearly, but not quite, the same. You find the same images almost, but not quite, repeating themselves as you go down through the scales.

Nor do you ever reach a point where you have explored the full complexity of the set, an ultimate particle below which you cannot go, because there are always lower levels to explore. The Mandelbrot set stands, therefore, as a visual metaphor for the insights offered by chaos theory, and its disruption of our traditional understanding of such ideas as order, disorder, global and local. As chaos's most resonant public image it traces the passage from disorder to chaos, and treads a path between global and local.

This relates in some ways – again metaphorical – to Mexico's approach to the territory 'between the zero and the one', discussed above. His statistical analysis of the rocket strikes on London gives him access to an understanding which Pointsman is denied by his strict concentration on the either–or dichotomy between one and zero. It is also rather similar to the sense we get at the end of *The Crying of Lot 49*, where Oedipa Maas is finally exiled into an excluded middle, 'walking among matrices of a great digital computer, the zeroes and ones twinned above'.[76]

However, in *Gravity's Rainbow*, the key notions which illustrate an interest in that which lies between the global and local come in Pynchon's treatment of the ideas of paranoia and anti-paranoia, the first of which represents a globalising impulse, and the second of which denotes a localising drive. Both of these ideas are shown to be untenable in *Gravity's Rainbow*, in relation to both the character of Slothrop, and the interpretative strategies by which the reader makes sense of the novel.

---

[76]   Thomas Pynchon, *The Crying of Lot 49* (1966; London: Picador, 1979), p. 125.

Paranoia is defined in the text as the discovery that '*everything is connected*, everything in the Creation [...].'[77] For Slothrop this amounts to the realisation that he is being controlled by outside forces, and that there is a mysterious connection between himself and the rocket, over which he has no control. This is an impossible situation in which to live because, without exception, everything becomes connected in a web that manipulates him. Paranoia implies a globalising impulse to Slothrop's understanding of the world, because everything must be connected in a coherent conspiracy against him.

Yet anti-paranoia is equally untenable because it implies the complete opposite to paranoia, a state in which 'nothing is connected to anything, a condition not many of us can bear for long'.[78] Towards the end of the novel Slothrop finds himself experiencing this, 'sliding onto the anti-paranoid part of his cycle',[79] and feeling that he does not belong anywhere in the world, and that there are no meaningful connections between different things. At least paranoia suggested that 'They have put him here for a reason'; the alternative is even more disturbing because it suggests that 'he's just here'.[80] In other words, only the local (he himself) has any relevance to him, and he does not fit into the larger, global scale of things.

Slothrop's eventual disintegration may illustrate the inadequacy of these sharp choices between paranoia and anti-paranoia, global and local, with which he is faced. For much of the novel his paranoia leads him to try to understand how he fits into the schemes of others. Yet it is impossible to comprehend this fully because the multitude of forces that serve to condition him do not slot together into one giant, coherent and totally unified scheme. As a result he finds himself playing a number of mutually exclusive roles (Plechazunga, the pig hero; Ian Scuffling, the war correspondent; and Rocketman, the comic-book hero, for instance). In other words it actually throws him into a kind of anti-paranoia, a schizophrenia in which he keeps flitting from one role to another, unable to connect between them, as he occupies the central position in different people's conceptions of him. Even when he seems to realise that he is losing track of himself, his attempt to recover his identity and hold on to a unified conception of himself becomes just another way of slotting himself into someone else's story, in this case the rigid structure of a private-detective film: 'Yeah! yeah what happened to Imipolex G, all that Jamf a-and that S-Gerät, s'posed to be a hardboiled private eye here, gonna go out all alone and beat the

---

77   Pynchon, *Gravity's Rainbow*, p. 703.
78   Pynchon, *Gravity's Rainbow*, p. 434.
79   Pynchon, *Gravity's Rainbow*, p. 434.
80   Pynchon, *Gravity's Rainbow*, p. 434.

odds, avenge my friend that They killed, get my ID back and find that piece of mystery hardware'.[81]

The constant changes of costume through which Slothrop goes in the course of the novel illustrate these shifting identities. Earlier on in the book, when he counter-conspires most successfully against 'Them', he chooses his own wardrobe, dressing, for instance, in garish clothes at Raoul's party: 'green French suit of wicked cut with a subtle purple check in it, broad flowered tie [...] brown and white wingtip shoes with golf cleats, and white socks'.[82] Yet most of the time his costumes – the pig-suit, the Rocketman regalia, and so forth – are chosen for him. Similarly, Slothrop's lack of control over himself, and the way in which he is forced to fit himself into a number of mutually exclusive paranoid schemes, are expressed through the lack of control he wields over his own voice. I noted that he adopts the voice of the private detective in trying to understand what he is doing in the Zone, towards the end of the novel. Similarly, he finds himself unwillingly adopting what can only be described as a John Wayne drawl, when he confronts Morituri, the Japanese Ensign, who has been watching him make love with Bianca: '"Yeah, I ... " why is Slothrop drawling this way? "saw ya watching ... last *night too*, mister. [...] W'l hell, Ensign ... why don'tcha just ... join in? *They're* always lookin' fer ... company."'[83]

Facing the world only with paranoia (as he impossibly tries to make everything fit into a single scheme, devoted to him) or the alternative, anti-paranoia (where he has no connection with anything else) Slothrop's attempts to make sense of his world are doomed to failure. Once the paranoid approach fails, he is sent to the opposite, anti-paranoid pole, and it is perhaps this that we can use to explain Slothrop's eventual disintegration at the end of the novel when he is 'Scattered all over the Zone'.[84] What the novel seems to suggest is the need for a middle ground, between global (paranoia) and local (anti-paranoia).

This can be seen not only in relation to Slothrop's attempt to make sense of his world, but also in relation to the reader's attempt to make sense of *Gravity's Rainbow*. Much has been made of the way in which the novel repudiates closure and resists the imposition of ordered meaning structures upon it. Lance Olsen, for instance, argues that 'the text abandons the Newtonian belief in cause-and-effect and drifts into a world of statistical probability',[85] and Robert D. Newman claims that 'the implication inherent [in

---

[81] Pynchon, *Gravity's Rainbow*, p. 561.
[82] Pynchon, *Gravity's Rainbow*, p. 244.
[83] Pynchon, *Gravity's Rainbow*, p. 473.
[84] Pynchon, *Gravity's Rainbow*, p. 712.
[85] Lance Olsen, 'Deconstructing the Enemy of Color: The Fantastic in *Gravity's Rainbow*', *Studies in the Novel* 18 (1986), p. 80.

the novel's refusal to coalesce into meaning structures] is that interpretation as a stay against confusion fosters entropic and delusory patterns in its effort to harness the flux of life'.[86] Both critics imply that the novel resists attempts to produce comprehensive interpretations of it, and that it will not yield to any overall explanation – for Olsen, any form of cause-and-effect is rendered implausible by the novel, and for Newman any interpretation that we produce is delusion, because it will not render the full reality of life. In other words, they imply that we must abandon a 'paranoid' criticism, which aims to make everything about the text yield up its meaning and fit into a grand interpretative structure.

This repudiation of 'paranoid' criticism (seeking a single explanation of the text) is fully justified, but Olsen and Newman seem to assume that by rejecting it, and by rejecting the text's closure, we necessarily have to go to the opposite extreme, and adopt an anti-paranoid approach which refuses to find any meaning in the text at all. If we reject any sort of cause-and-effect, and any sort of interpretation, then the novel just fragments, much as Slothrop himself does, into a renunciation of all meaning. This is, of course, as untenable for literary criticism as it is unpleasant for Slothrop. If we read, and especially if we write about, the novel, we necessarily find some meaning in it, and this is of course exactly what Olsen and Newman do in the remainder of their articles.

Gravity's Rainbow is not so much a rejection of all possibility of meaning, as of traditional meaning structures. Paranoia (connection and control) and anti-paranoia (complete lack of connection and control), are part of the same Enlightenment discourse which stresses that we must adopt one or the other of these. Pynchon's novel suggests that they need not be antagonistically opposed to each other, and fosters the production of interpretations which are never stable. By necessity we create meanings from the novel as we read it, but these meanings are always in flux, always exploring the scales between paranoia (where the text yields a single unitary meaning) and anti-paranoia (where the text dissolves into a series of disconnected episodes).

To return, at last, to the brief discussion about Lyotard with which this sub-section began, what both Slothrop and the reader find is the inadequacy of trying to construct either grand narratives, or just *petit récits*, to make sense of the world. When Slothrop is beset by paranoia, and sees himself as the product of a universal conspiracy, he is trying to construct a grand narrative which will make sense of everything. Similarly, when the reader tries to make the huge volume of information which constitutes *Gravity's Rainbow* cohere into a lucid, unitary meaning, he or she is also trying to construct a grand narrative

---

[86]   Robert D. Newman, *Understanding Thomas Pynchon*, Understanding Contemporary American Literature (Columbia: South Carolina University Press, 1986), p. 132.

that will make sense of everything within the text. Both are doomed to failure because there is too much information, and because there is a surfeit of plausible, but contradictory, explanations which make sense of it.

Conversely, when Slothrop is beset by anti-paranoia, he ceases trying to connect with the rest of the world, and in effect constructs a *petit récit* which is over-zealous in its embrace of the local (there is just him, and there is no link to the rest of the world). If the reader, despairing at the impossibility of making ultimate sense of the novel, does the same, and tries to disconnect the different pieces of information from each other, then he or she is in effect resolving the novel into a series of *petit récits*. This must fail as surely as a grand narrative will. Slothrop does fit into the wider scheme of things in some respects, and cannot exist on his own. Nor can the reader ever, for more than a moment, seriously entertain the notion that the novel is beyond interpretation – it is just that our interpretations stay in flux.

A grand narrative implies a rigid structure into which everything must fit, and *petit récits* imply no large structure at all. Neither option is viable for the production of a body of knowledge which aspires both to explain the world, and to be open to revision and refinement.

The links between literature and science in the form of the discourses discussed here are obviously open to questions about verification. If there is no direct series of links between the literature and the science – and therefore no possibility of absolute verification or falsification – how can the connection between the two realms ever be established? This is partly a product of the sort of culture which is under discussion here, and the inevitable constraints upon our inquiry into it. It is not being argued that the literature 'causes' the science, or that the science 'causes' the literature, in any obvious way: rather that they are both the manifestations of a more general postmodern perspective. This perspective is discussed in greater detail in chapter 6.

However, there are instances when the linking discourses between the literary and the scientific do produce more concrete correlations. The next case study provides an example. Here a specific metaphor – that of living things (including humans) as machines – crops up in both the literature and the science. Again, there is no direct passage from the literary to the scientific texts. However, both draw on the same stream and, indeed, both explore a characteristically late twentieth-century version of the metaphor: living things as *electronic* machines. In both cases the deployment of this metaphor inevitably raises questions about free will and determinism, about the relations between the mechanical and the organic, and about what it means to be alive.

Chapter 4

Discourses of Identity: Machines, Bodies and Information

And here I give particular emphasis to showing that, if there were such machines which had the organs and appearance of a monkey or of some other irrational animal, we would have no means of recognizing that they were not of exactly the same nature as these animals: instead of which, if there were machines which had a likeness to our bodies and imitated our actions ... we would still have two very certain means of recognizing that they were not, for all that, real men.[1]

In the *Discourse on Method*, quoted here and first published in 1637, René Descartes formulates human identity by comparing humans, animals and machines. He imagines two sorts of automata, the first of which is designed to mimic a monkey, and the second to imitate a human. He claims that there is no reason why, in principle, the first should not succeed in its purpose, convincing us that it is indeed a monkey. However, the second would fail for two interconnected reasons: it would be incapable of responding to the sense of anything said to it (even though it could be constructed to say particular phrases in response to being touched), and it would fail in any task that required it to act 'through knowledge' (even though it could conceivably perform certain predictable tasks better than people).

This defines human identity in terms of absolute difference (it is not just a distinction of degree) from machines and animals (which are seen as essentially similar). This difference is based upon the famous Cartesian split between mind and body, with the mind separated from the material world so that the 'reasonable soul ... could not in any way be derived from the power of matter'.[2] Humans have a mind and reason (it is significant that the first automaton is to be modelled on an 'irrational' creature), and this is what makes us special.

---

[1] René Descartes, 'Discourse on Method', *'Discourse on Method' and Other Writings*, trans. F.E. Sutcliffe (Middlesex: Penguin, 1968), pp. 73–4.

[2] Descartes, p. 76. The problem of how the mind might interact with matter to affect the body is a difficult one for Descartes which he eventually solves by suggesting that the pineal gland is the medium through which thoughts have material consequences.

What Descartes's anecdote about the two automata also does is enact a standard metaphor, with a long history, whereby the body is seen as a machine – it is a metaphor which is apparent whenever the heart is seen as a pump, or the lungs as bellows, or joints as levers. What this chapter focuses on is a contemporary reconfiguring of this metaphor, assimilating it into the postmodern posture toward the past. This new version of the metaphor takes machines peculiar to the late twentieth century – machines for processing information: computers and the information technology associated with them – and uses them to investigate human identity. This is significant because these new sorts of machines are used to understand what is at the heart of life – genetics – and what traditionally marks humans out from animals – the brain. The use of this metaphor, and the new understanding of life with which it is associated, therefore problematise the understanding of human identity formulated by Descartes. If our minds are machines, and if at the heart of life stands not a divine essence but the material world, then what is it exactly that makes us human (as opposed to animal), and what is it exactly that makes us alive? (Are we just machines that work instead of machines that do not work?)

David Porush has explored this idea in *The Soft Machine* where he argues that 'We live not in an information age but a cybernetic one. Our lives are dominated not only by the getting and sending of information, but the spin-offs from this technology'.[3] His book traces the genesis of a particular branch of postmodern fiction which he terms 'cybernetic'. The essence of his argument is that fiction has always dealt with the various metaphors of machines which are used to characterise humans, and that with the change of the predominant machine metaphor in recent years, fiction has also changed to reflect and contest these new metaphors.

This chapter is conceived in the spirit of Porush's study, in that it explores the disputed border between the natural and the artificial. Just as the last chapter showed how postmodern discourses of knowledge upset binary distinctions between order and disorder, and global and local, so this chapter will investigate the opening up of a territory between the natural and the artificial in postmodern discourses of identity. However, it departs from Porush's project by focusing directly on scientific texts at the same level as literary texts. Porush was concerned with a literary cybernetic discourse; this chapter is concerned with literary and scientific cybernetic discourses of identity.

Cybernetic fiction, Porush says, may deal directly with robots or computers, or explore the mechanisation of the human on a deeper,

---

[3]   David Porush, *The Soft Machine: Cybernetic Fiction* (New York: Methuen, 1985), p. 1.

metaphorical level.[4] Given this, William Gibson's trilogy of novels, *Neuromancer, Count Zero,* and *Mona Lisa Overdrive,* are obvious choices for a study hoping to explore cybernetic fiction. Gibson himself is a key figure in the development of 'cyberpunk' science fiction, and the novels' concern with a mechanised future, and with the interrelations of the human and the machine, clearly lend themselves to a study of this type. Whether they mirror their cybernetic themes self-reflexively in form and style, as they strictly should in order to qualify as cybernetic fictions,[5] is more questionable. Nevertheless, there is a conscious concern with the borders between the human and the machine which is, in many ways, representative of a wider cultural concern with the natural and the artificial.

At first glance Richard Dawkins's books about evolution are a much less obvious choice for a study of this type. Dawkins is interested in explaining a particular version of evolutionary theory – perhaps best summed up in the title of his book *The Selfish Gene* – to the reader, and is not concerned, as Gibson so obviously is, with exploring the relationship between people and technology. Moreover, while Gibson's work shows evidence of the influence of postmodernist writers like Thomas Pynchon, a similar intellectual history clearly does not lie behind the four works by Dawkins focused on in this study: *The Selfish Gene, The Blind Watchmaker, River Out of Eden,* and *Climbing Mount Improbable.* It is certainly not the intention of this chapter to read (or misread) Dawkins as a closet postmodernist. What it will do, however, is focus on one aspect of his work that is relevant: the metaphor of DNA as a digital information technology. This metaphor is relevant because, although the context is very different to that of Gibson's novels, it raises exactly the same questions as the exploration of the relationship between biology and technology does there.

In the work of both writers is a contemporary discourse of identity that works the natural–artificial divide. This chapter explores this discourse by establishing, first of all, the centrality of information (and therefore information technology) to the world views of both writers, and then goes on to see how ideas of machines and organisms are reconfigured through the use of the central metaphor.

Worlds of Information

It is important to begin by stressing the centrality of information, especially as it relates to information technology, to the radically different projects of

4   See Porush, *Soft Machine,* p. 17.
5   See Porush, *Soft Machine,* p. 17.

Gibson and Dawkins. It is vital in two ways, which I shall describe in detail in the course of this section: as a central aspect of the worlds described by the two writers; and, more directly, in terms of the information technology which appears in their texts. Information lies at the heart of the fictional world described by Gibson, because the economy and the lives of the protagonists are driven by exchanges of information; in Dawkins's work, it is important because it is at the centre of the natural world, where the informational content of DNA changes as evolution progresses and one generation succeeds another. Information technology appears in Gibson's novels as an imagined future technology, where current trends towards faster and faster processing of information, and greater interconnectedness of different computer facilities, have been exaggerated to the point where they dominate the cultural and economic worlds; in Dawkins's work it appears as an important metaphor to describe DNA and the creatures and plants which carry it. The emphasis upon these technologies serves to stress and heighten the informational aspect of the worlds the two writers describe. I will begin by exploring these informational characteristics, before going on to deal with the technology associated with them in more detail.

Gibson's stress upon the importance of information is apparent within all three novels, most particularly in his descriptions of 'cyberspace' or the 'matrix'. This is his key invention: a world which resides wholly within computer systems and which is constituted by an unimaginable complexity of data. Case, the central protagonist in *Neuromancer*, watches a child's introduction to cyberspace where it is described as a 'consensual hallucination experienced daily by billions of legitimate operators [...] A graphic representation of data abstracted from the banks of every computer in the human system. Unthinkable complexity. Lines of light ranged in the nonspace of the mind.'[6] Although it is a 'hallucination', this world constructed wholly of data is actually the fundamental reality posited in the novels. This is partly because it is not wholly disconnected from the physical world, with the matrix representing data concentrations that exist in economic centres, and therefore producing a contorted correlation between the largest and brightest structures in the matrix, and the busiest cities. It is also because much of the action takes place within the matrix. Case is a 'console jockey', a 'cyberspace cowboy' who is hired for his skill in navigating the matrix and penetrating restricted areas of it. Importantly, there is a direct feedback from the virtual world to the real world – get caught by defence systems in the matrix and the operator can

---

[6]   William Gibson, *Neuromancer* (1984; London: Grafton-HarperCollins, 1986), p. 67. My ellipses are put in square brackets to distinguish them from Gibson's.

die, a fate which nearly befalls Bobby Newmark, an aspiring cyberspace cowboy and the eponymous hero of *Count Zero*.[7]

However, information (and the technology associated with it) is not just important in providing the scene where the action takes place. It is much more than a mere high-tech, science-fiction backdrop because it is intrinsic to the motivations of Gibson's characters and the world in which they move. Examples which illustrate this centrality of information abound.

For instance, although Gibson only gives us a sketchy background to the short period of history between our own time and that he imagines, we learn that a significant feature of conflicts in this period is the battle for information. So, the three-week war with Russia that we learn about in *Neuromancer* (the novel was written before the end of the cold war) included a battle for and about information for the first time, with American combatants trying 'to burn this Russian nexus with virus programs'.[8] This operation is the forerunner of the culture Gibson invents where the protagonists are characters like Case and Bobby Newmark, who make their livings trying to break into protected sites and steal information on the matrix.

Similarly, the plot of *Count Zero* revolves around the attempts by one company, Hosaka, to ensure the successful defection of Mitchell, a highly-skilled expert from another company, Maas Biolabs. What they are fighting for here is expertise, the ability to manipulate information. Gibson takes the thriller genre, and blends it with a high-tech world. The future he imagines is one dominated by multinational companies, rather than nation states, and they have at their disposal immense resources. Indeed, they have acquired all the characteristics of (usually despotic) nation states, except for the ties to a specific physical territory. Instead of competing for land, they fight for, and deal in, information and technology.[9]

In *Mona Lisa Overdrive*, Britain is described as lagging behind in this shift from the nation state to the multinational corporation. However, this state of affairs is threatened by Roger Swain, who 'has recently come into possession of a very high-grade source of intelligence and is busy converting it into power'.[10] By the end of the novel we are to believe that Swain is deploying

---

[7] William Gibson, *Count Zero* (1986; London: Voyager-HarperCollins, 1995), p. 31.

[8] Gibson, *Neuromancer*, p. 39.

[9] This mirrors Lyotard's prediction that information will be the most valuable commodity in the future, possibly even replacing land as the key issue over which wars will be fought: 'It is conceivable that the nation-states will one day fight for control of information, just as they battled in the past for control over territory'. Jean-François Lyotard, *The Postmodern Condition: A Report on Knowledge*, trans. Geoff Bennington and Brian Massumi, Theory and History of Literature 10 (1979; Manchester University Press, 1986), p. 5.

[10] William Gibson, *Mona Lisa Overdrive* (1988; London: Voyager-HarperCollins, 1995), p. 207.

this information so that he can take over power in the country: 'He's bloody *changing* it [the government]. Redistributing power to suit himself. Information. Power. Hard data'.[11] Because information is so central to the fictional world that Gibson imagines, Swain is able to deploy it as a means of securing political control.

Information also figures prominently in Dawkins's work. Importantly, like Gibson, he concentrates upon information as it relates to information technology, presenting the DNA molecule as a sophisticated 'natural' information technology. The centrality of this metaphor to Dawkins's work (at times, because the informational content of DNA seems so intrinsic, this becomes more than metaphorical, as we shall see) derives from his view of evolution from the gene's point of view. The unit of natural selection which is most important, according to Dawkins, is not the species, or even the individual, but the gene – so 'survival of the fittest' means, in effect, survival of the fittest gene.[12] In effect he reverses the popular perception which sees DNA as the means by which species or individual organisms are preserved into the future, arguing that organisms are actually 'survival machines' built for the benefit of genes.[13] Genes which cooperate successfully with each other to build bodies with a greater likelihood of surviving and reproducing than their rivals, will be those which tend to survive into the future. Consequently, 'the basic unit of natural selection is best regarded not as the species, nor as the population, nor even as the individual, but as some small unit of genetic material which it is convenient to label the gene'.[14]

Information comes in as an important concept here because DNA is characterised, more than anything else, by its informational properties: 'DNA can be regarded as a set of instructions for how to make a body, written in the A,T,C,G alphabet of the nucleotides'.[15] With DNA described here as a set of instructions, what we have foregrounded is the idea of information. Dawkins carefully defines what he means by a gene: 'A gene is defined as any portion of chromosomal material that potentially lasts for enough generations to serve as a

---

[11]   Gibson, *Mona Lisa*, p. 268.

[12]   Arguments favouring the gene-centred view occur in all of Dawkins's books, but can perhaps be found most clearly explained in the third chapter, 'Immortal Coils', of *The Selfish Gene*. Richard Dawkins, *The Selfish Gene*, 2nd edn (1976; Oxford University Press, 1980), pp. 21–45.

[13]   This phrase recurs frequently in Dawkins's work – its first appearance is in the fourth line of the preface to his first book. Dawkins, *Selfish Gene*, p. v.

[14]   Dawkins, *Selfish Gene*, p. 39. Stephen Jay Gould articulates the argument against Dawkins's selfish gene theory in 'Caring Groups and Selfish Genes', *The Panda's Thumb: More Reflections in Natural History* (New York: Norton, 1980), pp. 85–92.

[15]   Dawkins, *Selfish Gene*, p. 22.

unit of natural selection'.[16] This definition emphasises information over everything else, because each gene is a meaningful piece of code occurring on chromosomes in different organisms. It is this informational quality which makes metaphors taken from information technology such potent ways of explaining how DNA works: the selfish gene is not so much a single strand of DNA as 'all replicas of a particular bit of DNA, distributed throughout the world', and it 'is trying to get more numerous in the gene pool. Basically it does this by helping to program the bodies in which it finds itself to survive and reproduce'.[17]

With information centred so prominently in the works of Gibson and Dawkins, it is not surprising that information technology, so ubiquitous in the late twentieth century, should itself figure prominently in their books. The centrality of this technology is self-evident in the case of Gibson, and will have been obvious from my earlier comments. What is worth mentioning in addition is that genetics itself also figures in his work. Indeed, it is highly significant that the two strands of science and technology which he extrapolates from their present status, to an imagined future level of sophistication, are information technology and genetics. Just as the data coded into computers is open to manipulation and reorganisation, so DNA is projected, in his novels, as being susceptible to recoding.

For instance, we are told in *Neuromancer* that although horses have been extinct for a few years, some people are still trying to 'code 'em up from the DNA',[18] albeit unsuccessfully, and that mink DNA is used to artificially manufacture fur.[19] Similarly, the novels feature characters who have had their bodies reshaped and remoulded in various ways, and who are adorned with prosthetics of various kinds (most obviously Molly, who features in the first and third books and has, among other attachments, steel blades which emerge from beneath her fingernails). Not only this, but the biological and the electronic are actually merged in various ways; these will be dealt with later on in this chapter because they are crucial to the view of identity which the novels offer us.

It has already been mentioned that information technology as a metaphor for DNA is central to Dawkins's work. Three of his best-known books have chapters devoted predominantly to DNA as an information technology: 'The

---

[16]   Dawkins, *Selfish Gene*, p. 28. This definition is taken from G.C. Williams. For a full citation see Dawkins, *Selfish Gene*, pp. 272–3.

[17]   Dawkins, *Selfish Gene*, p. 88. It should be noted that Dawkins is not, of course, suggesting that genes consciously try to get more numerous, but merely that those which are better at building bodies likely to survive and reproduce will be those which will, on the whole, prosper.

[18]   Gibson, *Neuromancer*, p. 113.

[19]   Gibson, *Neuromancer*, p. 149.

Gene Machine' in *The Selfish Gene*, 'The Power and the Archives' in *The Blind Watchmaker*, and 'The Robot Repeater' in *Climbing Mount Improbable*. In truth, however, the metaphor is not limited to these chapters, and runs right through all four works with which I am here concerned.

With DNA defined in Dawkins's work in terms of the information it encodes, it is important to note that he conceives of it as a digital, rather than an analogue, information technology. This distinction is described at various points by Dawkins – perhaps at greatest length in a four-page section of *River Out of Eden*[20] – but the key characteristics of a digital technology can be briefly summarised. Most importantly, by storing information in a number of discrete states (a digital system's 'fundamental elements are either definitely in one state or definitely in another state, with no half measures and no intermediates or compromises')[21] a digital information technology offers the perfect transmission of information not possible with analogue technology. It is precisely in terms of a digital technology that Dawkins describes genetics: 'the information technology of living cells uses four states, which we may conventionally represent as A, T, C and G. There is very little difference, in principle, between a two-state binary information technology like ours, and a four-state information technology like that of the living cell'.[22] It is because of this essential similarity between artificial and 'natural' technologies that Dawkins uses so many analogies from information technology – particularly from computing, which is the digital information technology *par excellence* – in order to describe how genetic information changes and evolves in the course of evolution.

As well as offering the possibility of high fidelity transmission of information, a digital information storage system also makes natural selection possible. When genes are mixed in reproduction each bit of genetic information comes either from one parent or from the other – it is not a mix of the two. This is important to natural selection because it means that populations do not grow more and more like each other, but diversity is maintained as beneficial traits can be preserved, without dilution, down the generations.[23]

However, not only does Dawkins suggest that information technology provides a convenient way of understanding how genes work. He even, in places, goes further, suggesting that it is much more than a convenient metaphor: information is so central to the business of DNA that it actually is, to all intents and purposes, an information technology. This is most apparent

[20]   Richard Dawkins, *River Out of Eden*, Science Masters (London: Weidenfeld and Nicholson, 1995), pp. 12–16.
[21]   Dawkins, *The Blind Watchmaker* (Harlow: Longman, 1986), p. 112.
[22]   Dawkins, *Blind Watchmaker*, p. 115.
[23]   For a lengthier description of the importance of digitalness to the theory of evolution see Dawkins, *Blind Watchmaker*, pp. 113–14.

at the beginning of chapter 5, 'The Power and the Archives', in *The Blind Watchmaker*: 'On the bank of the Oxford canal at the bottom of my garden is a large willow tree, and it is pumping downy seeds into the air ... It is raining instructions out there; it's raining programs; it's raining tree-growing, fluff-spreading algorithms. That is not a metaphor, it is the plain truth. It couldn't be any plainer if it were raining floppy discs'.[24]

DNA exists, in this view, as a series of instructions for building organisms, and also as a computer program for directing their behaviour: 'genes too control the behaviour of their survival machines, not directly with their fingers on puppet strings, but indirectly like the computer programmer. All they can do is set it up beforehand; then the survival machine is on its own, and the genes can only sit passively inside'.[25]

The further development of these analogies between genetics and information technology takes us into the whole issue of identity with which the rest of the chapter is concerned. It is where analogies with information technology are brought to bear upon the development of various organisms, that we find a discourse of information that taps the same streams as those which Gibson draws on. What Gibson and Dawkins do is call into question the natural–artificial divide, transgressing the border from both directions: there is a migration of things normally associated with the natural into machine territory, and vice versa. We will turn first to the latter of these transgressions, exploring the ways in which living things are described as, or supplemented by, artificial entities.

Border Disputes along the Natural–Artificial Divide (a): Electronic Organisms

It has already been mentioned that in Gibson's trilogy, physical changes are brought about by the various prosthetics with which characters supplement their bodies. The restrictions of the flesh can also be overcome by accessing cyberspace, with the body transcended, rather than supplemented, in a world where those with the requisite skills manipulate matterless streams of information.

The characters themselves are referred to, by Gibson and by each other, in technological terms (particularly those to do with information technology and electronic circuitry), and this is another means by which the natural is modified by the electronic. For instance, a drug that Case takes 'lit his

---

[24] Dawkins, *Blind Watchmaker*, p. 111.
[25] Dawkins, *Selfish Gene*, p. 52.

circuits',[26] Molly, in resignation, says that she sometimes hurts people because 'I guess it's just the way I'm wired',[27] and she tells Case that she knows 'how you're wired'.[28] This ties in with a more general preponderance of technological metaphors used to describe natural phenomena. The most dramatic and well known of these is the opening sentence of *Neuromancer*: 'The sky above the port was the color of television, tuned to a dead channel'.[29] As we begin reading the trilogy, we are immediately faced with a technological description of a natural phenomenon, made all the more poignant as we normally expect the sky to be associated with metaphors of freedom and escape. Indeed, there is an interesting twist upon the convention of pathetic fallacy here – as readers we are just about to meet Case, who has had his nervous system damaged by his former employers so that he can no longer have access to cyberspace. He had 'lived for the bodiless exultation of cyberspace' and this is the 'Fall' for him.[30] He feels imprisoned, 'tuned to a dead channel' like the sky above him.

For Case, the character with whom the reader is asked to identify in the first book, the natural body is restrictive. In comparison with the 'bodiless exultation' of cyberspace, the body itself becomes a hindrance: 'In the bars he'd frequented as a cowboy hotshot, the elite stance involved a certain relaxed contempt for the flesh. The body was meat. Case fell into the prison of his own flesh'.[31] Indeed, Case is characterised by his contempt for the flesh: 'Travel was a meat thing'[32] we are told, and when death threatens he mutters, 'Here comes the meat'.[33] Life without technological enhancement of some sort is unbearable for Case.

All these literal and metaphorical modifications of people by technology create an atmosphere in which the distinction between nature and artifice is of diminished importance. Perhaps the most important way in which these incursions from the artificial into the natural are made is through the 'constructs', which can be found in the form of Dixie Flatline, in the first book, and Finn, in the third. These allow Gibson to open up questions about what makes things alive, and what distinguishes the organic from the inorganic.

The constructs are coded, computer versions of dead people, 'a hardwired ROM cassette replicating a dead man's skills, obsessions, knee-jerk responses'.[34] This definition provides an interesting comparison to a passage in

26   Gibson, *Neuromancer*, p. 29.
27   Gibson, *Neuromancer*, p. 37.
28   Gibson, *Neuromancer*, p. 41.
29   Gibson, *Neuromancer*, p. 9.
30   Gibson, *Neuromancer*, p. 12.
31   Gibson, *Neuromancer*, p. 12.
32   Gibson, *Neuromancer*, p. 97.
33   Gibson, *Neuromancer*, p. 194.
34   Gibson, *Neuromancer*, p. 97.

The Blind Watchmaker, where Dawkins seeks to explain genetic information as a certain kind of computer memory: 'DNA is ROM. It can be read millions of times over, but only written to once – when it is first assembled at the birth of the cell in which it resides. The DNA in the cells of any individual is "burned in"'.[35] These quotations from Gibson and Dawkins illustrate why the pairing of genetics and information technology is so seductive – information technology provides the metaphor by which we know genetics, because it fits so neatly into our need to understand how information, encoded in DNA, can affect our bodies.

The pairing of the two raises questions about definitions of life and death, sentience and pure mechanical insentience. These questions are generally implicit in Gibson's novels, but become explicit in a number of passages relating to the constructs. When Case asks Dixie Flatline, one of the constructs, whether or not he is sentient, he receives this reply: 'Well it *feels* like I am, kid, but I'm really just a bunch of ROM. It's one of them, ah, philosophical questions, I guess ...'.[36] Even Dixie does not know if he is sentient or not – and even were he to claim that he was, it would raise the question of whether he (it?) had just been programmed to behave in a lifelike way, to the extent of claiming to be alive. In *Mona Lisa Overdrive*, Kumiko is similarly curious about the Finn, a character from the first and second novels, who is now dead but has had his personality coded into a computer in an armoured housing, standing in an alley: 'But did it wake, Kumiko wondered, when the alley was empty? Did its laser vision scan the silent fall of midnight snow?'[37]

There is a sense in which both these constructs are just reconstructions, imitations of dead people. Yet, they seem so convincing in their imitation of life that they are treated as though they are alive, and may perhaps be so. The question these episodes raise is about the level of complexity at which something ceases to be a clever imitation and becomes, to all intents and purposes, alive: at what point do these constructs pass across the border from the artificial to the sentient? Does the Finn only exist as a living thing for other people, or is it alive for itself, when it is alone and scans the 'midnight snow'? The other way in which Gibson's novels pose questions about life, death, sentience and insentience, is through the Artificial Intelligences that are at the heart of the mysteries in the novels, but these will be returned to in the next section of the chapter, which details the penetration of the artificial by the natural.

Dawkins's work also includes numerous examples of the incorporation of machines and technology into what we are used to thinking of as being

---

[35]   Dawkins, *Blind Watchmaker*, p. 117.
[36]   Gibson, *Neuromancer*, p. 159.
[37]   Gibson, *Mona Lisa*, p. 174.

naturally alive. Although the incorporation is in many of these cases metaphorical – things are described as machines in order to explain how they work – the issues that are raised (about determinism and the borders between the natural and the artificial) are remarkably similar to those broached by Gibson.

Most obvious is his description of organisms as 'survival machines' for genes. As mentioned earlier, he reverses the commonly-held assumption that genes are the means by which organisms ensure the continuation of the species into the future, and pictures the body as a machine built by genes in order to guarantee their survival down the ages. This is most dramatically stated in the paragraph that ends the second chapter of *The Selfish Gene*. After describing one theory of the initial evolution of life on earth (whereby an initial chance event leads to the existence of replicators, molecules capable of copying themselves, which gradually improve as the best ones survive at the expense of the others) he asks what has happened to the replicators now, answering this question with a statement which it is worth quoting at length:

> Now they swarm in huge colonies, safe inside gigantic lumbering robots, sealed off from the outside world, communicating with it by tortuous indirect routes, manipulating it by remote control. They are in you and in me; they created us, body and mind; and their preservation is the ultimate rationale for our existence. They have come a long way, those replicators. Now they go by the name of genes, and we are their survival machines.[38]

The analogy with robots is in some respects a metaphor. However, there is also a truth to it which works the natural–artificial divide. This is brought out in a fascinating endnote that appears in the second edition of the book, and deals with criticisms of the passage made by readers of the first edition. Here Dawkins tells us that the passage has been cited 'in gleeful evidence of my rabid "genetic determinism"'.[39]

Dawkins's response to this criticism is enlightening because it suggests that developments in information technology have produced a shift that the critics of the passage fail to see, making the outdated assumption that robots are 'rigidly inflexible morons'.[40] Since the dawn of 'the golden age of electronics', Dawkins says, robots have become capable of 'learning, intelligence, and creativity',[41] and should be viewed in a way that is more appropriate to these characteristics. What he draws our attention to here,

---

[38]   Dawkins, *Selfish Gene*, pp. 19–20.
[39]   Dawkins, *Selfish Gene*, p. 270.
[40]   Dawkins, *Selfish Gene*, p. 270.
[41]   Dawkins, *Selfish Gene*, p. 270.

therefore, are three things: firstly, the importance of the electronic age; secondly, that machines now have more of the characteristics normally associated with the 'natural' world; and thirdly, that the natural world is itself constituted by lots of highly complicated, biological machines. This last point is highlighted a little later on in his endnote, and it is again worth quoting this passage at length because it is central to the argument linking Dawkins with Gibson:

> People who think that robots are by definition more 'deterministic' than human beings are muddled (unless they are religious, in which case they might consistently hold that humans have some divine gift of free will denied to mere machines). If, like most of the critics of my 'lumbering robot' passage, you are not religious, then face up to the following question. What on earth do you think you are, if not a robot, albeit a very complicated one?[42]

This explicitly states the belief that the only difference between a machine and an organism is, ultimately, to do with the level of sophistication – the strict border between the two is not really maintainable. This is in direct contrast to Descartes's definition of the human cited at the beginning of this chapter. In pondering the differences between humans and automata he suggested that although bodies could be mimicked by machines, minds – the faculty of reason – could not. This position can no longer be sustained because we have electronic machines which can perform certain incredible acts of calculation. Although they might not be able to 'think' like humans, it is not inconceivable that they should do so in the future; at least, there is not such a gulf between human and machine that we cannot see that the machine mimics, at some level, the operations of the human brain.[43]

The other major contemporary departure from the belief of Descartes's days is that the harsh dividing line between species has been collapsed by Darwinism. Descartes saw reason as a faculty which not only separated humans from machines, but also from animals; now we have to acknowledge that the divisions between species are not so rigidly drawn, and that animals can be seen to have human faculties, albeit on a 'lower' level.[44]

---

[42]   Dawkins, *Selfish Gene*, pp. 270–71.

[43]   Bruce Mazlish gives an extended discussion of Descartes's conception of machines in which he makes a similar point to the one I am making here. He also contrasts the Cartesian machines with those described by Norbert Wiener, an issue I explore toward the end of this chapter. Bruce Mazlish, *The Fourth Discontinuity: The Co-Evolution of Humans and Machines* (New Haven: Yale University Press, 1993), pp. 19–26.

[44]   For example, in an article about the 1996 Tucson conference about consciousness, the *New Scientist* reported the work of various researchers who were exploring the language-forming skills of other species, commenting that 'recently the evidence has become much stronger that humans are not alone in using language and in forming abstract concepts'. Alun

When the natural–artificial boundary is called into question in this way, the determinism–free will border is almost inevitably contested as well. If we return to Dawkins's defence of the 'lumbering robot' passage in his endnote, we can see this very clearly. Misreadings of the passage, Dawkins notes, suggest it says that genes 'control' us, body and mind, rather than (as he actually wrote) that they 'created' us. The distinction is extremely important because it makes clear that although genes did indeed create us, they do not directly control us, and this leaves us a measure of independence from them: 'We effortlessly (well, fairly effortlessly) defy them every time we use contraception'.[45] These sentiments find further expression in the dramatic closing sentences to the first edition of *The Selfish Gene* (the second edition includes two extra chapters): 'We are built as gene machines and cultured as meme machines, but we have the power to turn against our creators. We, alone on earth, can rebel against the tyranny of the selfish replicators'.[46] There is a pay-off between free will and determinism here – it is, in the picture of life with which Dawkins presents us, not useful to talk of either as an absolute category, at least not in relation to humans.

All this shows how the natural is penetrated by images of information technology in Dawkins's work through the description of DNA as an information technology, but it should be noted that there is one further way in which this occurs in his descriptions of evolution. This is a more straightforward development from the traditional metaphors of bodies as machines (hearts as pumps, and so forth), focusing on minds as machines: 'Brains may be regarded as analogous in function to computers. They are analogous in that both types of machine generate complex patterns of output, after analysis of complex patterns of input, and after reference to stored information'.[47]

Here, again, because we are in the information age, we see the primary symbol of information processing, the computer, invoked as a way of understanding a natural process – the dominant machine metaphor is electronic rather than mechanical now.[48] As with his 'lumbering robot' passage, Dawkins

---

Anderson, Bob Holmes and Liz Else, 'Zombies, Dolphins and Blindsight', *New Scientist* 4 May 1996: p. 21.

[45] Dawkins, *Selfish Gene*, p. 271.

[46] Dawkins, *Selfish Gene*, p. 201. 'Memes' are invented by Dawkins as a way of talking about all the different things that make up culture ('tunes, ideas, ways of making pots', and so on), and how they are transmitted. For more about this see chapter 11 of Dawkins's book, 'Memes: The New Replicators'. Dawkins, *Selfish Gene*, pp. 189–201.

[47] Dawkins, *Selfish Gene*, p. 49.

[48] The metaphor of the brain as a computer has also informed work in cognitive psychology. For example, in an introduction to the field, Anthony J. Sanford writes that cognitive psychology often denotes a philosophical approach to the subject 'termed the *information processing* approach, and it has several important characteristics. First, it views

has found himself under attack for using this metaphor. Again he defends himself in a fascinating endnote:

> Statements like this worry literal-minded critics. They are right, of course, that brains differ in many respects from computers. ... This in no way reduces the truth of my statement about their being analogous in function. Functionally, the brain plays precisely the role of on-board computer – data processing, pattern recognition, short-term and long-term data storage, operation coordination, and so on.[49]

What the metaphor of the brain as a computer allows Dawkins to do, is to articulate in a powerful way the function that brains play in the survival of genes into the next generation: 'By dictating the way survival machines and their nervous systems are built, genes exert ultimate power over behaviour. But the moment-to-moment decisions about what to do next are taken by the nervous system. Genes are the primary policy-makers; brains are the executives'.[50] Computers provide compelling ways of understanding the processing of information. As a species which distinguishes itself from others in terms of brain size, it is hard to avoid the conclusion that we are, more than anything, information-processing creatures and therefore not dissimilar from the information-processing machines we create.

The difference between the metaphor used here, and that used to describe DNA as a digital information storage system, is that, in the earlier instance, there was something intrinsic to the way that DNA stores information that made the comparison more than a metaphor. Here, the metaphorical status of the 'brain as computer' is a little more obviously foregrounded: 'The basic unit of biological computers, the nerve cell or neurone, is really nothing like a transistor in its internal workings'.[51] Nevertheless, the difference between the thing being described and the metaphor used to describe it lies, again, only in the degree of sophistication: 'Certainly the code in which neurones communicate with each other seems to be a little bit like the pulse codes of digital computers, but the individual neurone is a much more sophisticated data-processing unit than the transistor. Instead of just three connections with

---

those activities which make up mental events as reflecting a flow of information. ... Secondly, such an approach implies a rather mechanistic view of the mind: it is seen as an automaton. The complexity of that automaton is very great, greater than the most flexible of modern computers, which many see as analogous to the mind'. Anthony J. Sanford, *Cognition and Cognitive Psychology*, Weidenfeld Psychology Ser. (London: Weidenfeld, 1985), pp. 1–2.

[49] Dawkins, *Selfish Gene*, p. 276.
[50] Dawkins, *Selfish Gene*, p. 60.
[51] Dawkins, *Selfish Gene*, p. 48.

other components, a single neurone may have tens of thousands'.[52] As with the descriptions of DNA, the comparison of brains with electronic technology seems, at times, to go beyond the purely metaphorical.

The relationship between humans and machines seems so much more complex and fraught, therefore, than in the view propounded by Descartes where there was an absolute and obvious distinction. If we understand ourselves as machines, what is free will? What makes us alive? These questions about ourselves find a close correspondence in the questions we might ask about our perception of machines, and it is these questions which are raised when we consider the other side of the process, when the artificial is penetrated by the natural.

Border Disputes along the Natural–Artificial Divide (b): Living Machines

The reverse process, whereby the artificial is penetrated by the natural, also takes place in both Gibson's and Dawkins's work. With Dawkins this is far less pronounced because he is seeking to explain to the lay reader how evolution works, and so is primarily concerned with what we normally think of as alive and natural, and not with machines. Nevertheless, in order to explain some points he draws out analogies between machines and organisms (some of which we have already seen), and in the process passes comment upon machines.

For instance, in a chapter of *The Selfish Gene* entitled 'Gene Machine', he draws out a number of analogies with various machines in order to make certain points. One of these is that organisms (survival machines) engage in apparent purposive behaviour – they act as if they are motivated by the conscious desire to achieve certain goals. Of course, we cannot know if animals are conscious or not, but Dawkins suggests it makes sense to talk about them as if they are, precisely because they engage in activities which seem to be motivated by a purpose. In this way the actual question of whether they are conscious or not can be left open. Dawkins illustrates this by an analogy with machines. It is useful, he says, to talk about machines as if they are conscious, even though we know they are not: 'it is easy to talk about machines that behave *as if* motivated by a purpose, and to leave open the question whether they are conscious'.[53] He then goes on to give the example of the Watt steam governor, which regulates the rate at which an engine works, shutting steam off when it goes too quickly, and increasing steam to it when it goes too slowly. It

---

52   Dawkins, *Selfish Gene*, p. 48.
53   Dawkins, *Selfish Gene*, p. 50.

is useful talk about it as if it *desires* to maintain an optimum speed, even though the process by which it does this is entirely mechanical. We can, therefore, make the same move in discussing the behaviour of animals. The justification for this proceeds in a curious (though entirely legitimate) way: because real machines behave in a way that seems to be conscious (even though we know that it is not), it is reasonable to talk about living things as though they are conscious (even though we do not really know whether they are), because they are like machines in this respect.

So, for an instant, we are asked to imagine that machines are conscious. Dawkins then goes on to show how more advanced machines (the examples he uses are guided missiles and chess computers) 'achieve more complex "lifelike" behaviour'.[54] There is never the implication that these actually are conscious or alive, and in this respect Dawkins cannot go as far as Gibson who in his fictions, as we shall see, imagines a future where machines really do achieve sentience. Nevertheless, although Dawkins does not invoke machines as living things ('The "desired" state of the Watt governor is a particular speed of rotation. Obviously it does not consciously desire it'),[55] he makes passing reference to the lifelikeness of machines in order to show how it is fruitful to think of organisms as purposeful machines. Natural and artificial are, to a degree, merged here.

The point is rather more forcefully made in *The Blind Watchmaker*. Dawkins's approach to evolution in this book is through William Paley's treatise of 1802, in which Paley argued that just as one assumes the existence of a watchmaker when one sees a watch, so we can assume the existence of a god-like creator when we find complexly-designed objects (living creatures) in the world. Dawkins's book is dedicated to showing how Paley was wrong, and that the theory of evolution is all that we need to explain the existence of life on Earth: the deity supposed by Paley is irrelevant to the question. He therefore starts off with a chapter 'Explaining the Very Improbable',[56] which shows how a religious explanation is unnecessary in accounting for the existence of complex life forms on Earth.

As part of this explanation he suggests a novel way of looking at machines: 'In this book they will be firmly treated as biological objects'.[57] Here machines are described as 'biological objects'; a few pages further on they are referred to as 'honorary living things'.[58] Dawkins's purpose is not, of course, to argue that these machines actually are alive – he is making a point about how we seek to explain things that appear to be consciously designed. Nevertheless,

[54]   Dawkins, *Selfish Gene*, p. 51.
[55]   Dawkins, *Selfish Gene*, p. 51.
[56]   Dawkins, *Blind Watchmaker*, pp. 1–18.
[57]   Dawkins, *Blind Watchmaker*, p. 1.
[58]   Dawkins, *Blind Watchmaker*, p. 10.

it is interesting that the natural and the artificial are used together in this way. Gibson, in his creation of a futuristic imaginary world, pushes this sense of living machines much further.

They crop up in two main ways in his novels: with technological artefacts coming to life, and with multinational corporations being treated as living entities. We will begin with the first of these because it offers the most direct route to an understanding of the border transgressions from the natural to the artificial in Gibson's work.

The 'constructs', which encode people's personalities, have already been discussed above. However, as well as viewing these as people who become machines, we could equally well see them as machines that come to life. This latter perspective is certainly apposite for making sense of the Artificial Intelligences (AIs) which lie at the heart of so many events in the novels. Indeed, if there is a common story which evolves over the course of the three books, it is a story about AIs – electronic machines – achieving sentience. One of the mysteries in *Neuromancer* is about who is in ultimate control of the sabotage operation in which Case and Molly are employed to take part. Initially it seems to be Armitage, who approaches them personally. However, they then discover that Armitage is merely a pawn being manipulated by an AI, known as Wintermute, and that Armitage's personality may even have been constructed for him by Wintermute.

As with the constructs, questions are raised about sentience and what distinguishes life from non-life. This comes across when Case and the AI, Wintermute, meet in a sort of virtual reality scenario. Wintermute tries to explain the enigma of its existence to Case, whilst revealing a little more of the mystery to him: '[I'm an] artificial intelligence, but you know that. Your mistake, and it's quite a logical one, is in confusing the Wintermute mainframe, Berne, with the Wintermute *entity* [...] I, insofar as I *have* an 'I' – this gets rather metaphysical, you see – I am the one who arranges things for Armitage'.[59]

This positing of an 'entity' separate from the physical hardware is evocative of Descartes's distinction between body and mind. There is something about the AI which Gibson wants to suggest really is, in some sense, alive. One could read the positing of this separate 'entity', or mind, as either conservative or radical in the extent to which it transgresses the binary distinction between the natural and the technological: it is conservative if one sees it as reinscribing the old mind–body dualism into these new living things; and it is radical if one sees it as transgressing the mind–body divide by suggesting that a living 'entity' arises spontaneously from the computing hardware and software.

---

[59]   Gibson, *Neuromancer*, p. 145.

Case, and his accomplice Molly, eventually find out that they are being used by Wintermute to launch an attack upon itself, cutting the safety devices that are meant to prevent it from getting any smarter, and allowing it to join up with another AI in Rio. When Case is briefly arrested by agents for the Turings, who police computer matters, one of them suggests that by cutting Wintermute's shackles Case will allow it to come alive in a dramatic way: 'You have no care for your species. For thousands of years men dreamed of pacts with demons. Only now are such things possible [...] What would your price be, for aiding this thing to free itself and grow?'[60]

The point about Wintermute's transition to a living status is made more forcefully in a later episode where Case again meets him in a virtual reality scenario. Wintermute picks up a vacuum tube from an old television and says, 'See this? Part of my DNA, sort of [...] You're always building models [...] Adding machines. I got no idea why I'm here now, you know that? But if the run goes off tonight, you'll have finally managed the real thing'.[61] The 'real thing' is presumably creating more than a model, something that is actually alive, because when Case expresses confusion Wintermute explains further: 'That's "you" in the collective. Your species'.[62] The description of a vacuum tube as a 'sort of' DNA reinforces this point.

Case and Molly's assault on the system is successful, but the second book, *Count Zero*, does not develop these ideas of sentience much further, except to introduce the 'biochip' (another merging of the artificial and the natural), the character of Angie (whom, we will discover in the final book, has been manipulated by an AI), and manifestations of strange, inexplicable occurrences on the matrix. These occurrences, interpreted in terms of the supernatural, as voodoo, suggest that the matrix is being seen as more than just an artificial construct and is, possibly, being invested with some lifelike properties.

It is indeed this last explanation which is provided in the final book of the series, *Mona Lisa Overdrive*. Angie, one of the principal characters, tries to find out about the time just after Case and Molly's assault on Wintermute when the matrix started behaving strangely, and known as 'When It Changed'. Angie finds that When It Changed is either an assumption that 'the cyberspace matrix is inhabited, or perhaps visited, by entities whose characteristics correspond with the primary mythform of a "hidden people"', or that it 'involves assumptions of omniscience, omnipotence, and incomprehensibility on the part of the matrix itself'.[63] In other words, the matrix seems to have

---

[60]   Gibson, *Neuromancer*, p. 193. The name of the computer police, the Turings, is a reference to Alan Turing, credited by some with inventing the first computer.
[61]   Gibson, *Neuromancer*, p. 204.
[62]   Gibson, *Neuromancer*, p. 204.
[63]   Gibson, *Mona Lisa*, p. 138.

become more than just a collection of computers. Molly recounts Case's theory about what happened to Wintermute: '[he] had this idea that it was gone, sort of; not *gone* gone, but gone *into* everything, the whole matrix. Like it wasn't *in* cyberspace anymore, it just *was*'.[64] Wintermute seems to have achieved lifelike properties, merging with the whole of cyberspace.

The operation for which Case and Molly were employed in the first book has freed the AI, which has gone into the matrix and achieved a sort of sentience, perhaps even a supernatural existence of some kind. The machine has become more than a machine, the biochip being the key component. This constitutes the thread of storyline which links the three novels: the erosion of the strict binary division between human and machine as the machine achieves sentience. The actual living experience of the machine is, however, always concealed from the reader, and only accessed through the attempts by the constructs or AIs to explain what it is to exist to the human characters – as though it is impossible to conceive of this other non-human intelligence. In this sense the 'mystery' of consciousness is preserved. The point at which the non-living becomes living is beyond comprehension, and Gibson resists the temptation to attempt explaining it.

The second way in which the natural–artificial divide is breached is through Gibson's presentation of the corporations which dominate his fictional world. They are almost living organisms themselves, taking on a life of their own which is independent of the people who populate them. In *Count Zero*, for example, Josef Virek's wealth has multiplied to the point where it seems to grow and pursue its own ends: 'Aspects of my wealth have become autonomous, by degrees; at times they even war with one another. Rebellion in the fiscal extremities'.[65] Virek himself only exists in a vat which keeps him alive, and his only contact with the 'real' world is through various forms of virtual reality. Looking at one of these virtual constructs, Marly senses the existence of a non-human life-form: 'And, for an instant, she stared directly into those soft blue eyes and knew, with an instinctive mammalian certainty, that the exceedingly rich were no longer even remotely human'.[66]

Similarly, in *Mona Lisa Overdrive*, the media corporation Sense/Net is found not to be run by its nominal human head, Hilton Swift, but by the AI Continuity. Continuity had initially appeared to be nothing more than a high-tech personal assistant but, it turns out, she actually controls Swift: 'Hilton Swift is obliged to implement Continuity's decisions. Sense/Net is too complex an entity to survive, otherwise, and Continuity, created long after the bright

---

[64]   Gibson, *Mona Lisa*, p. 175.
[65]   Gibson, *Count Zero*, p. 26.
[66]   Gibson, *Count Zero*, p. 29.

moment [When It Changed], is of another order'.[67] In an interesting echo of Dawkins's work, Continuity's motives are seen to be nothing more than self-perpetuation. This is the only 'purpose' which Dawkins allows us to subscribe to genes. The whole point of the selfish-gene theory is that those genes that act in a way which benefits their survival will be those which last longest – there is no conscious purpose here; it is just that those which are better at surviving will be those which, on the whole, tend to survive. This very point seems to be being made about Continuity, who runs things merely in order to continue in existence: 'Continuity is continuity. Continuity is Continuity's job ... '[68] This sentence could be applied to Dawkins's selfish genes – their purpose, as much as it can be described as such, is continuity.

In the *Neuromancer* trilogy, though, this presentation of corporations as self-perpetuating entities allows Gibson to produce a critique of multinational capitalism. For instance, when Case muses upon the biological nature of multinationals in *Neuromancer*, it opens up issues about the manipulation of individuals by corporate power structures:

> Power, in Case's world, meant corporate power. The zaibatsus, the multinationals that shaped the course of human history, had transcended old barriers. Viewed as organisms, they had attained a kind of immortality [...] [W]eren't the zaibatsus more like that ... hives with cybernetic memories, vast single organisms, their DNA coded in silicon?[69]

What makes the description of the corporations as alive so potent, is the equation that is made in this quotation, and throughout the books, between life (DNA), machine (silicon), and corporation (multinationals). The corporations have grown to such an extent that they act as though they really are alive, with an existence independent of (and more than that of) their individual human and machine parts.

Organisms and Machines: Concluding Remarks

Gibson imagines a world, then, where living things have become more like machines, and machines have become more like living things. He presents us

---

67   Gibson, *Mona Lisa*, p. 265.
68   Gibson, *Mona Lisa*, p. 265.
69   Gibson, *Neuromancer*, p. 242. The same point is made more explicitly in one of Gibson's short stories, 'The New Rose Hotel', in which Fox claims that the 'blood of a zaibatsu is information, not people. The structure is independent of the individual lives that comprise it. Corporation as life form'. *'Burning Chrome' and Other Stories* (London: HarperCollins, 1995), p. 129.

with a vision of permeable boundaries between the natural and the artificial, and there is no absolute definition to which we can aspire of what is and is not alive.

It makes sense to view this aspect of his work as postmodern because it necessarily involves a posture toward the past. This posture arises in the form of a rejection of the Cartesian conception of a mind sitting apart from the world of matter, linked to it only by the pineal gland. The observing mind does not exist outside the material world it observes. Indeed, mind very much is matter – minds are extended by electronic enhancements, and electronic machines give birth, in an emergent way, to minds.

This may seem a long way from the reality of our contemporary world, and from the descriptions of evolution which Richard Dawkins produces, where information technology is used as a metaphor to explain how DNA works. However, it is important to realise that his use of information technology is not just a literary conceit, used to explain a technical detail to the lay reader. There is something about DNA which makes it, in a literal sense, an information technology. A comment in *River Out of Eden* illustrates this beautifully, encapsulating the way in which our contemporary understanding reconfigures older definitions of life: 'There is no spirit-driven life force, no throbbing, heaving, pullulating, protoplasmic, mystic jelly. Life is just bytes and bytes and bytes of digital information'.[70] Life is not, in this understanding of it, imbued with any mystical qualities, and we need to alter our conceptions of it if we aspire to discuss these issues in an accurate manner.

This is important: the difference between the living and the non-living is not an essential one, but merely a difference in the level of complexity. What makes a living thing alive is that it is created by a highly complex digital information system. What Dawkins is trumpeting here is a change in the metaphors that we use to describe life – perhaps, indeed, it spells the end of attempts to imbue life with any mystical qualities, be they a soul, the detached mind proposed by Descartes, or the 'spark of being'[71] which Frankenstein is imagined to use to imbue his creature with life. In the cybernetic age, information, not mysticism, lies at the core of life:

> What lies at the heart of every living thing is not a fire, not warm breath, not a 'spark of life'. It is information, words, instructions. If you want a metaphor, don't think of fires and sparks and breath. Think, instead, of a billion discrete, digital characters carved in tablets

---

[70]   Dawkins, *River*, pp. 18–19.
[71]   Mary Shelley, *Frankenstein: Or, The Modern Prometheus* (1818; London: Penguin, 1985), p. 105.

of crystal. If you want to understand life, don't think about vibrant, throbbing gels and oozes, think about information technology.[72]

It is impossible to date this shift in conceptions of life precisely. However, it is reasonable to argue that it comes about in the second half of the twentieth century, and therefore ties in with Lyotard's claim, referenced in the last chapter, that postmodern discourses have arisen during the last fifty years. A key early text must be Norbert Wiener's *The Human Use of Human Beings*, first published in 1950. Wiener was prominent in developing the theory of communication and control mechanisms in both organisms and machines, and coined the term 'cybernetics' (which is of course picked up in Gibson's neologism of 'cyberspace').

The Human Use of Human Beings is a popularised version of Wiener's earlier work, *Cybernetics*, and in it we can find the sense of the equivalence of the electronic and the organic, which later flowers into Dawkins's and Gibson's presentations of the issue. Throughout the book, Wiener writes about notions of communication, control, and the processing of information, arguing that they are essentially the same whether we choose to consider them in relation to machines, humans or societies. He even addresses the problems of defining the word 'life' accurately, and the difficulties of using it to distinguish between humans and machines: 'Here I want to interject the semantic point that such words as life, purpose, and soul are grossly inadequate to precise scientific thinking ... Now that certain analogies of behavior are being observed between the machine and the living organism, the problem as to whether the machine is alive or not is, for our purposes, semantic'.[73] Wiener then goes on to describe the ways in which the new machines being developed during the middle of the twentieth century (the forerunners of computers), are like living things: they are islands of order, becoming more organised against a background of increasing entropy; they possess effector organs (similar to limbs) in order to carry out their tasks; they possess sense organs to monitor their environment; and as a result of these characteristics they are able, through feedback, to monitor and respond to the effects that they have on the local environment. Consequently, natural and artificial are fundamentally similar: 'the nervous system and the automatic machine are fundamentally alike in that they are

---

[72] Dawkins, *Blind Watchmaker*, p. 112.

[73] Norbert Wiener, *The Human Use of Human Beings: Cybernetics and Society*, 2nd edn (1950; London: Eyre and Spottiswoode, 1954), pp. 31–2. One of the examples that Wiener cites to illustrate this is the problem of whether viruses are, properly considered, alive, given that they only have some of the characteristics of living things. In recent years a mirror image of this dilemma has arisen in computing, where living metaphors are used to describe problems that beset computers – computer 'viruses' can 'infect' networks, and you can even get a disk 'doctor' to cure your machine.

devices which make decisions on the basis of decisions they have made in the past'.[74]

Furthermore, Wiener distinguishes between two kinds of machines. The older sort, which he terms Leibnitzian, 'saw the whole world as a collection of beings called "monads" whose activity consisted in the perception of one another on the basis of a pre-established harmony laid down by God'.[75] These are rather like the resolutely un-lifelike machines described by Descartes. They are predictable and similar to the primitive robots described as 'rigidly inflexible morons' by Dawkins. However, the second, newer sort of machines identified by Wiener (and being developed in the middle of the twentieth century) are more like living creatures. Wiener's presentation of them brings to mind the adaptive, growing machine intelligences of Gibson's *Neuromancer* trilogy, and Dawkins's emphasis on 'learning, intelligence, and creativity' in modern robots:

> Certain kinds of machines and some living organisms ... can, as we have seen, modify their patterns of behavior on the basis of past experience so as to achieve specific anti-entropic ends ... In other words, the organism is not like the clockwork monad of Leibnitz with its pre-established harmony with the universe, but actually seeks a new equilibrium with the universe and its future contingencies. Its present is unlike its past and its future unlike its present.[76]

It is therefore with the technological developments of the mid-twentieth century, and the new perception of humans and machines which they facilitated (and were facilitated by), that we can see the roots of the postmodern discourses discussed in this chapter.

Interestingly, Paul Davies and John Gribbin's presentation of contemporary science in *The Matter Myth* provides further evidence for this sort of paradigm shift – this new way of talking about what was previously seen as inanimate. Although they make no reference to postmodernism, their contention that the way of looking at the world, in the sciences, has changed, ties in with my suggestion in this chapter that the mechanical and the organic are becoming entwined in contemporary discourse. For instance, they label their final chapter, 'The Living Universe', and earlier on in their book contend that the language of science has shifted from a mechanical to an organic vocabulary:

---

[74]   Wiener, p. 33.
[75]   Wiener, p. 18.
[76]   Wiener, p. 48.

This burgeoning study of nonlinear systems is causing a remarkable shift of emphasis away from inert 'things' – lumpen matter responding to impressed forces – and towards 'systems' that contain elements of spontaneity and surprise. The old machine vocabulary of science is giving way to language more reminiscent of biology than physics – adaption, coherence, organization, and so on.[77]

These sort of changes do suggest a late twentieth-century reworking of our conceptions of the natural and artificial. Of course, such a reworking can lead either to a kind of mysticism (seeing that which is inanimate to be imbued with spirit), or a debunking of the mystical (that which was assumed to be divine or transcendent being shown instead to be just highly complex).

The final case study takes us into another area: the reworking of notions of time, and particularly of humanity's place in evolutionary time, in contemporary discourses. With this the shift to a 'postmodern' perspective is perhaps more dubious, and it may be argued that the posture of postmodernism actually repeats notions already at least implicit in the work of Charles Darwin in the nineteenth century.

---

[77] Paul Davies and John Gribbin, *The Matter Myth: Beyond Chaos and Complexity* (1991; London: Penguin, 1992), p. 55.

Chapter 5

Discourses of Time: Purpose and Absurdity

In recent decades, evolutionary biology has witnessed a shift, as it were, from modern romance to postmodern picaresque as the most compelling way to plot the history of life on this planet.[1]

In 'The End of Metanarratives in Evolutionary Biology', from which this quotation is taken, Eric White argues that many contemporary narratives of evolution are characterised by a postmodern attitude towards time. The cultural ethos of modernity stressed the 'attainability of perfection',[2] and so saw change over time as progress toward this perfect state. Postmodern narratives, on the other hand, suggest that there is no intrinsic direction to history, and therefore renounce this sort of progress: 'history, from the standpoint of modernity ... approximates to a comic romance in which the hero's final triumph is assured from the beginning of the tale. Postmodernity, on the other hand, entails the view that no fixed direction has been inscribed in history from its outset'.[3] White goes on to argue that these differences dictate that modernist narratives of evolution employ one of two narrative forms (comic romance, or tragic romance), both of which imply a mastery (either symbolic or actual) of nature, whereas postmodernist versions, which replace them, tend to adopt a picaresque form which eschews mastery.

This chapter explores this postmodern perception of time in contemporary literature and science writing. However, the argument differs from White's in three key ways. Firstly, it does not see a wholesale shift from 'modern' conceptions of time to 'postmodern' ones. Instead, it sees the contemporary view of time described by White as one of the postures toward the past that constitute postmodernism. In other words, there is a perception of time which ties in with the wider renunciation of the past apparent in postmodernism, but this is not (at least not necessarily) an actual reworking of previous positions. Postmodern discourses try to establish their importance by setting themselves up as doing things in a different way to those of the

---

[1] Eric White, 'The End of Metanarratives in Evolutionary Biology', *Modern Language Quarterly* 51 (1990): p. 64.
[2] White, p. 63.
[3] White, p. 63.

Enlightenment, and we find this occurring in the literary and scientific narratives discussed here, but they are not necessarily the radical reworkings they claim to be.

Secondly, whereas White suggests that the new narratives of evolution eschew mastery – that there is something more liberatory about them – this chapter claims that they very clearly are about mastery of a sort. The new stories about evolution are adopted not because they cease to make humans the goal of evolution, but because those who propose them believe that they are more accurate: the dethroning of humanity from the place at the pinnacle of evolutionary achievement is a consequence, not a cause, of the new perception.[4] Humans actually maintain mastery (the term is not being used perjoratively) because they strive to understand nature. White seems to imply that any attempt to rationalise the workings of nature implies a symbolic mastery of it. It is difficult to see how *any* narratives of evolution accord with a rejection of this sort of mastery, for Gould and others like him are as determined to understand nature as anyone else – we do get a very real sense of what White calls the 'consolation of intelligibility' from *Wonderful Life*.[5]

The third, and final, departure from White's perspective is a slight modification of the postmodern attitude toward time which he presents. He sees 'no fixed direction' inscribed in history at the outset, whereas the position taken in this chapter is that in the postmodern perspective, although there is no overall guiding direction, at any moment there are local factors which determine the immediate direction of change over time. We can make the way in which this departs from White's view a little clearer by further reference to White's argument. To establish what he means by there being 'no fixed direction', he makes reference to chaos theory: 'the end can no longer be said to reside in the beginning because stochastic departures from the past behavior of a system remain an ever-present possibility'.[6] This oversimplifies the presentation of chaos theory in science writing. It is not so much that the beginning does not affect the end, as White is claiming here, as that we cannot know the beginning in enough detail to predict what will happen at the end. Chaos theory stresses 'sensitive dependence on initial conditions', not 'no dependence on initial conditions' or even 'partial dependence on initial conditions'. To predict the behaviour of a chaotic system we would need infinite accuracy in our measurement of that system – that this is theoretically, as well as practically, impossible, does not mean that the beginning does not affect the end. What it

---

4   Note that the 'new' perception is new in the sense that its proponents set it up as new; it is actually consistent with viable interpretations of Darwin's *The Origin of Species*.

5   White, p. 69.

6   White, p. 64.

does mean is that our predictions of the end are fundamentally limited; indeed, that anything except short-term prediction may be impossible.

This is important for our appreciation of contemporary narratives of the history of life, because, whereas White stresses that evolutionary development is marked by chance, the reading of these narratives offered in this chapter is that evolution is not truly random, but that at each stage contingent circumstances may take it off in different directions: the end does reside in the beginning, but there is no way of knowing what that end will be. This chapter is therefore in agreement with White's broader point that contemporary narratives tend not to present a general direction in which evolution moves.

It should also be noticed, incidentally, that a further objection to White's reference to chaos theory may be made on the grounds that chaos theory and evolution are very different subjects, and it is inappropriate to suggest that the popularised findings of one somehow validate the popularised findings of the other. One might, alternatively, attempt a general reading of the presentation of these sciences in the culture which links them through their popularisations of broadly similar attitudes to time (such a reading is not attempted here), but it is important to make clear that there is no direct causal link between the different areas of professional science in which they reside, and we must therefore be careful not to conflate them in a careless way.

The scientific text for this case study is Stephen Jay Gould's *Wonderful Life: The Burgess Shale and the Nature of History*. White refers to Gould, and his collaborator Niles Eldredge, as scientists who have produced examples of the new postmodern discourse in their formulations of the theory of 'punctuated equilibrium', which stresses a view of natural history where evolution is not constituted by continual steady progress, but is composed instead of periods of relative equilibrium, interspersed with times of rapid change and speciation. Quite how revolutionary this is, is open to debate – for instance Richard Dawkins writes persuasive dismissals of the claims made by Gould to have produced a substantially new picture of evolution.[7]

However, as in the previous case studies, in order to avoid overstepping the boundaries of my expertise I will not be commenting upon the truth, or otherwise, of competing scientific claims. What is justifiable is to state that Gould is an important contributor to the public scientific discourses of evolution – whether punctuated equilibrium is 'right' or not – and *Wonderful Life* represents an intriguing articulation of his view of evolution. This chapter seeks to demonstrate that it has all the hallmarks of a postmodern discourse, and that it shares these hallmarks with postmodern literature.

---

[7]   Most recently, for instance, he has contested Gould's view in *Unweaving the Rainbow*. Richard Dawkins, *Unweaving the Rainbow: Science, Delusion and the Appetite for Wonder* (London: Penguin, 1998), pp. 193–203. See also note 10 below.

The literature dealt with in the case study is a sequence of Kurt Vonnegut's novels, selected to illustrate Vonnegut's return, again and again, to the issue of time: *Player Piano* (1952), *The Sirens of Titan* (1959), *Cat's Cradle* (1963), *Slaughterhouse-Five* (1969), *Breakfast of Champions* (1973) and *Galapagos* (1985). The chapter shows how Vonnegut arrives at a similar presentation of time and, in *Galapagos*, of evolution, independently of Gould.

This last novel, dealing directly with evolution as it does, is an obvious choice for a comparison with Gould's book – all the more so as Gould claims that 'I would (and do) assign it to students in science courses as a guide to understanding the meaning of contingency [in evolution]'.[8] Furthermore, in the novel Vonnegut refers to the twentieth century as '"the Era of Hopeful Monsters", with most of the monsters novel in terms of personality rather than body type'.[9] The phrase 'hopeful monsters' was coined by Richard Goldschmidt, who proposed nonconformist, saltationist views of evolution in the 1930s and 1940s, and whose reputation Gould and Eldredge have attempted to revive.[10] Vonnegut seems, therefore, to be allying himself very directly with a particular view of evolution: that described by White as postmodern.

This particular presentation of change over time does not only appear in *Galapagos*, in which Vonnegut deals directly and consciously with evolution. The genesis of these ideas about time, progress and teleology lies right back in Vonnegut's earlier novels, and evolves over the course of his *oeuvre*. What we are dealing with, therefore, is not just a writer responding directly to a scientific idea that he finds interesting, but the separate emergence of similar ideas about time in different areas of the culture. In other words, this case study, while interested in the second category of literature–science criticism identified in chapter 2 (the influence of science and technology on writers), is concerned predominantly, like the previous case studies, with the fifth category (shared metaphors and discourses). The direct link between science and literature in

---

[8]   Gould, *Wonderful Life: The Burgess Shale and the Nature of History* (1989; London: Hutchinson Radius-Century Hutchinson, 1990), p. 286.

[9]   Vonnegut, *Galapagos* (1985; London: Grafton-Collins, 1987), p. 78.

[10]   Saltationism proposed that evolution takes place in large-scale steps, rather than more gradually. For a more detailed description of the theory, and for Dawkins's arguments as to why it could not work, and why he thinks that Gould and Eldredge are not really, despite their claims, supporting saltationism, see chapter 9, 'Puncturing Punctuationism', in *The Blind Watchmaker* (Harlow: Longman, 1986). Here Dawkins's objection to Gould is not so much that he is wrong, as that he restates what evolutionary biologists have always known in terms which make the ideas appear to be revolutionary and new. It should be noted that Gould does not advocate an unqualified acceptance of Goldschmidt's views – see, 'Return of the Hopeful Monster', *The Panda's Thumb* (New York: Norton, 1980), pp. 186–93; and a reference to Goldschmidt in 'Evolution as Fact and Theory' (pp. 253–62) in *Hen's Teeth and Horse's Toes* (1983; London: Penguin, 1990), p. 260.

Galapagos emerges *after* the idea has developed separately in Vonnegut's fiction, and in science writing about evolution.

The study begins by demonstrating the ways in which Vonnegut's presentation of evolution in *Galapagos* is equivalent to that proposed by Gould in *Wonderful Life*. The point of this is to establish a fairly direct link between literature and science by showing how, in writing a novel about evolution, Vonnegut has responded to a specific contemporary scientific view of the subject. These similar views of evolution, although occurring in the different contexts of literature and science, raise similar questions about the place of people in the world.

However, although the study begins with this direct link, it then goes on to show how the view of time which is implied by this presentation of evolution has its roots not only in science, but also in Vonnegut's earlier novels. Its development is traced from *Player Piano* through to *Breakfast of Champions*, the novel which precedes *Galapagos* in the sequence of books discussed in this chapter. The point of doing this is to show that although it is reasonable to suppose a fairly direct link between *Galapagos* and Gould's views of evolution, the concept of time implied by both arises separately and, for Vonnegut, has its origins much earlier on in his work. The view of evolution that he gives us in *Galapagos* is therefore not something completely new, but is rather a means of expressing ideas about time that have been important to him throughout his writing career.

Equivalent Presentations of Evolution in Science and Literature: Stephen Jay Gould's *Wonderful Life* and Kurt Vonnegut's *Galapagos*.

It has already been established that specific references in Vonnegut's novel suggest that he draws on a view of evolution similar to that proposed by Gould. This section describes in detail the two main elements of this view of evolution: a rejection of a simplistic notion of progress; and its replacement by a sense in which development over time is determined by contingency.

The first, the rejection of a simplistic notion of progress, involves a posture toward the past, and a rejection of it, which ties in with a broader postmodern discourse, and is similar to the postures of rejection of older forms of knowledge, discussed in chapter 3, and older conceptions of identity, discussed in chapter 4. In it, evolution is reconfigured as simplistic notions of progress are supplanted by an emphasis on less straightforward drives.[11]

---

[11]   It should be noted that some dispute whether Gould's presentation of evolution is actually radically different to that apparent in the past. See note 10.

In Gould's work this comes out particularly strongly in a sub-section of chapter 1, 'The Ladder and Cone: Iconographies of Progress', which analyses popular representations of evolution, and includes a discussion of cartoon depictions of the march of evolution toward the emergence of humans. Gould's argument is that these popular depictions of evolution encapsulate a now outdated assumption that evolution is synonymous with progress: 'The march of progress is *the* canonical representation of evolution – the one picture immediately grasped and viscerally understood by all'.[12] Indeed, Gould argues, the idea that natural history is a history characterised by continuous onward and upward development is so broadly accepted that evolution 'becomes a synonym for *progress*'.[13]

This same rejection of progress also appears in Vonnegut's presentation of evolution in *Galapagos*. Like *Wonderful Life*, the novel implies a certain history of ideas, distancing itself from a previous position. Again, this prior position, rejected in the novel, is that evolution is about continuous and progressive development, with the emergence of humans as the pinnacle of evolutionary achievement.

This rejection of progress appears in the novel in a number of ways, most specifically in terms of the idea, derided by Vonnegut, that the human brain marks an evolutionary advance. Just as White suggests that older, 'modern' narratives of evolution were marked by their adherence to an intellectual, and actual, mastery of nature by human brains, so *Galapagos* mocks a similar viewpoint, relegating human brains from being the *telos* of evolution, to being just one among many evolutionary anomalies.

Two examples will suffice to illustrate this. Mary, a character who will eventually be stranded on the island of Santa Rosalia, along with the only other survivors of bacteria which wipe out human life elsewhere, is a school teacher. Vonnegut highlights the misconceptions about evolution as progress that she passes on to her students by contrasting her assertion that the human brain is a superb achievement by evolution, with the ways in which her own brain lets her down: 'Mary had also taught that the human brain was the most admirable survival device yet produced by evolution. But now her own big brain was urging her to take the polyethylene garment bag … and to wrap it around her head, thus depriving her cells of oxygen'.[14]

Secondly, and more importantly, the timescale of the novel, which runs from the present to a million years in the future, also serves to undermine the association of evolution with progress by taking the popular marker of

---

    [12]   Gould, *Wonderful Life*, p. 31.
    [13]   Gould, *Wonderful Life*, p. 32.
    [14]   Vonnegut, *Galapagos*, p. 30. Mary's classes on natural history do also contain elements which conform with the 'postmodern' view of evolution, as we shall see later on.

evolutionary progress – the brain – and showing how it ceases to be important to the human race. After the annihilation of the majority of mankind, humans evolve to survive on Santa Rosalia, the only location on earth on which they remain. In a million years' time this means their brains have shrunk, and they have evolved fur and flippers in order to catch fish. Surveying this change, the narrator of the novel, the ghost of Leon Trout, finds himself redefining humanity, realising that what links humans of the twentieth century with their descendants is not brains but fishing: 'In the beginning, as in the end, I find myself speaking of human beings, regardless of their brain size, as fisherfolk'.[15] At the beginning of the story, people made their living by fishing metaphorically for wealth; by the end they survive by catching real fish. The big brains of today have disappeared and with them has gone the idea that evolution involves steady onward and upward progress, toward increasing sophistication and intelligent life.

So both Gould and Vonnegut reject the idea of evolution as progress. However, this is not the only link between them. There is a second characteristic which their work – though written in different contexts and for different reasons – also has in common. This is the replacement that they find for the old equation between evolution and progress: a sort of 'determined chance' or, as Gould puts it, 'contingency'.

Neither writer suggests that rejecting progress also involves rejecting any meaning to change over time, or the embracing of the opposite of determinism, randomness. The new view involves treading a line between seeing the general course of evolution as either wholly determined or wholly undetermined. Gould states this succinctly when he says that rejecting traditional notions of strict, consistent determinism does not involve accepting complete randomness: 'Rejection of ladder and cone [iconographies of progress] does not throw us into the arms of a supposed opposite – pure chance in the sense of coin tossing or of God playing dice with the universe'.[16]

In this rejection of both complete determinism and its opposite, total chance, the 'postmodern' view necessitates the disruption of a binary opposition, just as the case studies in the previous chapters did. To explain the history of life as either progress towards a goal, or its opposite, total randomness, is inadequate and fails to do justice to the complex factors that drive change over time. The disruption of this binary opposition may not have the 'soundbite' quality of the order versus disorder, global versus local, or human versus machine conflicts discussed in other chapters in this book, but it is of a fundamentally similar character.

---

[15]   Vonnegut, *Galapagos*, p. 51.
[16]   Gould, *Wonderful Life*, p. 50.

The rejection of one pole of this opposition, determinism (in the sense of progress toward the evolution of intelligent life), in *Galapagos* and *Wonderful Life*, has already been discussed. Both books deny that the emergence of intelligence was inevitable once evolution got going: humans are not the *telos* of natural history. In order to see how Gould and Vonnegut avoid accepting the opposite pole, complete chance, instead, we need to explore the mechanisms of natural selection they posit to replace the old view.

For Gould, the reigning, determining factor in evolution is contingency. We can see why this is stressed by considering the general argument put forward in his book. *Wonderful Life* is concerned with the Burgess Shale in British Columbia, an important fossil locality discovered by Charles Doolittle Walcott in 1909. Gould describes how Walcott's original analysis of the Burgess Shale fossils placed all of the organisms into existing, known categories of fauna, 'viewing the fauna collectively as a set of primitive or ancestral versions of later, improved forms'.[17] The assumption with which Walcott approached the evidence was that 'fossils fall into a limited number of large and well-known groups, and that life's history generally moves toward increasing complexity and diversity'.[18] In other words, it was an assumption that there is a definite progress underpinning the history of life on earth: a small number of species groups, early on in evolution, would inevitably give rise to a larger number of more complex forms later on.

What *Wonderful Life* charts is the process by which the revision of this viewpoint can be seen in the reinterpretation of the Burgess Shale fossils. Rather than assume that the Burgess fossils represent a large number of fauna belonging to a few well-known groups, the new approach to the Shale suggests that the fossils in fact represent many groups, many of which have now become extinct. In other words, evolution has not been a process of steady diversification and increasing complexity of life forms, but has involved the mass extinction of many groups of organisms. Furthermore, Gould suggests, it is not possible to say, from the evidence we have, which organisms were best fitted to survive into the future. There seems to have been a large element of luck involved.

This is where contingency comes in, because Gould does not mean that luck should be understood, in this case, to refer to complete chance. There are reasons for what happens – it is just that these reasons cannot be understood in terms of a steady, unchanging sequence of factors that would allow us to divine what is going to happen in advance. Rather than a general rule of development which would always produce the same evolutionary result (progress toward intelligent life), Gould suggests that the particular pathways

---

[17]   Gould, *Wonderful Life*, p. 24.
[18]   Gould, *Wonderful Life*, p. 111.

that evolution takes are a response to a multitude of local, individual conditions. In other words, history is admitted into science as a valid explanatory form. This, Gould suggests, offers an alternative to the strict choice between determined, predictable progress and 'coin tossing' referred to above:

> This third alternative represents no more nor less than the essence of history. Its name is contingency – and contingency is a thing unto itself, not the titration of determinism by randomness. Science has been slow to admit that different explanatory world of history into its domain ... Science has also tended to denigrate history, when forced to a confrontation, by regarding any invocation of contingency as less elegant or meaningful than explanations based directly on timeless 'laws of nature'.[19]

The implication of this is brought out most dramatically in a thought experiment that Gould proposes, in which we are asked to imagine the history of life on Earth as a tape recording. If we rewind the tape to the beginning and let history run again, what will happen? According to Gould, we will not see evolution repeat itself. Instead, a whole new natural history will emerge: 'a replay of life's tape would yield a substantially different set of surviving anatomies and a later history making perfect sense in its own terms but markedly different from the one we know'.[20]

Interestingly, these new interpretations of the Burgess Shale, which ran counter to Walcott's initial classification of the fossils, did not involve the discovery of any new evidence, but the rereading of existing evidence. This suggests that a new intellectual climate facilitated the new understanding and, indeed, Gould argues – without resorting to relativism – that both old and new interpretations of the Burgess Shale fossils are the products of particular intellectual climates.

For example, in discussing the old view of evolution he suggests that Darwin was influenced by Victorian notions of progress: 'Progress was the watchword of his surrounding culture, and Darwin could not abjure such a central and attractive notion. Hence, in the midst of tweaking conventional comfort with his radical view of change as local adjustment, Darwin also

---

[19]   Gould, *Wonderful Life*, p. 51. Quotations like this inevitably recall similar statements which are associated with chaos theory – both sciences seem to be partaking of a postmodern discourse through these sorts of insights.

[20]   Gould, *Wonderful Life*, p. 304. The current patterning of life is determined, in Gould's view, by periods of mass extinction when survival is either random, or dependent on different rules than prevail under normal conditions. For a longer description of the thought experiment described here, see Gould, *Wonderful Life*, pp. 48–50.

expressed his acceptance of progress as a theme in life's overall history'.[21] Similarly, as he approaches the new view of evolution, Gould hints that it is a changed intellectual climate which prompts Professor Henry Whittington to revise traditional classifications of the Burgess Shale fossils with a monograph in 1971: 'We have a reasonably well-controlled psychological experiment here. The data had not changed, so the reversal of opinion can only record a revised presupposition about the most likely status of Burgess organisms'.[22]

Whatever the reason for these new interpretations, we are being presented with a view of change over time that is very different to one in which straightforward progress toward a goal provides the core evolutionary drive. Teleology is all but absent from this view of life although it does persist, in a greatly denuded form, as short-term adaptation to local environmental conditions. In the long term, present life forms record 'the few fortunate survivors in a lottery of decimation, rather than the end result of progressive diversification by adaptive improvement'.[23] The future is not an improvement upon the past, then; it is just different to it. We can see this, and Gould's view of contingency, mirrored in *Galapagos*.

Gould focuses on periods of mass extinction, but Vonnegut deals with a calamity which affects just one species, the human race, which is all but wiped out by a bacterium which eats human eggs. The question we need to ask in order to understand whether or not Vonnegut's view of evolution accords with that of Gould is, what determines human survival into the future? What factors lead to the continued existence of human life on the island of Santa Rosalia and shape the form which that life eventually takes?

Intelligence is certainly not a factor. I have already shown how Vonnegut mocks the effects of the human brain upon the species' prospects for survival, and throughout the novel he focuses on the absurdities of human behaviour to suggest that we are anything but the rational creatures we like to imagine ourselves to be.

What does determine human survival in the novel is a series of accidents, and it is through these that Vonnegut admits a view of evolution which is akin to the contingency invoked by Gould. The history of the Gálapagos islands, South America, and the individuals involved is constantly referred to as a sequence of lucky chances by Vonnegut. We are told that the islands were discovered when a ship was blown off course in 1535,[24] and that their transformation by Darwin into something worthwhile was '*magical*'.[25] This led to the tourist boom on the islands and, ultimately, to the 'Nature Cruise of the

---

[21]   Gould, *Wonderful Life*, pp. 257–8.
[22]   Gould, *Wonderful Life*, p. 172.
[23]   Gould, *Wonderful Life*, p. 304.
[24]   Vonnegut, *Galapagos*, p. 23.
[25]   Vonnegut, *Galapagos*, p. 24.

Century', which brings a number of crucial people to Guayaquil in Ecuador. They are joined on their ship, the *Bahia de Darwin*, by others who arrive there because of a series of chance events involving, among other things, the accidental extermination of most of the Kanka-bonos tribe by insecticides, and civil unrest occasioned by a worldwide financial crisis. None of these people – the future ancestors of all humanity – act consciously to escape the impending plague, and even their arrival on the island of Santa Rosalia is the fortunate consequence of the captain's incompetence. They are not 'fitter' than the rest of humanity; lacking exceptional physical prowess, intelligence or ingenuity, they are lucky. They are, in Gould's phrase, 'fortunate survivors in a lottery of decimation'.

Importantly, though, Vonnegut stresses determinism in the operations of chance that he describes. Outside forces shape what happens to the characters, determining their lives, but there is no overriding purpose which moulds these forces. Events are not expressions of a drive towards anything; they just happen. This is remarkably similar to the view of evolution stressed by Gould. During unusual periods, when a new and serious threat troubles the species, and for which it cannot possibly have evolved, chance events determine who survives and what evolutionary conditions they will face in the future. After that, we return to a more normal period when the evolutionary pressure is constant, and the direction of evolution is therefore more readily determined by predictable factors. This 'normal' phase is also represented in *Galapagos*, in that when the lucky few have improbably, and fortuitously, reached Santa Rosalia, a more predictable sort of determinism reasserts itself. This is because the eventual evolution of humans into fishing creatures is almost certain given the local, contingent conditions which prevail on the island:

> But in the long run, I don't think it would have made much difference which males did the impregnating, Mick Jagger or Dr Henry Kissinger or the Captain or the cabin boy. Humanity would still be pretty much what it is today.
> In the long run, the survivors would still have been not the most ferocious strugglers but the most efficient fisherfolk. That's how things work in the islands here.[26]

In the long run, though, contingency rules. This embrace of contingency, and rejection of progress, involves, in both *Galapagos* and *Wonderful Life*, an erosion of the concept of teleology. Without progress, there can be no journey toward a goal; with contingency, chance events can always throw the course of evolution onto a different path. This raises questions about purpose and meaning.

---

[26] Vonnegut, *Galapagos*, p. 167.

Is there *any* purpose which we can find to the history of life? Certainly not in terms of a human-centred teleology. Progress toward intelligence, or anything else which we might use to distinguish humans from the rest of the natural world, is rejected as a driving force in evolution by both Gould and Vonnegut. If there is a purpose it is only that of persistence, and if there is a goal it is only that of survival. Gould's proposal that contingency is so important perhaps makes the achievement of this goal rather haphazard and short term; with changing conditions determining survival, there is no telling what form of life will be best suited to persist into the future. Indeed, a form which favours continued existence at one time, may mitigate against it at another time. Nevertheless, it is a form of purpose.

It is not so different from the only sense of purpose which Dawkins allows us in his descriptions of evolution: short-term adaptation, with no long-term view. Those genes which happen to favour survival at one time will be those genes which happen to persist into the future. In the face of a world shaped by these sorts of short-term evolutionary trends, both science writers find, instead of purpose, fascination in the history of life. They celebrate a kind of existentialist freedom to appreciate the world in all its indifferent complexity. For instance, Gould ends his book with the following observation:

> The survival of *Pikaia* [oldest ancestor of humans] was a contingency of 'just history'. I do not think that any 'higher' answer can be given, and I cannot imagine that any resolution could be more fascinating. We are the offspring of history, and must establish our own paths in this most diverse and interesting of conceivable universes – one indifferent to our suffering, and therefore offering us maximal freedom to thrive, or to fail, in our own chosen way.[27]

What Gould is suggesting here is that we cannot look for meaning in nature; we can only find it within ourselves. A human-centred meaning to life is not going to be a meaning which has a reality outside of a human frame of reference. Similarly, Dawkins argues in his latest book that the 'feeling of awed wonder that science can give us is one of the highest experiences of which the human psyche is capable ... It is truly one of the things that makes life worth living and it does so, if anything, more effectively if it convinces us that the time we have for living it is finite'.[28]

For Gould the knowledge that there is no overall purpose to life – except to keep on living – leads him to suggest that we must find a purpose within ourselves. It is precisely this dilemma, about human purpose in an indifferent universe, that Vonnegut uses evolution to explore in *Galapagos*. He, too,

---

[27]   Gould, *Wonderful Life*, p. 323.
[28]   Dawkins, *Unweaving the Rainbow*, p. x.

acknowledges that if evolution is not about progress, but mere survival, then there is a real problem with ascribing meaning to the world. Purpose, for all the species that are described in the novel, is merely self-perpetuation, and they are not even conscious that this is their purpose.

This comes across most strongly in Vonnegut's descriptions of the courtship dance of the blue-footed boobies, a species of bird which populates Santa Rosalia. The elaborate ritual which they go through, Vonnegut suggests, is just part of how they are determined, and how they go about getting a mate – we cannot ascribe any artistic expression or freedom to the dance: 'As for the meaning of the courtship dance of the blue-footed boobies: The birds are huge molecules with bright blue feet that have no choice in the matter. By their very nature, they have to dance exactly like that'.[29] Like the evolution of life, the courtship dance begs an explanation, but any human-centred interpretation that desires to find a higher meaning in it, is going to be wrong. Blue-footed boobies do what blue-footed boobies do – they are 'molecules' that have to behave in a certain way. There is no higher purpose to their lives.

The importance of this dance to Vonnegut's wider discussions of purpose and teleology in evolution is made explicit elsewhere. Mary asks her students to write a poem or an essay about the courtship dance, and her favourite response comes from Noble Claggett:

> Of course I love you,
> So let's have a kid
> Who will say exactly
> What its parents did;
> 'Of course I love you,
> So lets have a kid
> . . . .'
> Et cetera.[30]

The purpose of the dance is purely to mate, and have offspring which will also dance and, in their turn, mate to produce further offspring. Trout tells us, from his position far in the future, that the dance 'has not changed one iota in a million years'.[31] The birds dance solely because they are descendants of birds who dance.

Whether perpetuation of the species is also the sole purpose of human life, is a question which Vonnegut explores in the novel, and to which he produces an ambiguous response. This comes out in a paragraph that follows his description of the blue-footed boobies as molecules forced to do a dance:

[29]   Vonnegut, *Galapagos*, p. 102.
[30]   Vonnegut, *Galapagos*, p. 100.
[31]   Vonnegut, *Galapagos*, p. 102.

'Human beings used to be molecules which could do many, many different sorts of dances, or decline to dance at all – as they pleased'.[32] His description of humans as 'molecules' suggests a machine-like quality which accords with issues raised in my exploration of the human–machine dichotomy in the last chapter: humans are machines that do what humans are programmed to do. However, the suggestion that they can choose to do different dances is more ambiguous – does this mean that they do have freedom, or does it just mean that the restriction on their freedom is more carefully hidden?

This dilemma about whether humans have a higher purpose, or whether they are at the mercy of their role in meaningless cycles of reproduction, also emerges in Leon Trout's description of his ancestry. His inheritance from his mother suggests that there is something exceptional about his ancestry and therefore about his life, because she proudly tells him that he is descended from French noblemen. However, when Leon questions his cynical father, Kilgore, about his noble blood, the response he gets is much more down to earth: "'My boy," he said, "you are descended from a long line of determined, resourceful, microscopic tadpoles – champions every one."'[33]

Leon's mother reveals a conventional conviction that noble blood can determine status, and implies that there is a purpose in evolving ancestries. His father reveals the possibility of an almost purposeless world – all there is to be proud of in the progression of the family through the generations is that each one was able to reproduce.

The eventual evolution of humans into seal-like creatures whose only purpose is to fish and survive long enough to reproduce, suggests that Vonnegut sees the purpose of humanity purely in terms of persistence as well: that he sides with Leon's father rather than his mother. However, there are one or two suggestions in the novel that Vonnegut is not stating this as the truth of the matter, but just playing with the possibility that this is the truth. Vonnegut forces us to face the dreadful possibility that human life is meaningless, but does not confirm that this is the case.

For instance, Leon Trout's continuing fascination with humans – and his refusal to go into the afterlife until he has seen what happens to them – suggests that there was something meaningful and interesting about humans in the era of big brains, even though we cannot find meaning in evolution itself. A

---

[32]   Vonnegut, *Galapagos*, p. 102.

[33]   Vonnegut, *Galapagos*, p. 144. This celebration of 'champion tadpoles' is reminiscent of Dawkins's insistence at the beginning of *River Out of Eden* that the only purpose of life is to keep living: 'All organisms that have ever lived ... can look back at their ancestors and make the following proud claim: Not a single one of our ancestors died in infancy. They all reached adulthood, and every single one was capable of finding at least one heterosexual partner and of successfully copulating'. Richard Dawkins, *River Out of Eden*, Science Masters (London: Weidenfeld and Nicholson, 1995), p. 1.

million years in the future – when all they do is fish – Trout expresses a sense
of loss. Even though his narration has, for the most part, presented the
evolution of humans into fisherfolk as a process of the species being forced to
accept its humble status among the other creatures of the earth, there is a sense
in which big-brained humans brought something interesting to the planet:

> I can expect to see the blue tunnel [to the afterlife] again at any time.
> I will of course skip into its mouth most gladly. Nothing ever happens
> around here any more that I haven't seen or heard so many times
> before. Nobody, surely, is going to write Beethoven's Ninth
> Symphony – or tell a lie, or start a Third World War.
>   Mother was right: even in the darkest times, there really was
> still hope for humankind.[34]

'Hope', here, might mean hope that despite wars and deceit, great music could
be produced by humans; or it might merely mean that there was always the
hope that humans might be able to evolve away from their big-brained,
cataclysmic successes and failures.

This dialogue between purpose and lack of purpose, and progress and
mere change, is what Vonnegut uses evolution to explore in *Galapagos*. Life,
for both Vonnegut and Gould, seems in many ways to be a theatre of the
absurd: meaningless but fascinating. Although there is a direct link to
contemporary presentations of evolution in *Galapagos*, however, the same
themes have their roots much earlier in Vonnegut's work. In order to
demonstrate that equivalent views of time arose separately in literature and
science, before Vonnegut made the explicit link between the two in *Galapagos*,
the remainder of the case study will now explore the development of the idea
by working through the relevant novels in chronological order.

The Development of a Postmodern View of Time in the Novels of Kurt Vonnegut

(a) Machines Against Humans: 'Player Piano'

Although this early novel does not dwell upon time as one of its themes, by
dealing with a conflict between humans and machines it marks Vonnegut's
concern, at the beginning of his career as a writer, with issues which were to
develop into the explicit treatment of evolution that he produces in *Galapagos*.

---

[34] Vonnegut, *Galapagos*, p. 236. Perhaps Trout's fascination with humans mirrors
Gould's and Dawkins's fascination (in response to the lack of any other purpose to our
existence) with life in general, discussed on page 144.

This is because the human versus machine conflict is also a conflict between free will and determinism. This has obvious consequences for how we view change over time: if we have free will, then the future is not set, but if we are part of a machine-like universe then the future is unalterable.

Vonnegut imagines a society with a three-fold structure, which is given geographical expression in the splitting of Ilium, where the action takes place, into three sectors: the south, Homestead, for the menial workers and those displaced by society; the northwest for the managers, engineers, civil servants and professional people; and the northeast for the machines which run the country. This strict physical segregation of Ilium provides the template upon which a rigid social order is constructed, with the machines determining the lives of individuals, and regulating the type of work that they do.

The novel deals with an uprising against this rigid social stratification, and the allied mechanisation, of the country. In charting the failure of this revolution, it also charts a failure to achieve an ideal society where machines have a limited, useful role, simultaneously allowing for individuality and self-expression among the citizenry. This is made apparent by the three counts on which the revolution fails in the eyes of Paul Proteus, one of the revolutionaries: it is crushed by the security forces but, more importantly, rioters smash useful as well as useless machines, and people's curiosity drives them to start trying to remake machines from the wreckage of those that have been destroyed.

The novel actually bemoans the lack of a middle ground between the possibilities of a machine society and a non-machine society, mourning the existence of a stark binary choice between determinism and free will. People will either smash everything, or they will thoughtlessly reconstruct the machines. With the failure of the revolution, society will revert to its wholly mechanised form, with the individual's role in life determined purely by his or her performance in tests at a young age. The choice, as Proteus comes to see it, is between an overly mechanised society, where the machines determine everything that people do, and complete anarchy – either the needs of the individual are wholly subordinated to those of society, or there ceases to be anything approximating to a society because individual actions are in no way curtailed by the needs of other members of the community.

The centrality of this notion to the novel is made clear by the references to the 'player piano' of the title. A player piano is one which plays a pre-programmed tune, depressing its keys automatically. The tune is therefore machine-determined, rather like the meaningless dance of the blue-footed boobies, the 'molecules' of *Galapagos*, who go through their absurd motions again and again over millions of years. Vonnegut's novel offers an alternative to these pre-set tunes, but it is one which is a renunciation of any ordered musical form: Ed Finnerty, one of the revolutionaries, overrides the mechanism that controls the piano, playing his own 'hellish' music instead.[35] The options, in this symbolic gesture, are between determinism (automatic music) and anarchy (Finnerty's 'hellish' music). Vonnegut's adoption of the player piano as a guiding motif for the novel introduces a theme which is of importance throughout his career, and which is allied to the human–machine one: the role of art in an indifferent universe.

What we have here, then, are the seeds of the dilemma about time which Vonnegut explores in *Galapagos*: are things determined, or is there room for free will to shape the course of history? These ideas find more complex expression in *Sirens of Titan*. If *Player Piano* bemoans the lack of a middle ground in the conflict between determinism and free will, *Sirens of Titan* develops this idea by making the determinism it treats a universal condition, rather than something isolated within a particular society. It also introduces distortions of chronological time as a central motif of the novel.

(b) Human Purpose in a Machine Universe: 'Sirens of Titan'

The extent to which our lives are determined by outside forces is again explored in *Sirens of Titan*, where it occurs on a number of levels. Our first introduction to this theme is through Malachi Constant, the luckiest man on earth, who inherits from his father a method for amassing a vast fortune from an irrational and wholly fortuitous scheme of investments, based on matching biblical text with the initials of companies. Although he considers himself to be free, he finds out that he is under the control of Niles Rumfoord.

Rumfoord's control of Malachi, and of human life in general, is the first level on which determinism is explored in the novel. Along with his dog Kazak, Rumfoord gets caught in a 'chrono-synclastic-infundibula' (the ridiculous name indicates the humour with which Vonnegut treats the scientific ideas he invents – the science he presents in his science fiction is wholly fantastical). This leaves him existing in the form of waves that flow across the solar system, materialising on different planets at different times, and on Titan, a moon of Saturn, continually. It also allows Rumfoord to see into the past and the future. Given the possibility of manipulating events, and being able to see the consequences of this manipulation, he decides to improve life on Earth.

He does this by kidnapping people, brainwashing them, and forming them into a fanatical but utterly ill-equipped Martian army to attack earth. Earthlings are forced to wipe them out and, overcome with guilt, they renounce violence, and any form of divine authority, believing only in a god who is supremely indifferent: there is no purpose to life. This indifferent universe is

---

[35]   Kurt Vonnegut, *Player Piano* (New York: Delacorte, 1952), p. 91.

markedly similar to that toyed with in *Galapagos*. Malachi Constant features because he is also kidnapped by Rumfoord, and is later offered to Earthlings as proof that if there is a creator, he is wholly indifferent to them.

It is here that we get a treading of the middle ground between determinism and chance, and a view of change over time which is recognisably similar to that proposed in *Galapagos*. Events are determined by an outside force, but they have no meaning. The religion that results from Rumfoord's interventions illustrates this, and also presages the central tenets of Bokonism, a religion that Vonnegut creates in *Cat's Cradle*. In order to impress the efficacy of his artificial religion upon Earthlings, Rumfoord prophesies Malachi's exact actions and words when he arrives back on earth. Bewildered by the enthusiastic welcome he receives, Malachi (or Unk, as he is now known) finds himself acting exactly in the way that the Earthlings have been led to expect by Rumfoord's predictions. His first words are the words Rumfoord has told everyone he will say, and a central text in the new religion: '"I was a victim of a series of accidents," he said. He shrugged. "As are we all," he said'.[36]

The impression that we are all victims of a series of accidents – that we are determined by what happens to us, but that there is no purpose to this – is very similar to the history of the human race as it appears in *Galapagos*, where the characters are also victims of a series of accidents. However, although it is similar when this plot strand is considered on its own, it is not identical because there is at least some meaning to the manipulation of lives that takes place. This meaning might only be Rumfoord's attempts to make life more pleasant, but it is a meaning of sorts, nevertheless.

The second level on which the novel explores determinism, however, removes even this sense of meaningfulness from life. This is because it is revealed that not only does Rumfoord manipulate human affairs, but he himself is being manipulated and controlled. Moreover, there is no human-centred purpose to this determination of his life. He, and in fact all of human history, have been manipulated in order to convey messages to Salo, a Tralfamadorian who is stranded by his faulty spaceship on Titan. Events in earth's history, and Rumfoord's life, convey messages to him from Tralfamadore. The Great Wall of China, for instance, is really just a message meaning '*Replacement part being rushed with all possible speed*', and the Moscow Kremlin means '*You will be on your way before you know it*'.[37]

On a third level, Salo himself is also being manipulated because he is sent on a mission which, it turns out, is meaningless. Nor is there any higher

---

[36]   Kurt Vonnegut, *The Sirens of Titan* (1959; London: VGSF-Gollancz, 1989), p. 161.
[37]   Vonnegut, *Sirens*, p. 190. Vonnegut's italics.

purpose to either the second-level manipulation of Rumfoord, or the third-level manipulation of Salo. Salo's mission is to celebrate the anniversary of the Tralfamadorian civilisation, by conveying a message from Tralfamadore to the most far-flung alien culture he can reach. Yet, grand and purposeful though this seems, when Salo opens the message against orders, and at Rumfoord's insistence, he finds that it is essentially meaningless. It simply says, *'Greetings'*.[38]

So we have a sense of the universe as a purposeless machine here. Just as, in the novel, humans go through a crisis concerning the reason for their existence, so we find that the Tralfamadorians, too, have faced such a crisis in their history. Obsessed with the idea that everything had to have a purpose, and that some things had a higher purpose than others, creatures on Tralfamadore committed themselves to finding and understanding the higher purpose. Each time they discovered what it was, it seemed so low that they felt disgusted and ashamed and, rather than serve it, they created machines to serve it, while they themselves looked for a still higher purpose. This carried on, we are told, until the machines were asked to find out what the purpose of the creatures themselves was: *'The machines reported in all honesty that the creatures couldn't really be said to have any purpose at all'*.[39] An orgy of killing ensues, as the creatures dislike purposeless things more than anything else, but even this has to be finished off by the machines which are much more efficient at the job.

As a result, Salo and all the other Tralfamadorians are nothing more than machines, appropriate life-forms for a meaningless machine-like universe. This also ties in with the issues raised by the subversion of the human–machine dichotomy which was explored in chapter 4. The implication, which is picked up in Vonnegut's later fiction, is that there may be no real distinction between machines and people.

Cat's Cradle pushes further the notion that events are both determined and meaningless. It also includes another religion, Bokonism, which is about reconciling us to the meaninglessness of life.

(c) Inventing a Purpose to Explain the Machine: 'Cat's Cradle'

The central notion of Bokonism, the fictional religion created by Vonnegut in *Cat's Cradle*, is that we are placed where we are by outside forces. Individuals are placed and determined by the complexities of life, just as people in *Sirens of Titan* are the 'victims of a series of accidents', and the characters in *Galapagos* are placed on Santa Rosalia by events outside their control: *'Busy,*

---

[38]   Vonnegut, *Sirens*, p. 210.
[39]   Vonnegut, *Sirens*, pp. 192–3. Vonnegut's italics.

busy, busy, is what we Bokonists whisper whenever we think of how complicated and unpredictable the machinery of life really is'.[40]

The idea of a 'machinery' of life emphasises determinism, but the purpose of this machinery is always concealed by complexity and, therefore, unpredictability. For instance, as early as the second chapter, we are told that Bokonism preaches the unknowability of life. One of the many terms which Vonnegut coins for his religion, *karass*, means the team of people who are connected to an individual and affect his or her life. There is no hope, however, of finding out how the *karass* operates: 'Nowhere does Bokonon warn against a person's trying to discover the limits of his *karass* and the nature of the work God Almighty has had it do. Bokonon simply observes that such investigations are bound to be incomplete'.[41]

In the face of this unknowability, Bokonists passively accept that things are bound to happen, writing off events in their lives with the phrase 'as it was *supposed* to happen',[42] rather than 'as it happened'. In the face of this overwhelming drive, there seems to be little that individuals can do to shape their own lives, and the religion seems to countenance the passive acceptance of this state of affairs.

Yet the explanation that is offered for life – the purpose that lies behind it – is much the same in Bokonism as it is in Rumfoord's artificial religion in *Sirens of Titan*. Although it invokes God, Bokonism does not really hold out the possibility that a divine force shapes events. This is because it undercuts itself by admitting that it is nothing but lies. The title page of *The First Book of Bokonon* has a warning on it: 'Don't be a fool! Close this book at once! It is nothing but *foma!* [lies]'.[43] This leads us to the 'cruel paradox of Bokonist thought, the heartbreaking necessity of lying about reality, and the heartbreaking impossibility of lying about it'.[44]

Vonnegut's explanation of purposelessness here goes one stage further than it does in *Sirens of Titan*. This is because Bokonism is used to explore more directly the systems of interpretation that we have to invent to make sense of a meaningless universe. Our descriptions of it are always going to be inadequate, are always going to be lies, and yet they will also always have some sort of 'truth' about them, because they will be more accurate than a complete refusal to articulate the world. Bokonism presents things 'as they are', yet the explanations it offers inevitably lack, like Rumfoord's artificial religion in *The Sirens of Titan*, the ability to find any purpose to life.

---

[40]   Kurt Vonnegut, *Cat's Cradle* (1963; London: Gollancz, 1974), p. 61.
[41]   Vonnegut, *Cat's Cradle*, p. 15.
[42]   Vonnegut, *Cat's Cradle*, p. 76, p. 77, p. 191.
[43]   Vonnegut, *Cat's Cradle*, p. 214.
[44]   Vonnegut, *Cat's Cradle*, p. 229.

This lack of purpose suggests that individual actions are meaningless when set against the huge framework of events that constitute history. As in many of Vonnegut's novels, we are presented with a huge force which cannot be stopped, and which overwhelms individual lives. In *Cat's Cradle* this is 'ice-nine', a substance which, once it comes into contact with water, will turn it into ice. However, although ice-nine eventually destroys the world, Vonnegut does offer a glimmer of hope that individual actions may have value on a local scale. For instance, after one of the first times it is used, Newt, Angela, Frank and the narrator work to rectify the trouble that ice-nine has caused: 'In a messy world we were at least making our little corner clean'.[45] Although this is a futile action, it is also a hopeful one, and it does at least signal defiance in the face of the inexorable march of events.

Similar small gestures of defiance occur in *Sirens of Titan* and *Galapagos*. The former ends with Salo depositing the dying Malachi Constant back on earth. Before he goes, Salo hypnotises him 'so that he would imagine, as he died, that he saw his best and only friend, Stony Stevenson'.[46] In the latter, Captain von Kleist tries to put his ship in order after an orgy of looting has stripped it: 'The shower in the head was dripping, and he turned it off right. That much he could make right, anyway'.[47] These are gestures of kindness and hope in a universe that is indifferent to the human plight. The questioning of the value of these individual, small-scale actions, in the face of the huge historical events which overwhelm them, is the central theme of *Slaughterhouse-Five*. As we shall see, Vonnegut focuses not so much on writing an anti-war novel, as on the impossibility of writing an anti-war novel. Yet, at the same time, he expresses dissatisfaction with absolute resignation in the face of the large-scale forces which shape our lives. Again, in *Slaughterhouse-Five*, there is a sense of small-scale actions having some value: 'I have told my sons that they are not under any circumstances to take part in massacres, and that the news of massacres of enemies is not to fill them with satisfaction or glee'.[48]

Cat's Cradle also anticipates *Slaughterhouse-Five* by making form intrinsic to content in a way which was not apparent in the earlier novels. The simplistic style of writing is crucial to the themes that Vonnegut is attempting to explore, expressing the difficulty of rendering the world adequately. This is perhaps what was meant in the assertion that the central paradox of Bokonism is that it is impossible to tell the truth about reality, and it is impossible to lie about it. What can be said about reality can be stated in bald, bland sentences,

---

[45]   Vonnegut, *Cat's Cradle*, p. 200.
[46]   Vonnegut, *Sirens*, p. 223.
[47]   Vonnegut, *Galapagos*, p. 177.
[48]   Kurt Vonnegut, *Slaughterhouse-Five: Or, The Children's Crusade: A Duty-Dance with Death* (1969; London: Vintage, 1989), p. 14.

much as, at the beginning of *Slaughterhouse-Five*, Vonnegut says everything he wants to about the nastiness of massacres in a few words which, because they are so simple, fail to convey the full reality of the Dresden bombing. In *Cat's Cradle* we are presented with a narrator who uses a lot of very simple sentence constructions. After most humans have been wiped out by ice-nine, there is nothing the characters can say which will adequately express the scale of the devastation, and their lives shrink into irrelevance beside it. Faced with events that are beyond expression, they fall back on a series of clichés: 'Don't shoot the cook. He's doing the best he can'; '"Save our soullllls," Hazel intoned, singing along with the transmitter'; 'You'll be one of a long, long line'; 'I like a good laugh'; 'Each person here has some speciality, something to give the rest'; 'Many hands make much work light'; 'let's keep their memory alive'; 'No use crying over spilt milk'.[49] The phrases, rendered almost meaningless by their over-familiarity, reflect the characters' alienation from a world they cannot possibly comprehend.

So, while *Cat's Cradle* recalls the sense of a world ruled by purposeless determinism that we found in Vonnegut's earlier novels, it also develops these ideas by using Bokanism to explore humanity's need to re-imagine reality, in order to make sense of it, and by making all of these ideas intrinsic to the novel's form. This relationship between language and reality finds expression in the references to cat's-cradles in the book. Newt, for instance, holds up his hands with a cat's-cradle entwined between his fingers, and says that kids 'grow up crazy' looking at the X's of string: *'No damn cat, and no damn cradle'.*[50] Any expression of reality – the metaphor of the cat's cradle – has to be a transformation of it, and therefore a fiction.

This is tied up with the purposelessness of life, summed up in the childlike rhymes of the Bokonist song which recalls Noble Claggett's poem about the dance of the blue-footed boobies in *Galapagos*:

> We do, doodley do, doodley do, doodley do,
> What we must, muddily must, muddily must, muddily must;
> Muddily do, muddily do, muddily do, muddily do,
> Until we bust, bodily bust, bodily bust, bodily bust.[51]

We are beings who do what we must till we bust, just as, in *Galapagos*, blue-footed boobies live and reproduce purely to create other blue-footed boobies that will, in turn, live and reproduce.

Slaughterhouse-Five returns to the manipulations of chronology in *Sirens of Titan*, developing the ideas about purpose, free will and determinism, by

49   Vonnegut, *Cat's Cradle*, pp. 224–5.
50   Vonnegut, *Cat's Cradle*, p. 137.
51   Vonnegut, *Cat's Cradle*, p. 216. For Noble Claggett's poem see note 30.

making time and time travel into central features of the plot. It also explores these ideas through form, narrating the novel through a fragmented chronology.

(d) Finding the Middle Ground Between Free Will and Determinism: 'Slaughterhouse-Five'

With time travel a central feature of the novel, and a more developed use of form, *Slaughterhouse-Five* explores the free will–determinism and organism–machine boundaries. Tralfamadorians again feature as an alien life-form, and although it is not obvious whether they are the same machines as appeared in *Cat's Cradle*, they certainly represent a view of the universe which is machine-like. Their ability to see in four dimensions – time as well as space – allows them to educate Billy during the rather pleasant kidnapping that they arrange for him, and they teach him the view, which we have already found in Vonnegut's earlier novels, that things are determined but there is no purpose to them.

This comes out explicitly in their response to Billy's question about why they have kidnapped him rather than someone else: 'That is a very *Earthling* question to ask, Mr. Pilgrim. Why *you*? Why *us* for that matter? Why *anything*? Because this moment simply *is*. Have you ever seen bugs trapped in amber? ... Well, here we are, Mr. Pilgrim, trapped in the amber of this moment. There is no *why*'.[52] This suggests that our explanations of why things change over time are meaningless – or, at least, highly problematic. The difficulty of expressing this lack of any meaning is brought out by the use of italics in the above passage: there is nothing to say beyond a blank statement that things are as they are. Yet this fact that there is nothing meaningful to say is itself very important and has to be emphasised through the use of italics: the moment *is*, there is no *why*.

This does not only express a belief about the universe. It also necessarily suggests a way of acting (or rather, as we shall see, not acting) in the universe. Again, the Tralfamadorians explain this to Billy: 'All time is all time. It does not change. It does not lend itself to warnings or explanations. It simply *is*. Take it moment by moment, and you will find that we are all, as I've said before, bugs in amber'.[53] Taking life moment by moment is precisely what Billy does, even though the moments of his life do not occur in a linear order because of his uncontrolled time travelling. Like many of Vonnegut's protagonists he is

---

[52] Vonnegut, *Slaughterhouse-Five*, p. 55. Vonnegut's hope that the Tralfamadorians are wrong in this, is neatly expressed by the fact that the response of a German guard to a prisoner who complains at being unfairly beaten, is exactly the same as the Tralfamadorian's response to Billy: 'Vy you? Vy anybody?' The Tralfamadorian view, and that of the guard, allow for a complete abnegation of individual responsibility.

[53] Vonnegut, *Slaughterhouse-Five*, p. 62.

a passive victim of circumstances, doing little to control the course of events in which he is caught. Believing that history is set, he sees no need to attempt to change it.

It is because of this that the integration of a science fiction novel with one about war is such an imaginative and successful venture on Vonnegut's part. To understand why this is the case, we need to take a short detour into the issues that Vonnegut raises in the first chapter of the book, where he writes about the background to *Slaughterhouse-Five*. It is here that he himself struggles with the questions raised by adopting a philosophy akin to that of the Tralfamadorians, because as a writer of a war novel he too is caught up in the problem of whether individual actions have any influence upon the unfolding of large-scale events. For instance, the (fictional?) movie-maker Harrison Starr asks him why he does not write an anti-glacier book instead of an anti-war book, a rhetorical question which Vonnegut interprets as meaning that anti-war books are futile ventures: 'What he meant, of course, was that there would always be wars, that they were as easy to stop as glaciers. I believe that, too'.[54]

However, just as there was no final judgement on the question of whether there is any meaning to human life in *Galapagos*, so Vonnegut leaves the question of whether individual actions have meaning unanswered in *Slaughterhouse-Five*. On the one hand, there is the view of the Tralfamadorians that all things are as they are, and cannot be changed. Further support for this view comes from the disjointed form of the novel, the short, staccato feel imposed by frequent breaks and jumps reinforcing the sense of being flung backwards and forwards in time with Billy, unable to control anything. Repeated phrases also reinforce this sense of powerlessness. The constant response in the novel to death – 'So it goes' – suggests resignation in the face of the events which shape and end lives.

Yet the constant repetition of 'so it goes' (106 times – on nearly two out of every three pages – by my calculations) also implies the inadequacy of this viewpoint. Vonnegut has told us that he wants to write an anti-war book, but then presents us with indifference in the face of death. This suggests an ironic stance, and also an attempt to draw our attention to the dehumanising effects of war and the fact that language is inadequate to express such horror, much as the characters in *Cat's Cradle*, finding themselves incapable of expressing what had happened to their world, fell back on cliché. As Vonnegut puts it early on in *Slaughterhouse-Five*, '[this book] is so short and jumbled and jangled ... because there is nothing intelligent to say about a massacre'.[55] Reality, in all its complex and terrible immensity, outstrips attempts to represent it.

---

54   Vonnegut, *Slaughterhouse-Five*, p. 3.
55   Vonnegut, *Slaughterhouse-Five*, p. 14.

What Vonnegut seems to be doing, then, is writing about the problems of writing about events like wars. The alien philosophy of the Tralfamadorians is used to represent the view that nothing will change, regardless of what we do and what we write. By counterpointing two genres – science fiction and war fiction – Vonnegut makes us question the values of each. War fiction often presupposes the efficacy of individual actions. If it portrays war as an adventure, then it assumes that individuals' actions have a purpose which can be realised; and if it adopts an 'anti-war' stance, then it assumes that writing about the experience of war may help to change people's attitudes toward it. The Tralfamadorians deny any validity to this view of the potency of individual actions in their re-education of Billy, and their presence in the novel also serves to undercut that staple of science fiction, the hyper-intelligent alien race who have learnt to overcome the problems that still face mankind – all the Tralfamadorians can offer is the knowledge that our actions are meaningless. The juxtaposition of two such antithetical genres also makes suspension of disbelief extremely difficult for the reader, and forces us to think about the status of the novel as fiction, even though it is based upon Vonnegut's own experiences.

A very different reading of the novel, which retains the elements dealing with Billy's life during and after the war as 'real' events, but makes the science fiction episodes into fantasies of Billy's, is of course possible. Yet this possibility that Billy is mad still takes us to a reading of the novel which makes it about the difficulty of writing about events like war, rather than just about the bombing of Dresden. In this reading, too, the novel searches for a way of saying something about a massacre which does have meaning, when placed in the context of the grand march of history. If Billy is mad then the novel is about the effects of the war upon him. How does our reading of the story evolve in this case?

After going to war and witnessing the bombing of Dresden as a prisoner of war, Billy returns to America and establishes a normal life for himself as an optician and family man. However, his experience in Dresden still affects him, though he does not realise it, and he often finds himself silently weeping out of all proportion to the circumstances.[56] Events in his life take him back to his war experiences, and it is these which he interprets as time travel: the black and orange tent at his daughter's wedding recalls the black and orange paint on the train wagons used to transport the prisoners of war;[57] when he cries in the present he 'time travels' to the past where the wind is making his eyes water;[58] when he is cold his 'blue and ivory' feet recall those of corpses during the

---

[56]   Vonnegut, *Slaughterhouse-Five*, pp. 44–45.
[57]   Vonnegut, *Slaughterhouse-Five*, p. 50, p. 52.
[58]   Vonnegut, *Slaughterhouse-Five*, p. 46.

war;[59] and the first thing Billy does when he arrives in the German prison camp and on Tralfamadore is take off his clothes.[60] As well as time travelling, he also constructs an escape scenario for himself in the form of a fantasy of being kidnapped by Tralfamadorians and mated with the film star, Montana Wildhack, in a zoo on Tralfamadore. Here, also, there are echoes of his real life: Billy has seen Montana Wildhack in a film being shown in a porn shop,[61] and elements of his experiences on Tralfamadore echo the science-fiction story, *The Big Board*, by Kilgore Trout, a writer to whom Billy is introduced by Eliot Rosewater.

However, he begins to gain awareness of the profound psychological effects of the war upon him when he is moved to tears by a quartet of singing opticians, the Febs (Four-Eyed Bastards), at his eighteenth wedding anniversary: 'Here was proof that he had a great big secret somewhere inside, and he could not imagine what it was'.[62] For the first time, he does not 'time travel' back to the past but imagines it, realising that the sight of the men's mouths opening and closing as they sing is the same as that of the German guards when they were first confronted with the full horror of the aftermath of the Dresden bombing.

It is only now that Billy is able to confront what happened to him, albeit in the safe fantasy of his idyllic existence with Montana Wildhack in the Tralfamadorian zoo. Immediately after he makes the connection between the singers and the guards, she asks him to, 'Tell me a story'.[63] For the first time Billy speaks about his war experiences. His story starts in a cold, matter-of-fact tone: '"Dresden was destroyed on the night of February 13, 1945," Billy Pilgrim began'.[64] However, it is not long before we get to the climax of Billy's tale, and Vonnegut's, which is the effort to clean up Dresden by the American prisoners of war and the surviving Germans, followed by the only piece of suffering with which Billy is really able to connect: the discomfort of the ill-shod horse for which he weeps.

In this reading the book is about Billy coming to terms with, and confronting, his experience at Dresden. He is unable to tell his wife, in the real world, about his war experiences, but finally manages to give expression to them in the safe environment of his fantasy life with Montana Wildhack.

---

[59]   For example, Vonnegut, *Slaughterhouse-Five*, p. 47, p. 52.

[60]   Vonnegut, *Slaughterhouse-Five*, p. 60.

[61]   Vonnegut, *Slaughterhouse-Five*, p. 149.

[62]   Vonnegut, *Slaughterhouse-Five*, p. 126.

[63]   Vonnegut, *Slaughterhouse-Five*, p. 130.

[64]   Vonnegut, *Slaughterhouse-Five*, p. 130. The fact that 13 February is the date on which Billy thinks he will die adds further weight to the argument that he imagines his time-travelling experiences, and that they are not real. The narrator also presages the year of Billy's 'imagined' death by saying that he looks like the central character in a parody of the painting, 'The Spirit of '76'.

Billy's voicing of these experiences, and the way in which he finally manages to connect with some of the suffering – the horse's pain for which he bears some of the blame – finally bring us back to Vonnegut's own problems with writing about the war, which he told us about in the first chapter of the novel. So, in its final pages, the novel comes full circle.

In the first chapter Vonnegut told us about drinking into the night and ringing old girl friends, or war colleagues, after his wife had gone to bed, with his breath smelling like 'mustard gas and roses'.[65] In the final chapter we are told that Billy and the other prisoners of war work to pull bodies out of the 'corpse mines' of Dresden, and we are reminded of this smell: 'But then the bodies rotted and liquified, and the stink was like roses and mustard gas'.[66] This suggests that the novel is as much about Vonnegut coming to terms with Dresden (and the reader making the link between the smell of his breath, and that of the corpses), and writing his story through a fantasy, as it is about Billy himself coming to terms with his experience and expressing it through a fantasy. Just as *Catch-22*, despite its dislocations of chronology, slowly and carefully builds to the cathartic, full description of Snowden's death which appears near the end, so *Slaughterhouse-Five* moves deliberately (and about 500 pages more quickly) to a description of the corpse mines of Dresden.

Of course, it is equally legitimate to read the novel as really being about time travel. Although this rather dramatically changes our reading of the details of the story, it does not change our more general perception of it. The story is still about the individual being moved by larger forces, and the deeper meaning of many episodes remains unchanged. For instance, there is the incident when, caught behind enemy lines, 'One scout hung his head, let spit fall from his lips. The other did the same. They studied the infinitesimal effects of spit on snow and history'.[67] Whether Billy later goes mad or not, this still expresses the overwhelming force of the march of events. Similarly, just as Vonnegut does write his war novel and does tell his sons to disassociate themselves from massacre machinery (something that Billy fails to do, given that his son joins the marines and fights in Vietnam), so, too, does Billy express his experiences of Tralfamadore, eventually speaking about them in public and, possibly in a fantasy, addressing a large crowd before his death with his message. He does,

---

[65]   Vonnegut, *Slaughterhouse-Five*, p. 3, p. 5.
[66]   Vonnegut, *Slaughterhouse-Five*, p. 157.
[67]   Vonnegut, *Slaughterhouse-Five*, p. 35. A similar point, about grand forces dictating individual actions, is made by a transgression of the natural–artificial boundary which is similar to, though less pronounced than, that in Gibson's work. A boxcar seems to be alive to the German guards that patrol outside it, 'a single organism which ate and drank and excreted through its ventilators' (p. 51). Conversely, the prisoners become inanimate objects, equatable with a boxcar here, and later on as 'a liquid which could be induced to flow slowly toward cooing and light' (p. 58). In these examples, individual actions cease to have meaning because the prisoners do not exist as individuals to the guards.

therefore, eventually take positive action. Paradoxically, the message Billy wants to communicate, when he finally takes this positive action and gives his speech, is about passivity and accepting what will happen, but it is, precisely because of this paradox, entirely fitting for the novel.

As in his other novels, Vonnegut is exploring change over time through the tension between self-determination and the individual's powerlessness in the face of larger forces. Some sort of ideal middle ground between the two is proposed in the novel, and is expressed in the prayer that is framed on Billy's office wall, and inscribed on a locket around Montana Wildhack's neck: 'God grant me the serenity to accept the things I cannot change, courage to change the things I can, and wisdom always to tell the difference'.[68] When, early on in the novel, we discover that this hangs on Billy's office wall, we are told that 'Among the things Billy Pilgrim could not change were the past, the present, and the future'.[69] In other words he is, at this stage, completely powerless. The second appearance of the prayer signals a change, though, and by the time it reappears in the novel Billy does have some control over his life: after we are told about Montana's locket, we come to the final chapter where we run through the story about the corpse mines, and finish the book with Billy about to ride into the city on the wagon drawn by the maltreated horse. The first event, the bombing of Dresden, Billy cannot change. The second event, the cruelty to the horse, he can (and, as we know, does not). He fails to discern this difference, but at least Vonnegut himself, by putting the prayer into the novel, manages to give expression to the existence of a mid-point between the individual being free to take action, and the individual being completely at the whim of determining outside forces.

Slaughterhouse-Five is then, if anything, a protest at the 'so it goes' attitude of the Tralfamadorians. Just as *Galapagos* offers the awful possibility that human life is meaningless, that the world is unforgiving, and that there is no teleology or purpose to the history of life, so *Slaughterhouse-Five* raises the fear that our actions are not our own, offering itself as a sincere hope that the actions of the individual – the writer – do have meaning and do have an effect.

(e) The Author as a Deterministic Force in the Fictional Universe of the Novel: 'Breakfast of Champions'

Although *Breakfast of Champions* drops time travel as a plot device, it still explores the same themes in much the same way. What distinguishes this novel from the others, though, is that it incorporates a self-reflexive drive.

---

[68]   Vonnegut, *Slaughterhouse-Five*, p. 44, p. 153.
[69]   Vonnegut, *Slaughterhouse-Five*, p. 44.

Admittedly, there are important elements of self-reflexivity in *Slaughterhouse-Five*, which will have been apparent from the discussion of it above. However, there is little *direct* contact between Vonnegut and the fictional world he creates, apart from one late-night telephone call that Billy receives from a drunk (presumably Vonnegut) whose breath smelt of 'mustard gas and roses'.[70]

In *Breakfast of Champions* the author figures much more prominently in the fictional world that he creates, and Vonnegut uses this to explore the way in which he acts to determine the lives of the characters he creates, robbing them of free will. The notional plot of the novel is driven by the events leading to the meeting between Kilgrore Trout and Dwayne Hoover on the eve of an Arts festival in Midland City, and the violent rampage Dwayne goes on after becoming convinced that he is the central character in a Kilgore Trout science fiction novel. However, the real plot drive is the one that leads Kilgore Trout into a meeting with Kurt Vonnegut, and the discussion they have in which Vonnegut reveals to Trout that he is just a character in a novel.

How does this self-reflexive drive develop the idea that a meaningless determinism shapes the course of events as they take place over time? Most importantly, it provides a context in which Vonnegut can explore the writing of novels and the control that he wields over his characters. It also allows him to make clear how he hopes his fiction differs from that of other writers.

Just as *Galapagos* and *Wonderful Life* create an intellectual history for themselves, by distancing their accounts of evolution from past versions of the theory, so Vonnegut creates a similar history for himself in *Breakfast of Champions*, by distancing himself from realist novels. He does this by creating a fictional novelist, Beatrice Keedsler, who is in Midland City for the Arts festival, and who represents writers of the sort of fiction of which Vonnegut disapproves. He has 'no respect' for Keedsler, whom he accuses of joining 'hands with other old-fashioned storytellers to make people believe that life had leading characters, minor characters, significant details, insignificant details, that it had lessons to be learned, tests to be passed, and a beginning, a middle, and an end'.[71]

He can then contrast his own writing style with this 'old-fashioned' kind. Keedsler works by creating order out of disorder. Vonnegut, on the other hand, does the opposite. He claims that individuals are mistreated because, influenced by conventional storytelling, governments are used to viewing them as disposable bit-part actors. His writing therefore tries to shun literary convention (even more so in this novel, where so much space is taken up by child-like drawings, than in the others):

---

[70]   Vonnegut, *Slaughterhouse-Five*, p. 53.
[71]   Kurt Vonnegut, *Breakfast of Champions* (London: Jonathan Cape, 1973), p. 209.

> Once I understood what was making America such a dangerous,
> unhappy nation of people who had nothing to do with real life, I
> resolved to shun storytelling. I would write about life. Every person
> would be exactly as important as any other. All facts would also be
> given equal weightiness. Nothing would be left out. Let others bring
> order to chaos. I would bring chaos to order, instead, which I think I
> have done.
>   If all writers would do that, then perhaps citizens not in the
> literary trades will understand that there is no order in the world
> around us, that we must adapt ourselves to the requirements of chaos
> instead.[72]

There are obvious parallels here with the writing I discussed in chapter 5,
which detailed the privileging of chaos over order in contemporary fiction.
Passages like this suggest that there is a common postmodern discourse that
not only runs between the work of Vonnegut and Gould, discussed in this
chapter, but also from here to the disruptions of the chaos–order distinction
which I explored in the works of Gleick, Prigogine, and Pynchon in chapter 3.

There is also a strong link to the disruption of the human–machine
dichotomy, discussed elsewhere in relation to the work of Dawkins and
Gibson. *Breakfast of Champions* presents many of its characters as machines,
and brings to the fore the transgression of the natural–artificial boundary that
we found in the earlier novels: black prostitutes 'had grown up in the rural
south of the nation, where their ancestors had been used as agricultural
machinery';[73] 'in the interests of survival, they [women] trained themselves to
be agreeing machines instead of thinking machines';[74] and in a phrase which
recollects the central premise of *Player Piano*, Bunny is a 'piano controller'[75]
rather than a piano player.

This treatment of people as machines ties in with the idea of Vonnegut as
a dictatorial controlling force in the fictional world. This becomes apparent
when a self-reflexive aside leads Vonnegut into a general discussion about
fiction:

> I had come to the conclusion that there was nothing sacred about
> myself or about any human being, that we were all machines, doomed
> to collide and collide and collide. For want of anything better to do,
> we became fans of collisions. Sometimes I wrote well about collisions,
> which meant I was a writing machine in good repair. Sometimes I
> wrote badly, which meant I was a writing machine in bad repair.[76]

---

[72]   Vonnegut, *Breakfast of Champions*, p. 210.
[73]   Vonnegut, *Breakfast of Champions*, p. 72.
[74]   Vonnegut, *Breakfast of Champions*, p. 136.
[75]   Vonnegut, *Breakfast of Champions*, p. 181.
[76]   Vonnegut, *Breakfast of Champions*, pp. 219–20.

Vonnegut here gives vent to the idea that we are all nothing more than deterministic machines. He also appreciates that this can be a highly dangerous notion, because it can have disturbing ramifications for how we view our fellow humans, and the responsibility we take for our actions. Just as the guard in *Slaughterhouse-Five* uses an appeal to determinism to justify hitting a prisoner for no apparent reason,[77] so Dwayne Hoover finally goes mad, and embarks on his violent spree, when he thinks that Kilgore Trout's novel is telling him that everyone is a machine, without free will, except him: 'He then socked Beatrice Keedsler on the jaw. He punched Bonnie MacMahon in the belly. He honestly believed that they were unfeeling machines'.[78]

As with the earlier novels, however, Vonnegut does hold out the hope that we are more than machines – or at least a mixture of the machine-like and the human. This hope comes from the abstract artist Rabo Karabekian, who expresses an alternative (or at least an addition) to the idea that people are machines. Vonnegut initially despises Karabekian as much as he does the novelist Beatrice Keedsler. However, he is redeemed in Vonnegut's eyes when he takes the trouble to explain his painting, *The Temptation of Saint Anthony*, to the people. His painting, a huge green rectangle with a vertical stripe in dayglo orange reflecting tape at one end, is crucial to the novel. Karabekian explains it like this:

> the picture ... shows everything about life which truly matters, with nothing left out. It is a picture of the awareness of every animal ... A sacred picture of Saint Anthony alone is one vertical, unwavering band of light. If a cockroach were near him, or a cocktail waitress, the picture would show two such bands of light. Our awareness is all that is alive and maybe sacred in any of us. Everything else about us is dead machinery.[79]

It is this which offers the hope in the novel that we are more than machines, and that we have an awareness, a consciousness, which cannot be reduced to machine-like terms.

This novel goes further than the previous ones, because Vonnegut does not only explore the consequences of the universe being nothing more than a machine, he also explores the idea that fictional universes are machines created by despotic writers, and so casts himself in a role which is that of a huge, external, determining force on the lives of his characters. Yet the awareness that is represented by the orange stripe in Karabekian's painting offers the hope that we can become more than machines. It also offers the hope that

---

[77] See note 52.
[78] Vonnegut, *Breakfast of Champions*, p. 259.
[79] Vonnegut, *Breakfast of Champions*, p. 221.

Vonnegut's novel can become more than a machine created by him, because he is himself more than a machine: 'And this book is being written by a meat machine in cooperation with a machine made of metal and plastic ... And at the core of the writing meat machine is something sacred, which is an unwavering band of light'.[80]

If the hope that Vonnegut expresses here is borne out, then we are fusions of machine and independent awareness, able to have some control over the deterministic processes that shape our lives. In expressing this hope, Vonnegut is forced to concede that he cannot control his characters completely, and that he must grant them some freedom to control their world: 'Here was the thing about my control over the characters I created: I could only guide their movement approximately, since they were such big animals. There was inertia to overcome ... [It was] as though I was connected to them by stale rubberbands'.[81]

This is the climax of the evolution of the ideas about free will and determinism that I have traced through this selection of Vonnegut's work. He proposes here a fusion of free will and determinism – of the machine and the unwavering band of light – that puts into practice the prayer inscribed on Montana Wildhack's locket in *Slaughterhouse-Five*, and offers the middle way between humans and machines first called for in *Player Piano*. This is not by any means a comfortable resolution, because the unwavering band of light is offered more in hope than in reality. Nevertheless, it is at least there as a possibility – something which cannot be said of much of the earlier fiction.

By the time we get to *Galapagos*, Vonnegut has become a little more cynical again, and there is a sense in which human fate is determined purely by outside forces, even though a little hope is expressed that we have some purpose in this world. In a view of evolution which is identical to that proposed by Gould, he finds an apt means for expressing the idea of the individual life, shaped by an indifferent universe, which has obsessed him throughout his career. The idea of time that he proposes in this novel does not therefore come solely from the scientific concept with which he deals. The notion of free will pitted against determinism, which I have traced through this sequence of novels, leads him to explore a view of change over time that mirrors one arrived at, seemingly independently, in presentations of evolution by scientists: things are determined, but with no reason (beyond the laws of physics) and to no purpose. This suggests that he does not so much take an idea from science, but that he sees in science a means of expressing those ideas that he has arrived at independently. In the light of this, it is not unreasonable to suggest that the sense of time that renounces teleology, identified by White,

---

[80]   Vonnegut, *Breakfast of Champions*, p. 225.
[81]   Vonnegut, *Breakfast of Champions*, p. 202.

is indeed characteristic of postmodern discourses. Despite the close parallels between evolution as it is presented in *Wonderful Life*, and as it is presented in *Galapagos*, the really interesting connection between the two books is not that Vonnegut should have used contingency in his novel, but that the foregrounding of this notion should accord with wider postmodern discourses of time.

The rather troubled and problematical notion of time is actually central to postmodernism. It is this that is picked up in the next chapter, which formulates an understanding of postmodernism that identifies it with a particular set of histories. The discussion of postmodernism that follows offers a justification for retaining the term, despite Sokal and Bricmont's objections to it described in chapter 2.

Chapter 6

Histories: Postmodernism, Literature and Science

The vexed subject of the past haunts postmodernism. It has frequently been observed that there is a paradoxical relationship between postmodern culture and history. On the one hand, postmodernism is often presented as the erasure of a sense of history, conceived of as a linear unfolding of a sequence of events. Much is made of the tendency in postmodern culture both towards pastiche, whereby cultural forms from the past are mixed and matched in an eclectic fashion, and the renunciation of Enlightenment metanarratives, driving us toward some future goal.[1] On the other hand, the term itself – *post*modernism – suggests something which comes after modernism and which is, therefore, very clearly situated historically. As Steven Earnshaw comments, 'It is the case that postmodernism would rather not be "in history" if it can help it … [But if] history is narrative, then the very word "postmodernism" cannot avoid being in history, and history in a very strong teleological sense'.[2]

This issue of postmodernism's relationship to history is one that will be addressed in this chapter. As will have been apparent from the three preceding case studies, the definition of postmodernism which seems to me to make most sense is one which acknowledges the way in which it is historically situated. What links the diverse issues and texts that were presented as postmodern in chapters 3, 4 and 5, is their replacement of an established category or concept (defined, implicitly, as modernist or belonging to the Enlightenment) by another. This chapter argues that this is the defining feature of postmodern discourses: their identification of themselves with the rejection of the past. This rejection may be based on an authentic overturning of the past, or it may involve the construction of a partial and distorted view of the past in order to make the present position appear revolutionary. This latter possibility – that

---

[1]   Jean-François Lyotard's celebration of the timelessness of narrative knowledge (emphasising repeated rhythm over linear narrative developments), and his attempt to expose science's reliance on teleological Enlightenment metanarratives of freedom and knowledge, are perhaps the most frequently cited examples. Jean-François Lyotard, *The Postmodern Condition: A Report on Knowledge*, trans. Geoff Bennington and Brain Massumi, Theory and History of Literature 10 (1979; Manchester University Press, 1986).

[2]   Steven Earnshaw, *Postmodern Surroundings*, Postmodern Studies 9 (Amsterdam: Rodopi, 1994), p. 54.

in order to present itself as radical, postmodernism constructs an unnecessarily narrow definition of modernism – is neatly phrased by Steven Connor: 'the modernist canon is thus no longer in place so as to foster ancestor-worship, but in order that it may be subverted, or surpassed. But the spectacular parricide announced by postmodernism can only take place as long as a false father is laid (repeatedly) upon the sacrificial slab'.[3]

In discussing the relationship between postmodernism and history, this chapter will also discuss the relationship between postmodernism and truth. One of the notable features of the science wars, which we are currently supposed to be waging, is the way in which the term postmodernism has focused the conflict. Indeed, if Alan Sokal and Jean Bricmont are concerned with the abuses of science by the humanities, it is partly because they see it to be subject to the misconceptions of a group of intellectuals who practice a postmodern philosophy. Chapter 2 endorsed Sokal and Bricmont's objection to the misuse of science in the humanities, arguing that we should use their illumination of the dangers of speaking beyond one's expertise to draw some of the borders for a mature literature–science criticism. However, their characterisation of postmodernism as a simplistic relativist philosophy will be strongly contested in this chapter. There are, undoubtedly, those who both advocate postmodernism and preach relativism, but these voices distort the postmodern culture they claim to portray. To polarise the discussion into a conflict between scientists and postmodernists simplifies a complex debate, just as the theorists objected to by Sokal and Bricmont misread and simplify one or two trends in science, generalising them beyond the boundaries of their applicability. Moreover, objecting wholesale to postmodernism robs us of a useful term for characterising some distinctive trends in late twentieth-century culture.

Therefore, while one of the central contentions in this book is that Sokal and Bricmont's sharp reprimand is instructive for literature–science criticism, and should be paid careful attention to in the humanities, it is also claimed that their misconceptions about postmodernism need to be interrogated (even though they acknowledge the slightly arbitrary nature of their use of the term).[4] Postmodernism will be characterised in this chapter as a phenomenon which brings us up against the limits of our knowledge, but without rejecting all foundations for it. The chapter will begin with a discussion of Sokal and Bricmont's presentation of postmodernism, indicating some of the ways in which their definition of it is unnecessarily narrow (whilst their application of

---

[3]   Steven Connor, 'The Modern and the Postmodern as History', *Essays in Criticism* 37 (1987): pp. 186–7.

[4]   Alan Sokal and Jean Bricmont, *Intellectual Impostures: Postmodern Philosophers' Abuse of Science* (London: Profile, 1998), pp. 11–12.

this definition to whole swathes of the humanities is dangerously broad). It will then go on to propose a definition which is both consistent with other conceptions of the postmodern, and that enables us to analyse the links between cultural science (see chapter 2 for a definition of this) and literature.

Sokal and Bricmont: Postmodernism as Relativism

As noted above, Sokal and Bricmont's characterisation of their opponents as postmodernist acknowledges that the concept is being used as a somewhat convenient umbrella term to identify a trend in the humanities which links the various theorists they discuss, and they openly draw our attention to the limitations of their use of the term. These are that they analyse only one aspect of postmodernist thought – the characterisation of science ('We make no claim to analyse postmodernist thought in general'); that not all of the theorists they discuss would think of themselves as postmodernists ('It is true that the French authors discussed in this book do not all regard themselves as "postmodernist" or "poststructuralist"'); and that there is not a unified postmodernist agenda linking the theorists ('the intellectual abuses criticized in this book are not homogenous').[5] Following these disclaimers, a two-fold justification of the use of the term is offered: writings on postmodernism make frequent reference to these theorists ('all the authors analysed here are utilized as fundamental points of reference in English-language postmodernist discourse'), and the style and content of these theorists' writings ('obscure jargon, implicit rejection of rational thought, abuse of science as metaphor') are 'common traits of Anglo-American postmodernism'.[6]

The authors discussed by Sokal and Bricmont are, indeed, often used as points of reference in postmodernist discourse, but neither they, nor the aspects of their work discussed by Sokal and Bricmont, are fundamental to postmodernism. There is in existence a large body of cultural artefacts (including those of cultural – though not necessarily professional – science) which are, to a lesser or greater degree, postmodernist, and the opinions of various theorists do not alter the existence or otherwise of this postmodern culture. Postmodernism is a term which is used in a number of ways, and here there are two distinct uses at issue: postmodernism as an adjective to describe the culture; and postmodernism as Sokal and Bricmont use it, as an adjective to characterise a certain philosophy of, or approach to, knowledge. Although they do, as noted, acknowledge that they use the term in a narrow way, it is important to stress that it is a concept integral to our understanding of

---

5   Sokal and Bricmont, p. 4, p, 11, p. 11.
6   Sokal and Bricmont, p. 12.

contemporary culture, and so should not be reduced to an easy shorthand for an unrepresentative relativist philosophy.

This is not to deny that some of the writers they object to do feature prominently in debates about postmodernism. Crucially, however, though their opinions are prominent, they are not fundamental. For instance, Jean-François Lyotard is by far the most influential figure, in terms of his perception of postmodernism, discussed by Sokal and Bricmont (even though he does not merit a chapter on his own in *Intellectual Impostures*). True to the limits of their project, Sokal and Bricmont concentrate upon Lyotard's description of science, and perceptively unpick his possibly wilfully over-literal extrapolation (to a claim that there is a 'postmodern' science) from the observation that the density of gas is dependent upon the scale at which it is observed.[7] This is a reasonable objection to Lyotard's use (or abuse) of science, but as an objection to postmodernism it is fundamentally limited. Firstly, other aspects of Lyotard's work (for example, his discussion of the information society) are left untouched; secondly, Lyotard is hardly accepted uncritically in the humanities; and thirdly, if there is a postmodern culture, discrediting Lyotard's opinion of it hardly denies the existence of that culture. Of course, Sokal and Bricmont claim they are trying to do none of these things, but it is as well to remind ourselves of the boundaries of their project, so that the acceptance of the pertinence of their observations in chapter 2 of this book is not read as a rejection of the validity of postmodernism as a concept.

Sokal and Bricmont's further objections to postmodernist discourse – as jargon-laden, dismissive of rational thought, and abusive of science as metaphor – deserve further discussion. The obscurity of postmodernist discourse may well be a cause for concern, and certainly it does no harm to remind ourselves of the benefits of clarity. However, this does not invalidate the postmodern as a concept. It is also worth adding that Sokal and Bricmont's arguments should not be extrapolated to apply automatically to those whom they do not discuss, and that, whilst impenetrable prose may be a symptom of muddled thought, or a way of obscuring banality, it is also the case that complex arguments, or attempts to formulate difficult ideas, can sometimes lead to unjust accusations of wilful obscurity.

The exposure of the abuse of science as metaphor is one of the primary targets of *Intellectual Impostures*, and it is a target which, as chapter 2 claimed, Sokal and Bricmont hit. However, equating this with postmodernism is too simplistic. It is, indeed, the case that many of those discussed by Sokal and Bricmont are equated, if not directly then by association, with a postmodern perspective. Moreover, literature–science criticism in general is also strongly associated with this perspective. However, this does not mean that

---

[7]   Sokal and Bricmont, p. 126.

postmodernism and the abuse of science as metaphor are directly equivalent. Aspects of, and extrapolations from, postmodernism may well be at the heart of the abuses of science to which Sokal and Bricmont object, but these abuses are not at the heart of postmodernism.

This ties in with the remaining objection to postmodernist discourse that Sokal and Bricmont formulate, that it is dismissive of rational thought. There are those who see postmodernism as a reaction against a strict Enlightenment rationalism which goes so far as to embrace extreme relativism, but there is a sustainable definition of postmodernism that does not follow this line. While there is no homogenous postmodern philosophy, it is reasonable to characterise the central thrust of postmodernist thought as antifoundational. However, critically examining the assumptions of our knowledge does not necessarily entail renouncing that knowledge out of hand.

This is an observation which is endorsed by a number of writers on postmodernism. For example, Stuart Sim, the editor of a volume which seeks to bring together the central tenets of postmodernism, *The Icon Critical Dictionary of Postmodernism*, writes about it as a critical philosophy which, though unliveable, clears the decks for a more positive philosophy in the future: it may be that the scepticism of postmodern thought has served a 'purpose in drawing attention to the weaknesses of certain philosophical positions, and that a less negatively oriented philosophical programme can take its place for the immediate future'.[8] Similarly, Patricia Waugh, in the introduction to *Postmodernism: A Reader*, writes that 'I suspect that Postmodernism will increasingly come to be seen as a strategy for exposing oppressive contradictions in modernity, but I would wish to resist the idea that we have all embraced it as an inevitable condition'.[9] Rather like Sim, she suggests it might function as a 'strategy of disruption', leading us to question ideas that would otherwise be taken unthinkingly as natural. Steven Connor also acknowledges that postmodernism's assault on the foundations of our knowledge does not lead to the renunciation of the possibility of knowledge, but rather to a critical questioning of its grounds: 'questions of value and legitimacy do not disappear, but gain a new intensity [when the grounds of value are questioned]; and the struggle to generate and ground legitimacy in the contemporary academy is nowhere more intense than in the debates produced by and around postmodernism'.[10] Linda Hutcheon's description of postmodernism as 'not so much a concept as a problematic' also suggests this sense that it does not function as a prescription for how to understand the

---

[8]   Stuart Sim, 'Postmodernism and Philosophy', *The Icon Critical Dictionary of Postmodernism*, ed. Sim (Cambridge: Icon, 1998), p. 14.
[9]   Patricia Waugh, introduction, *Postmodernism: A Reader* (New York: Routledge, 1992), p. 9.
[10]   Steven Connor, *Postmodernist Culture* (Oxford: Blackwell, 1989), p. 8.

world, so much as a means of questioning and thinking about the terms on which our understanding of the world is based.[11]

It may be useful to sketch in more detail exactly how postmodernism is being seen here, as this forms part of the justification for making the links between the literary and popular scientific texts discussed in chapters 3, 4 and 5. This definition rejects the expulsion of postmodernism from history in the work of some theorists, and places postmodernism in a particular era of cultural development.

Defining Postmodernism: History and Canons

It has already been noted that the issue of history is one that is bound up with that of postmodernism. The definition of postmodernism that makes most sense is one which acknowledges its historicity. Even though much postmodern culture is characterised by a pastiche of styles and genres from the past, seemingly disruptive of linear stylistic development, and therefore marked by a profound sense of the current moment without regard to a really-existing past, there are a number of ways in which history is very palpably present.

Firstly, the playful mixture of styles, the challenge to the distinctions between low and high culture, and all the other elements which are commonly cited as postmodern, are characteristic of contemporary culture in a way in which they are not characteristic of previous periods. Although it is naïve to assume that history was somehow more authentic in the past, and that the repackaging of history is an entirely contemporary phenomenon, it is reasonable to claim that the degree and intensity with which elements from previous periods are mixed together is characteristic of late twentieth-century culture. If contemporary culture can be distinguished in this way from earlier cultures, then it is distinct from them, and this denotes historical development.

Secondly, and more importantly, postmodern culture is marked by the specific historical factors that surround its rise. Those elements which characterise late twentieth-century life – the mixing of cultures that results from rapid communications and the growth in travel, the predominance of electronic media, and a consumer economy marked by service, rather than manufacturing, industries – are all factors which shape postmodern culture. Sometimes these factors are the explicit subject of postmodern culture (for instance, Pynchon's concentration in *Gravity's Rainbow* on the global cartels which transcend the national divisions of the Second World War), and

---

[11]   Linda Hutcheon, *The Politics of Postmodernism*, New Accents (London: Routledge, 1989), p. 15.

sometimes they are much smaller elements in projects which are notably different (for instance, the discussion of humans and machines which is just one part of Richard Dawkins's presentation of evolution). Postmodernism need not, then, be an 'all or nothing' concept: cultural artefacts may contain just one or two elements that are recognisably postmodern.

The primary element in a definition of postmodernism is this sense of history, whether explicit or hidden: the way in which something announces itself as *post* modern. 'Modern', in this sense, is given a broad meaning, referring to those characteristics of Western culture, or of thought, which have been prevalent since the Enlightenment. Defining these characteristics is itself somewhat problematical. The key requirement is not so much that the postmodern text in question should succeed in identifying and refuting an element from the Enlightenment, but that it should announce itself as doing so. In other words, it is postmodern if it is truly revolutionary, or if it merely carries the appearance of being revolutionary, constructing a false modernity from which it then distances itself.

The dispute over chaos theory illustrates this neatly. As has been established, there is a body of popular science writing that presents chaos theory as a revolutionary approach to the world, involving the rethinking of some fundamental Enlightenment categories. While the question of whether this is, or is not, a correct assessment of the importance of chaos theory, is clearly very important, it does not affect the postmodernity, or otherwise, of these texts. Postmodernism is a way of thinking about the contemporary moment, an attitude; it is not a concrete thing (although it may well have concrete effects in terms of the way people behave, or even in the form of postmodern architecture). These texts display a postmodern attitude by seeing the subject matter – chaos theory – as *post* a-particular-entrenched-Enlightenment-sort-of-science. Of course, these writers do not need to label themselves as postmodernists for their texts to function in this way – by virtue of suggesting that chaos theory rejects ideas which are associated with a long-established way of doing things, they are inevitably aligned with the broader rejection of the Enlightenment apparent in contemporary culture that we call postmodernism.

Another way of conceptualising this issue is to consider postmodern culture as invoking a canon of ideas or texts which are defined as its intellectual predecessors. This may be explicit, with the author drawing our attention to the 'modern' tradition from which his or her postmodern work distances itself, or it may be more implicit – for instance when a work of literature has characteristics which tie it to other postmodern literature that is itself frequently seen to reject realist and modernist positions. This kind of canon-forming will have been apparent in the suggestion that the texts in the case studies are postmodern because of their rejection, to some degree, of an Enlightenment past. A brief consideration of this, in relation to science and literature, may be useful.

Perhaps the most obvious sense of a canon comes in the descriptions of chaos theory which chapter 3 dealt with. For instance, it was established that Nina Hall's introduction to *The New Scientist Guide to Chaos* produced a brief summary of the history of science which places chaos theory in a revolutionary position: in Hall's presentation, the assumptions of an Enlightenment, Newtonian science go through a period of crisis in the early twentieth century with quantum mechanics, before chaos theory produces a wholesale revision of those assumptions.[12] Hall does not obviously conceive of chaos theory as postmodernist, but the type of history she presents, and the canon of preceding ideas she invokes, tie in very directly to postmodern postures elsewhere in contemporary culture.

One of the figures whom Hall associates with Enlightenment science, Pierre Simon de Laplace, is frequently invoked in 'postmodern' histories of science and it may therefore be worth considering his role in a little more detail here, in order to establish just how his work fits into the canon of ideas invoked by postmodernism. The most frequently cited passage from Laplace's work, because it makes explicit what a lot of people associate with Enlightenment science, is the following:

> Given for one instant an intelligence which could comprehend all the forces by which nature is animated and the respective situation of the beings who compose it – an intelligence sufficiently vast to submit these data to analysis – it would embrace in the same formula the movements of the greatest bodies of the universe and those of the lightest atom; for it, nothing would be uncertain and the future, as the past, would be present to its eyes.[13]

For our present purposes it does not really matter how representative of Laplace's general ideas this passage really is. What does matter is that it is frequently taken, in the 'postmodern' histories of science, to epitomise the viewpoint of Enlightenment scientists. For instance, Stephen Toulmin claims that 'the intellectual ideal of Science which Laplace had inherited from Descartes and Newton was captured in the image of an Omniscient Calculator'.[14] The emphases which are placed in these sorts of readings of this

---

[12]   See the discussion of Nina Hall's introduction to *The New Scientist Guide to Chaos* on page 80.
[13]   Pierre Simon Laplace, *A Philosophical Essay on Probabilities*, trans. Frederick Wilson Truscott and Frederick Lincoln Emory, 6th edn (1819; New York: Dover, 1951), p. 4.
[14]   Stephen Toulmin, *The Return to Cosmology: Postmodern Science and the Theology of Nature* (Berkeley: University of California Press, 1982), p. 243.

passage are its stress on determinism, predictability and (sometimes, in slightly more extreme readings), control: the development of the universe is entirely determined, it is therefore predictable, and it can be controlled.

This does not, of course, mean that Enlightenment scientists necessarily thought that it would, in future, be possible to predict everything that would happen in the universe. Nevertheless, the basic faith underpinning the Newtonian paradigm in these readings of the history of science is that this complete knowledge is theoretically possible. Although Laplace's 'Omniscient Calculator' was not a reality, it was an idealisation that reveals, for those who take his words to epitomise the ideals of Newtonian science, a central Enlightenment truth: the only handicap to our knowledge is lack of information and lack of processing power.

The important passage cited from Laplace may even remind us of a similar passage, which reveals a similar perspective, from René Descartes (another key figure who is often taken to epitomise Enlightenment ideals):

> These long chains of reasonings, quite simple and easy, which geometers are accustomed to using to teach their most difficult demonstrations, had given me cause to imagine that everything which can be encompassed by man's knowledge is linked in the same way, and that, provided only that one abstains from accepting any for true which is not true, and that one always keeps the right order for one thing to be deduced from that which precedes it, there can be nothing so distant that one does not reach it eventually, or so hidden that one cannot discover it.[15]

Although there is a difference between the two formulations – Laplace sees the need for reason to act upon information, whereas Descartes places greater stress on reason alone – they are bonded by the assumption that absolute knowledge can, at least in theory, be acquired.

It is these sorts of viewpoints that the contemporary histories of science characterised in this book as postmodern, use to establish an Enlightenment perspective from which they then distance twentieth-century science. Certain ideas from twentieth-century science – Heisenberg's uncertainty principle and chaos theory are popular choices – are used to denote a changed understanding, revealing of theoretical limits to our knowledge. For instance, as will have been apparent from the discussion in chapter 3, science writing about chaos theory frequently establishes it as a paradigmatic contemporary science by emphasising its application across a vast range of disciplines, and then

---

15   René Descartes, 'Discourse on Method', *'Discourse on Method' and Other Writings*, trans. F.E. Sutcliffe (Middlesex: Penguin, 1968), p. 41.

distances it from earlier science by drawing the reader's attention to the limits to prediction which it exposes.

There is, then, a process of canon-formation going on here which creates a particular history: in describing sciences like chaos theory, certain texts invoke a canon of ideas which serve to position contemporary science historically. By establishing the present as a thorough-going interrogation and reworking of Enlightenment ideas, they invoke a postmodern discourse.

Although this is the way in which postmodern discourses invoke a broad history of science, as will have been apparent from the case studies, some texts fit into a postmodern perspective in a different way. For example, Dawkins and Gould do not, by any stretch of the imagination, suggest a history of science like that implied by popular presentations of chaos theory. Their texts partake of postmodern discourses in smaller ways – not broad discourses of knowledge but, respectively, more specific discourses of identity and time.

To return to the broader discourse of knowledge, of course none of the discussion in chapter 3 of James Gleick and others like him proves anything about the true significance of chaos theory in relation to the development of science; nevertheless, it does demonstrate that it is invested with a meaning which ties it in with other aspects of postmodern culture. The primary function of a literature–science critic is to describe the intersection of literature and science in the culture. The manifestation of chaos theory in the culture is, partially, postmodern in the sense described above, and it is entirely legitimate to describe it as such, drawing out the points at which its concerns bisect those of other texts. However, the extent to which this postmodernism is indicative of a genuine scientific revolution is another matter entirely, and though extremely important, one on which a literature–science critic can comment with less, if any, authority.

Indeed, the extent to which the broader postmodern culture is genuinely revolutionary might be open to question. This is not because so much postmodern culture relies on a pastiche of previous styles – combining things in a novel way can be as innovative as a more conventional originality – but because, despite its strong antifoundationalist attack on the Enlightenment, there are areas where postmodernism struggles to provide anything to replace it. Rather than picturing postmodernism's rejection of the Enlightenment as a swift revolution, then, it is more like ongoing trench warfare. There are one or two areas where breakthroughs occur but in other areas, despite the vast numbers of texts and critics hurling themselves over the top to proclaim the revolution, there is no more than a wavering of the opposed lines.

Just as the use of the term 'postmodern' can be justified for manifestations of cultural science which invoke a canon of ideas or texts constituting a history that culminates in the rejection of a loosely defined

'Enlightenment' science – as in the presentations of chaos theory discussed above – so the term 'postmodern' also serves as a useful concept for the understanding of a significant body of contemporary fiction. This is a much less controversial use of the term, and it is a commonplace to talk about postmodern literature. Again, the idea of the canon gives us a profitable means of understanding this postmodern literature because it suggests that it exists in relation to a body of other texts – that postmodern literature contests ideas associated with earlier literature, and thus, again, implies a particular history for itself.[16]

For instance, Brian McHale's contention in *Postmodernist Fiction*, that postmodernist literature can be distinguished from modernist because it raises ontological, rather than epistemological, questions, would suggest the formulation of a canon of texts, charting the move from modern to postmodern, which produces a history rather similar to that implied by the presentations of chaos theory discussed above.[17] Just as Hall's and Gleick's texts construct chaos theory as asking questions of traditional science, so McHale suggests that foundational questions are posed by postmodernist literature, extending the less exacting questions asked of realist literature by the modernists.

This sense of an implied history for postmodernist literature can also be drawn from attempts to sum up literary history for general readers. This can be clearly seen in *The Oxford Companion to English Literature* which offers T.S. Eliot, Ezra Pound, James Joyce, Virginia Woolf, W.B. Yeats, Ford Madox Ford and Joseph Conrad as examples of writers with whom modernism is 'particularly associated'[18] – in other words, it tentatively offers these writers' works as a canon of modernist literature. It then goes on to say that a 'sense of cultural relativism is pervasive in much modernist writing' and that it is also marked by 'an awareness of the irrational and the workings of the unconscious mind'. Because these statements home in on states of mind, and perceptions of reality, they imply a foregrounding of epistemological questions that chimes with that identified by McHale in modernist literature. Indeed, some of the techniques employed by the writers cited in the entry – the streams of consciousness used by Woolf and Joyce, focusing the reader upon characters' perceptions of the world, instead of the world itself, for instance – would seem to emphasise this aspect of modernist literature.

The *Oxford Companion* goes further, though, because it also defines modernism backwards, by virtue of its difference from previous literary forms, particularly realism. Modernism 'rejected the traditional ... framework of

---

[16] This is not, of course, the only definition of postmodern literature – some readings do not see postmodern literature as renouncing the precepts of earlier literature, but as continually revisiting the modernist moment.

[17] Brian McHale, *Postmodernist Fiction* (New York: Methuen, 1987), pp. 9–10.

[18] 'Modernism', *The Oxford Companion to English Literature*, 1991 edn.

narrative, description, and rational exposition' and is 'based upon a sharp rejection of the procedures and values of the immediate past'. In this reading it is a significant shift in literary history, and the implication is that there was a literary tradition, preceding modernism, which focused more on an external, rather than a psychological, world.

Turning to the entry on realism in the *Oxford Companion*, we find this point reiterated. It acknowledges the difficulty of defining realism, but nevertheless offers a series of definitions that place it as an antecedent to the modernist enterprise. For instance, Sir Paul Harvey, the compiler of the first *Oxford Companion to English Literature*, is quoted thus: 'truth to the observed facts of life'.[19] This assumes, of course, that the 'facts of life' are the same for all observers – that reality is commonsensical and accessible. A similar point is made by reference to the French realist school of the nineteenth century which, we are told, 'insisted on accurate documentation, sociological insight, [and] an accumulation of the details of material fact'. Interestingly, the entry on literary realism is preceded by one on realism in scholastic philosophy which defines it as 'the doctrine that attributes objective or absolute existence to universals'.

So the *Oxford Companion* defines modernism backwards, albeit in a rather guarded fashion, by virtue of its difference from realism. Realism, despite the difficulties of definition acknowledged by the *Companion*, is associated with a more universal, easily accessible version of reality. Modernism complicates this view by asking questions about how different individuals perceive reality, and by focusing upon a particular sort of psychological world (because it emphasises a fragmentary series of different views of the world).

All this is pertinent to our understanding of postmodernism because, although the 1991 edition of the *Oxford Companion* intriguingly omits to include an entry on postmodernism, the definitions of realism and modernism provide a canon of ideas and texts that provide a history – and definition – of postmodernism. It is logical to assume that if we pursue the implications of the observations just made – that modernism complicates the commonsensical presuppositions of realism – then postmodernism (that which comes after and goes beyond modernism) will exacerbate and heighten the interrogative stance of the preceding modernists.

What is being suggested, then, is that postmodernism, in literature and in science, can be understood in terms of its historical situation. What is crucial is the history which is constructed by the canons of texts or ideas, explicitly cited or implicitly postulated, as antecedent to the postmodern artefacts. In the discussion that appears immediately above, it will be noticed that these histories are three-phase in both literature and science: a broad realism,

---

[19]   'Realism', *The Oxford Companion to English Literature*, 1991 edn.

challenged by early twentieth-century developments (modernism, quantum physics), and overturned (it is suggested) by late twentieth-century culture (postmodern literature, presentations of chaos theory). Two further issues relating to these canons need to be addressed before we can move on from the historical situation of postmodernism.

Firstly, the broad equivalence of two separate histories in literature and science, with developments related to the Enlightenment, being challenged and then surpassed in the twentieth century, might suggest that there is a causal link between literary and scientific developments. Indeed, the formulation of such a link is highly seductive, particularly if one is seeking to challenge the complete separation of literature and science implied by the two cultures perspective. However, we need to proceed with caution.

The justification for making a link such as this is presumably that a world view associated with, say, the early twentieth century is shared by writers and scientists, and predisposes people toward particular outlooks and an interest in particular issues. One could hypothesise, for instance, that for whatever reason (the cumulative impact of urbanisation and industrialisation; the waning of belief in divine authority; the challenge to Victorian myths of progress) there was a greater tendency to acknowledge multiple or alternate perspectives in the early twentieth century than in preceding decades, and that this might account for a greater interest in subjective perspectives in such diverse areas as literature (streams of consciousness and other challenges to omniscient narration), and science (Einstein's theories of relativity; Heisenberg's uncertainty principle).

The dangers of such an approach are that it smothers differences (presumably both relativity theory and the uncertainty principle are as objectively verifiable as preceding scientific theories); it ignores the influence of distinct disciplinary traditions (might Heisenberg not have been responding to the status of scientific knowledge at the time and, whatever the cultural influences, could he have formulated his ideas without a certain body of established scientific developments on which to build?); it ignores the possibility of coincidence (how do we distinguish between chance patterns of similarity between science and literature, and ones genuinely indicative of connection between the two?); and it only accounts selectively for literature and science (what about other scientific developments, and the continuing realist and naturalist traditions in literature? – how valid is it to propose a connection between literature and science when we simply seek out data which confirm our theories, and ignore everything which might challenge them?).

It is for these reasons that in studying postmodernism in contemporary literature and science, a focus on the idea of the canon is so important: it allows us to conceive of the way in which postmodern culture projects its own history, and thereby formulates its own identity. When we are faced with seemingly parallel histories of literature and science, therefore, although these might be indicative of direct connections between literature and science (or not), they clearly do indicate a linked perspective on intellectual history, and it is the particular conception of themselves, and of their relation to the past, which makes them postmodernist.[20]

The second issue which needs to be addressed is that of the questions which might arise when it is noticed that the three-phase history discussed here is not entirely identical with the two-phase history suggested by the case studies in chapters 3, 4 and 5. In each of these chapters it was suggested that a 'postmodern' link between literature and science (a new conception of knowledge in chapter 3, a different conception of human identity in chapter 4, and a challenge to the notion of linear progress in chapter 5) was based around the rejection of an implicitly or explicitly defined Enlightenment category. Where, it might be asked, does the third (middle) element come from in the canons of history and science briefly outlined above?

In fact this does not pose the dilemma it may at first seem to. The case studies focused on the distance between the rejection of one set of concepts (broadly defined as Enlightenment) in favour of another (equated, in a general sense, with a postmodern perspective). Because the important issue in each instance is the distance between these two opposing perspectives, there was a tendency not to direct attention on the intermediate, transitional phase. In fact, if a canon is constructed charting the history of the movement from one state to another, there should by implication be a moment of transition (a middle phase). Sometimes this may be passed over completely (either because it is so swift as to merit no mention, or because it is just not as important as the other two phases), but at other times it may be dealt with in more detail – as, for instance, when popularisers of chaos theory construct a history of science

---

[20]   It is worth pointing out that in addition to these histories of literature and science, one could also tie in a history of literary theory which is remarkably similar to that described for literature and science, with a 'realist' approach (trying to recover the 'meaning' of the text), challenged by a structuralist perspective, and finally surpassed by poststructuralism. Evidence for the importance of this history of literary theory can be gleaned from an analysis of 'readers' in literary theory which construct a history of the subject from a canon of key texts. Even those aspects of literary criticism – say feminism and Marxism – which might seem to lie outside the bounds of this history are often presented as having their own histories which tie in with this development in approach. A long discussion of the subject is omitted from this book in order to maintain its coherence, but it is discussed in chapter 4 of my PhD thesis. Daniel Cordle, 'Literature and Science Writing in Contemporary Culture: The Challenge to History in Post-Enlightenment Discourses of Literature, Science and Literary Theory', diss., University of Leicester, 1996. It should be noted that as the title may indicate, the ideas expressed in the thesis follow a cruder line (in their less critical acceptance of the standard literature–science perspective) than those expressed here.

which proposes a series of challenges to 'Enlightenment' science preceding the impact of chaos theory.

It might also be mentioned that alternative constructions of the history of literature and science may alter the canon a little, but retain the same essential movement from the Enlightenment to the present. For example, if postmodernism is seen as no more than the continuous recapitulation of the modernist position, it may well be that the shift to a 'post-Enlightenment' perspective is located at the beginning, rather than the end, of the twentieth century. Importantly, though, this maintains a contemporary perspective which defines itself by virtue of its difference from an Enlightenment stance.

Throughout this discussion, what has not been mentioned is the very different set of histories which might be used to explain literature and/or science, and which do not see the contemporary moment as a renunciation of the past. One example of this would be the potent and convincing explanation of scientific development as essentially cumulative and progressive. It is not the intention to denigrate these histories, nor to suggest they are necessarily incorrect, by ignoring them. They are not the subject of the case studies because one of the purposes of this book is to recoup a sense of the relations between science and literature in postmodern culture. As one of the defining features of postmodernism is its rejection of the past, the postmodern culture discussed here tends not to be concerned with other histories. It takes on the characteristics which are peculiar to it precisely because it conceives of itself as having a particular relationship to the past.

While this is fairly straightforward (although not entirely uncontroversial) in relation to postmodern novels, which are often seen as distinct from their realist and modernist forbears, or in relation to popularisations of chaos theory, where a particular history of science is often made explicit, it may seem less convincing in relation to some of the other texts used in the case studies. For instance, it would be both absurd and unjust to label Richard Dawkins a postmodernist: there is no sense in which the view of evolution which is the main subject of his books is presented as having an intellectual ancestry analogous to that of, say, the postmodern novel. What is being argued is that one, perhaps rather minor, aspect of his work chimes with other postmodern developments which do intimate the sort of history described above. Because this is an important point, and potentially the source of much contention, it will be returned to in more detail later on in the chapter, when the three case studies are discussed in more detail in relation to the comments made about postmodernism here.

Although these remarks provide us with the first element in our definition of postmodernism (as that which implies a particular history for itself), they are, on their own, clearly insufficient. However, a second angle of

approach, when combined with the first, will enable us to move from a weak to
a strong definition. This involves a consideration of the way in which the
concepts, defined as belonging to the Englightenment, are interrogated.

Defining Postmodernism: The Antifoundational Impulse

It has already been established that postmodernism is strongly associated with
an antifoundational impulse. When this is conjoined with its place in history,
produced by the retrospective construction of canons of texts and ideas
discussed above, we can move toward a stronger definition of postmodern
culture: that which sees itself as different to a (crudely defined) culture of the
Enlightenment or modernity, by virtue of its interrogation of those categories
which are (crudely defined as) foundational to that Enlightenment. How exactly
are these categories interrogated?

In the case studies I focused on the overturning of categories of binary
oppositions: chaos and order, global and local, human and machine, nature and
artifice, and free will and determinism. This is a standard 'postmodern' ploy
and it might be objected that a study which is attempting, among other things,
to describe objectively some of the claims to postmodernity in contemporary
culture, ought to steer clear of those ways of speaking which are themselves
entwined with postmodern perspectives. However, the justification for this
approach lies in the definition of postmodernism formulated in this chapter:
what makes something postmodern is that it either consciously sees itself as
postmodern, or it perceives itself in a way which is identifiably similar to other
postmodern artefacts. Postmodernism is, thus, not anything which is
concretely 'out there', but is rather an attitude, a posture. It should not be
surprising, then, that in those texts which adopt a postmodern posture we
should also find the contesting of binary oppositions that is also associated
with a postmodern perspective.

Furthermore, if postmodern culture is partially defined by its
antifoundational stance then it should not merely reconfigure or add to
Enlightenment knowledge, but it should interrogate the very assumptions and
categories on which that knowledge is based. Any interrogation of categories
will inevitably involve a transgression of the boundaries between concepts and,
therefore, binary divides. It must be remembered that it is not being argued that
postmodern culture necessarily invalidates Enlightenment knowledge, but
merely that it involves an interrogation of it. It is examples of these
interrogations that were explored in chapters 3, 4 and 5.

How might the binary divides investigated in these chapters be justified
as being intrinsically tied to the Enlightenment? In order to answer this

question we must, yet again, come back to the idea of canons. The texts imply a position from which they are distanced – a history for themselves which lies at the root of their identity – and it is by placing certain categories and concepts as anterior to the postmodern that they are made, in this sense, Enlightenment. Those aspects of contemporary culture investigated in the case studies therefore produce a double definition: the postmodern is defined by those points on which it differs from the Enlightenment, and the Enlightenment is defined in terms of its distance from the postmodern. This inevitably produces a hardening of the categories of Enlightenment and postmodern, and a strengthening of the borders between the two.

The Enlightenment is at issue in these case studies, then, purely in terms of how it is defined by those texts in ways that are typical of postmodern culture more generally. Because the object of study is limited to these texts, the very important, but more general, question of how accurate a representation of the Enlightenment this constitutes, is therefore put to one side. We can understand the intersection of discourses from literature and cultural science – the focus of these studies – without needing to broach the issue of the accuracy of those discourses. The point in this book is to understand ways in which literature and science may be linked, not to open up wider disputes about the accuracy of postmodern conceptions of the past (though such debates are undoubtedly important).

Clearly, three case studies cannot comprehensively cover the postmodern attack upon the Enlightenment past from which it distinguishes itself. However, the subjects of the case studies were selected in order to provide a concentration on key issues: knowledge, identity and time. In each case established categories are transgressed: the notion that knowledge can exist independently of those who formulate and use it is contested in *Gravity's Rainbow* and Gleick's popularisation of chaos theory; the idea of the human subject as unambiguously distinct from machines and animals is interrogated by Dawkins's work and Gibson's novels; and the notion that change over time is either simplistically progressive or entirely random is interrogated by Gould's and Vonnegut's presentations of evolution.

By drawing together the separate case studies, in the light of this chapter's discussion and definition of postmodernism, it may now be possible to reach more general conclusions about postmodernism.

Postmodernism: Contemporary Postures in Literature and Science

Although the texts in all three case studies can be linked, as has been suggested, by the posture they adopt in relation to their own history, and although this posture displays the hallmarks of a postmodernist attitude, it will also be noticed that there are some fundamental dissimilarities and areas of disagreement between them. These areas of contradiction are instructive, for they indicate both the tenacity of the term postmodernism, and some of the problems with it.

Let us recap briefly in order to draw these out. Postmodernism is characterised by the explicit rejection of the Enlightenment (or modernity), or a more subtle and implicit renunciation of concepts or ideas commonly associated with the Enlightenment. This rejection may involve the actual overturning of notions that have held sway for 300 years, or it may simply entail a revolutionary posture – a stance that seems radical, but which in reality fails to live up to this promise.

Gravity's Rainbow and *Chaos* are the texts, discussed in the case studies, which most explicitly renounce a prior form of knowledge, for Pynchon's novel is clearly a book about the origins of contemporary culture, and Gleick's science writing cites Thomas Kuhn's notion of paradigm shifts in order to establish the basis for chaos theory as a wide-ranging conceptual revolution in science. At the other end of the scale, Dawkins's work can only be justified as aligning with other postmodern postures in terms of one aspect – its problematising of the idea of the human as entirely distinct from animals and machines – and it ends up doing this almost by default. There are two interlinked grounds for seeing this aspect of Dawkins's work in this way, despite his (understandable and convincing) hostility to the notion of postmodernism: the idea of living creatures, including humans, as machines clearly conflicts with the Cartesian notion of a mind unencumbered by material considerations which is (rightly or wrongly) strongly associated with the Enlightenment; and ideas of the 'posthuman', which echo some of Dawkins's comments, are increasingly popular, and tend to be strongly associated with postmodernist discourse.

Although these postures link the various texts I have discussed, it will also be noticed that there are some areas of fundamental contradiction between them. Perhaps most obviously, two of the science writers I discuss are directly at odds with one another on a number of points. As the case studies acknowledged, Dawkins and Gould disagree about the fundamental unit of selection in evolution (whether it is the individual or the gene) and, perhaps more significantly, also about whether the speed of evolutionary change should be seen as 'gradualist' or as one characterised by 'punctuated equilibrium'. As it has already been established that texts need be postmodern in only one or two aspects in order to participate in the contemporary postmodernist discourse, this would not pose a problem were Dawkins and Gould's disagreement limited to the 'non-postmodernist' areas of their work. However, my characterisation of Gould's *Wonderful Life* as, in a sense, postmodern relies on a discussion of his view of change over time, and therefore of punctuated equilibrium, as a rejection of a previous perspective on this issue. How can Dawkins's work be related to postmodernism if he adheres to a view, the rejection of which is central to the definition of Gould's work as postmodern?

Crucially, the works of these two science writers are postmodern in different ways – Dawkins's in terms of its reappraisal of human identity; Gould's in terms of its reworking of a notion of change over time – and there is no need for other aspects of their work to chime either with each other, or with other postmodern discourses. However, highlighting this contradiction does draw our attention to one of the fundamental problems with postmodernism: it is not a single, unified philosophy. This may account for both its potency and its tenacity. However, although it launches an antifoundationalist attack on Enlightenment thought, and although the study of it gives us an effective means of conceptualising the ways in which contemporary culture sees itself as distinct from its predecessors, postmodernism itself does not offer any means of proposing better sorts of knowledge beyond the rejection of modernity.

This is not to say that individual writers, or texts, do not suggest new ways of knowing – to stick with the current examples, both Gould and Dawkins reject one point of view in order to assert another. In each case postmodernism aligns itself with these new points of view, but because postmodernism is defined by the process of rejection, it does not admit (as both Dawkins and Gould are willing to do) that there might be means of establishing the truth which can appeal beyond the limits of cultural specificity (say, by reference to a fossil record or, more broadly, to a stable aspect of nature which remains the same regardless of cultural perspective). There is a sense, then, in which postmodernism survives by performing a series of acts of terrorism, hijacking an eclectic bunch of cultural artefacts, branding them postmodern, and then jumping ship before it has to commit to a unified agenda.

The objection that might be made to this argument is that if postmodernism hijacks the texts and ideas discussed in this book's case studies, it is only because it has been made to do so: a circular argument has produced a skewed definition of postmodernism, included texts that conform to that definition, and then criticised the inconsistencies revealed when the definition and the texts are brought together. This hypothetical objection would be reasonable were it not the case that the texts used for each case study are either located explicitly as postmodernist or, alternatively, do display characteristics frequently cited as part of postmodernist discourse.

As long as we acknowledge that postmodernism is a discourse rather than a concrete thing (though a discourse which has concrete effects), and as long as our understanding of discourse conforms to the definition offered in chapter 2 –

as a narrative that gives meaning to other narratives – then we can produce a sustainable analysis of postmodern culture. The image of discourse offered in chapter 2 was as a narrative underpinning other narratives; so, if the experience of the reader, in encountering the words of the text, is seen as a horizontal line, then discourses appear as vertical lines, bisecting the text's narrative and giving meaning to it. The discourse of postmodernism therefore reveals itself, in the narratives used in the case studies, in terms of an eruption into the text of contemporary concerns with distinguishing the present from the past: a whole set of concepts – the merging of chaos and order; the posthuman; a move from an understanding of teleological development as inherently meaningful – are established as, in some sense, revolutionary.

It is this which links the three case studies, although in some the eruptions are more prominent than in others, and in some they take on notably different characteristics. Most obviously, although the view of living organisms, particularly humans, proposed by Dawkins is in opposition to that apparent in the Enlightenment, Dawkins is not suggesting that his view is culturally specific but rather that it is true (or, at least, objectively better than earlier views, whatever deeper understandings may follow in the future). It is overtly situated in a history characterised by progress (a history about the cumulative nature of scientific understanding, building better and better pictures of the universe) which is at odds with the suggestion, often associated with postmodernism, that all claims to truth are actually dependent on unverifiable cultural assumptions. Despite this conflict Dawkins's view of humans, and extended use of the machine metaphor, does ally with other – identifiably postmodern – rejections of the free Enlightenment subject. Dawkins's work is, therefore, very much of its late twentieth-century culture even though it also appeals (with success) beyond that culture to a more general truth.

It should be noted that although it is being argued that postmodernism reveals itself in a wide variety of aspects of contemporary culture, and is even linked here with writers who may recoil with horror at any kind of association with postmodernism, it is not being imbued with mystical characteristics, somehow manipulating writers to endorse a postmodern perspective against their will. Rather, as it is a good shorthand term for those aspects of late twentieth-century culture that resist Enlightenment ideals and beliefs, it worms its way into writers' work when they consciously reject the Enlightenment past, or when their works include aspects which readers are likely to associate with other contemporary rejections of Enlightenment ideals.

The use of the term postmodernism in this book is, therefore, markedly different from its use by Alan Sokal and Jean Bricmont in *Intellectual Impostures*, where it means a philosophy characterised by extreme relativism.

As this chapter will have made apparent, it is being used here to characterise an influential strain of contemporary culture. It is a descriptive term and does not, of itself, imply a value judgement: one can acknowledge the existence and significance of postmodern culture whether one embraces or rejects that culture. Indeed, it is of course legitimate to adopt a sophisticated stance in relation to postmodern culture, acknowledging a contemporary discourse linking various rejections of the Enlightenment, but embracing only some of those objections for the (very un-postmodern) broadening of our understanding they may give. Postmodernism is a posture, an oppositional stance, and it is reasonable to claim that although some of its revolutionary fervour is legitimate protest, in others ways the gesture of denial is empty.

Conclusion:
Advancing Together?

Two distinct aims have shaped this project. The first was to assess the shift in the perceived relationship between literature and science as we have moved from the two cultures debate to the science wars. This shift has been accompanied by a rapid growth in literature–science criticism, and the overriding purpose of this aspect of the book was to produce a viable model of culture and identify the methodologies that are legitimately available to the literature–science critic. This model, and these methods, are described in detail in chapter 2. The second aim was to define postmodernism in such a way that postmodern culture could be debated fruitfully without swiftly falling into declarations of being for or against it. This definition is drawn upon in the case studies, and discussed in detail in chapter 6.

Having twin aims like this is dangerous: in shooting at both targets, one might miss both. However, it is impossible to ignore postmodernism when considering the relationship between literature and science. The science wars have produced an atmosphere in which a consideration of the cultural aspects of science is almost inevitably taken as the unthinking endorsement of a postmodern perspective: one is either for science and against postmodernism, or one is for postmodernism and against science. The question is how to break out of this cycle of accusation, counter-accusation, and general recrimination.

One way is to acknowledge the expertise of colleagues on the other side of the disciplinary fence. The does not necessarily mean bowing down uncritically before the authority of science; nor does it involve the rather more absurd, if rather appealing, image of everyone kneeling to deify the wisdom of literary critics. Surely, indeed, the greatest form of respect is neither to accept unthinkingly nor reject out of hand, but to approach in a spirit of interested and sceptical inquiry. If this is to be more than a platitude then that scepticism needs also to be turned on one's own practice.

This book has attempted to take the first step along this road by fixing some boundaries. These are not like the old boundaries of the two cultures debate, simplistically dividing the literary from the scientific. Instead, they are boundaries that channel the routes between literature and science as carefully as possible. It would be presumptuous to assume that the seven routes identified in chapter 2 can form a blueprint for literature–science criticism, but they are at least a move toward such a blueprint, regardless of whether, in the end, some of these roads are closed off, or new ones opened up. As much as anything they make clear what is being implied when literature and science are linked. For instance, the case studies in chapters 3, 4 and 5 are highly conventional pieces of literature–science criticism, but the context of the methodology enunciated in chapter 2 should establish exactly what can be claimed by such a criticism. The studies do not presume that the science they discuss is just discourse, and they do not assume that popularisations of science are necessarily representative of science itself. However, they do claim that science writing has an equivalent cultural function to other more conventionally-studied pieces of writing. It is for this reason – clarity of objectives – that the distinction between cultural and professional science made in chapter 2 is so important.

If such a distinction is viable, then the links between the literature and the science made in the case studies should convince in theory, even if not in practice. Even if the studies are rejected in terms of their detail – through, for instance, different interpretations of the texts (though I stand firmly by the interpretations offered here) – they do at the very least provide a model for how literature and science might be joined together.

The question of whether they represent postmodern culture is another issue. One might make specific connections between literary and scientific texts, but these are going to be particularly important if they are somehow representative of broader cultural trends. The trends focused upon in this book, because they are so relevant to the science wars debates, are those of postmodernism but – again – one does not need to accept this part of the argument in order to accept other aspects of the book.

There are, then, attached to the twin aims of the book, four levels of argument on which it tries to convince the reader, although the rejection of any one of these need not involve the rejection of the others. The first is the proposal of a literature–science methodology; the second is the putting into practice of that methodology in the case studies; the third is the definition of postmodernism; and the fourth is the exemplification of that definition through the case studies.

There is, perhaps, also a fundamental point at which the twin aims of the book are connected: postmodernism is responsible, at least in part, for the shift in perspectives that has produced the sort of literature–science criticism that is at the heart of the science wars. Postmodernism's stress upon reality as existing in our perception of it – and as, therefore, something which is constituted by the stories we tell about it – has produced an interest in narrative which has broadened out to an interest in the narratives of science. However, this does not mean that we need accept postmodernism in order to explore science's role in the culture. Postmodernism may have sparked the contemporary interest in the place of science in the culture, but the sense that science is a big cultural player is not dependent on accepting the broader postmodernist agenda.

We need to acknowledge how science shapes our attitudes, and how its place in the culture is also shaped by those attitudes. The idea of discourse provides a useful means of conceptualising the links between different cultural phenomena, including those of science, and although postmodernism is perhaps responsible for this idea of discourse, we do not have to accept the extreme position that reality is just discourse.

Science's role in our culture is very important; if we fail to understand this role we fail to understand the culture. Yet we do not have to resort to an absolute cultural determinism, whereby all knowledge is seen to be the product of culture alone, without reference to physical reality. Postmodernism is a posture toward the past. It rejects the Enlightenment heritage, and by doing so allows us to interrogate the assumptions we have inherited from the past. Yet, while using the posture of rejection to produce this sort of interrogation, we can also refuse to accept that postmodernism is anything more than a radical critical philosophy, and refuse to accept that the Enlightenment is necessarily all bad. The absolute logical consequence of postmodernism might be relativism, but the practical consequence should surely be provisionalism: a knowledge that both confidently asserts its view of the world, whilst embracing sceptical interrogation and reorganisation of that perspective.

Such a project might reorientate us from the postmodern posture of denial toward the past, to Aldous Huxley's vision of practitioners of science and letters advancing together into the future. This is idealistic, but far from impractical when we are willing to rework and update such a vision. Hopefully, this book has shown that the strict division of science from literature, invoked by Huxley, is untenable: if we advance together it will not be into entirely separate, albeit parallel, territories; it will be into the same space.

Bibliography

Amrine, Frederick, ed. *Literature and Science as Modes of Expression*. Boston Studies in the Philosophy of Science 115. Dordrecht: Kluwer Academic Publishers, 1989.

Anderson, Alun, Bob Holmes and Liz Else. 'Zombies, Dolphins and Blindsight'. *New Scientist* 4 May 1996: 21

Appleyard, Bryan. *Understanding the Present: Science and the Soul of Modern Man*. 2nd edn. 1992. London: Picador-Pan, 1993.

Argyros, Alexander J. *A Blessed Rage for Order: Deconstruction, Evolution, and Chaos*. Ann Arbor: University of Michigan Press, 1991.

'Narrative and Chaos'. *New Literary History: A Journal of Theory and Interpretation* 23 (1992): 659–73.

Aris, Rutherford. 'Ut Simulacrum Poesis'. *New Literary History: A Journal of Theory and Interpretation* 23 (1992): 323–40.

Arnold, Mathew. *Poetry and Prose*. Ed. John Bryson. Vol. 3. London: Rupert Hart-Davis, 1954.

Aronowitz, Stanley. 'The Politics of the Science Wars'. *Social Text* 46–7 (1996): 177–98.

Bacon, Francis. *Bacon's 'Advancement of Learning' and 'The New Atlantis'*. 1605, 1627. The World's Classics. London: Oxford University Press, 1906.

Barthes, Roland. 'Science Versus Literature'. *Times Literary Supplement* 28 Sept. 1967: 897–8.

S/Z. Trans. Richard Miller. 1970. London: Jonathan Cape, 1975.

Beer, Gillian. *Darwin's Plots*. London: Routledge, 1983.

Open Fields: Science in Cultural Encounter. Oxford: Clarendon Press, 1996.

Benjamin, Marina, ed. *A Question of Identity: Women, Science, and Literature*. New Brunswick: Rutgers University Press, 1993.

Birch, Charles. 'Eight Fallacies of the Modern World and Five Axioms for a Postmodern Worldview'. *Perspectives in Biology and Medicine* 32.1 (1988): 12–30.

Borgmann, Albert. *Crossing the Postmodern Divide*. University of Chicago Press, 1992.

Bradbury, Ray. *Ray Bradbury*. The Pegasus Library. London: Harrap, 1975.

Broderick, Damien. *Reading by Starlight: Postmodern Science Fiction*. Popular Fiction Series. London: Routledge, 1995.

Bronowski, J. *Science and Human Values*. 1958. London: Penguin, 1964.

Bruce, Donald and Anthony Purdy, eds. *Literature and Science*. Rodopi Perspectives on Modern Literature 14. Amsterdam: Rodopi, 1994.

Bukatman, Scott. 'Gibson's Typewriter'. *South Atlantic Quarterly* 92 (1993): 627–45.

Burrow, John. 'Making a New Science'. *New Scientist* 26 May 1988: 73–4.

Carey, John, ed. *The Faber Book of Science*. London: Faber, 1995.

Carroll, Joseph. *Evolution and Literary Theory*. Columbia: University of Missouri Press, 1995.

Christie, John and Sally Shuttleworth, eds. *Nature Transfigured: Science and Literature, 1700–1900*. Manchester: Manchester University Press, 1989.

Connor, Steven. 'The Modern and the Postmodern as History'. *Essays in Criticism* 37 (1987): 181–92.

Postmodernist Culture. Oxford: Blackwell, 1989.

Coomb, Rosemary J. 'Encountering the Postmodern: New Directions in Cultural Anthropology'. *The Canadian Review of Sociology and Anthropology* 28 (1991): 188–205.

Darwin, Charles. *The Origin of Species by Means of Natural Selection: Or the Preservation of Favoured Races in the Struggle for Life.* Ed. J.W. Burrow. 1st edn. 1859. Middlesex: Penguin, 1982.

　The Voyage of Charles Darwin. Ed. Christopher Ralling. London: British Broadcasting Corporation, 1978.

Davies, Paul and John Gribbin. *The Matter Myth: Beyond Chaos and Complexity.* 1991. London: Penguin, 1992.

Dawkins, Richard. *The Blind Watchmaker.* Harlow: Longman, 1986.

　Climbing Mount Improbable. Somerset: Viking, 1996.

　The Extended Phenotype: The Gene as the Unit of Selection. Oxford: Freeman, 1982.

　River Out of Eden. Science Masters. London: Weidenfeld and Nicholson, 1995.

　The Selfish Gene. 2nd edn. 1976. Oxford: University Press, 1980.

　Unweaving the Rainbow: Science, Delusion and the Appetite for Wonder. London: Penguin, 1998.

Descartes, René. *'Discourse on Method' and Other Writings.* Trans. F.E. Sutcliffe. Middlesex: Penguin, 1968.

Drabble, Margaret, ed. *The Oxford Companion to English Literature.* Oxford: Oxford University Press, 1991.

Dusek, Val. 'Philosophy of Math and Physics in the Sokal Affair'. *Social Text* 50 (1997): 135–8.

Earnshaw, Steven. *Postmodern Surroundings.* Postmodern Studies 9. Amsterdam: Rodopi, 1994.

Eco, Umberto. *Foucault's Pendulum.* 1988. London: Picador-Pan, 1990.

Eliot, T.S. *Selected Prose of T.S. Eliot.* Ed. Frank Kermode. London: Faber, 1975.

Ferré, Frederick. 'Religious World Modeling and Postmodern Science'. *Journal of Religion* 62 (1982): 261–71.

Feyerabend, Paul. *Against Method.* 3rd edn. 1975. London: Verso, 1993.

Fraiberg, Allison. 'Of AIDS, Cyborgs, and Other Indiscretions: Resurfacing the Body in the Postmodern'. *Postmodern Culture: An Electronic Journal of Interdisciplinary Criticism* 1.3 (1991): File: 'Fraiberg 591'.

Franklin, Sarah. 'Making Transparencies: Seeing Through the Science Wars'. *Social Text* 46–7 (1996): 141–56.

Friedl, John. *Cultural Anthropology.* New York: Harper's College Press, 1976.

Gardner, Martin, ed. *'The Sacred Beetle' and Other Great Essays in Science.* Rev. edn. Oxford University Press, 1985.

Fuller, Steve. 'Does Science Put an End to History, or History to Science?' *Social Text* 46–7 (1996): 27–42.

Garvin, Harry R. and James M. Heath, eds. *Science and Literature.* Lewisburg: Bucknell University Press, 1983.

Gere, Ronald N. 'Philosophy of Science: An Enlightened Postmodern Perspective'. *Noûs* 24 (1990): 291–2.

Gibson, William. *'Burning Chrome' and Other Stories.* London: HarperCollins, 1995.

　Count Zero. 1986. London: Voyager-HarperCollins, 1995.

　Mona Lisa Overdrive. 1988. London: Voyager-HarperCollins, 1995.

　Neuromancer. 1984. London: Grafton-HarperCollins, 1986.

Gleick, James. *Chaos: Making a New Science.* 1987. New York: Penguin, 1988.

　Genius: Richard Feynman and Modern Physics. London: Little, 1992.

Gould, Stephen Jay. *Dinosaur in a Haystack: Reflections in Natural History.* London: Cape, 1996.

　Hen's Teeth and Horse's Toes. 1983. London: Penguin, 1990.

The Panda's Thumb: More Reflections in Natural History. New York: Norton, 1980.
Wonderful Life: The Burgess Shale and the Nature of History. 1989. London: Hutchinson Radius-Century Hutchinson, 1990.
Gross, Paul R. and Norman Levitt. *Higher Superstition: The Academic Left and its Quarrels with Science.* 2nd edn. 1994. Baltimore: Johns Hopkins University Press, 1998.
Hall, Nina, ed. *The New Scientist Guide to Chaos.* London: Penguin, 1992.
Halliday, M.A.K. and J.R. Martin. *Writing Science: Literacy and Discursive Power.* London: Falmer, 1993.
Hankins, Thomas L. *Science and Enlightenment.* Cambridge History of Science. Cambridge University Press, 1985.
Haraway, Donna. 'Enlightenment@science_wars.com: A Personal Reflection on the Sokal Affair'. *Social Text* 50 (1997): 123–30.
Harding, Sandra. 'Science is "Good to Think With"'. *Social Text* 46–7 (1996):15–26.
Harker, W. John. 'Information Processing and the Reading of Literary Texts'. *New Literary History: A Journal of Theory and Interpretation* 20 (1989): 465–81.
Hawking, Stephen W. *A Brief History of Time: From the Big Bang to Black Holes.* London: Bantam, 1988.
Hawkins, Harriet. *Strange Attractors: Literature and Chaos Theory.* New York: Prentice-Harvester Wheatsheaf, 1995.
Hawthorne, Jeremy. *A Concise Glossary of Contemporary Literary Theory.* London: Edward Arnold, 1992.
Hayles, N. Katherine. *Chaos and Order: Complex Dynamics in Literature and Science.* University of Chicago Press, 1991.
    'Chaos as Orderly Disorder: Shifting Ground in Contemporary Literature and Science'. *New Literary History: A Journal of Theory and Interpretation* 20 (1989): 305–22.
    Chaos Bound: Orderly Disorder in Contemporary Literature and Science. Ithaca: Cornell University Press, 1990.
    The Cosmic Web: Scientific Field Models and Literary Strategies in the Twentieth Century. Ithaca: Cornell University Press, 1984.
    'Postmodern Parataxis: Embodied Texts, Weightless Information'. *American Literary History* 2 (1990): 394–421.
Heisenberg, Werner. *The Physicist's Conception of Nature.* Trans. Arnold J. Pomerans. 1958. Westport: Greenwood, 1970.
Hirschkop, Ken. 'Cultural Studies and Its Discontents: A Comment on the Sokal Affair'. *Social Text* 50 (1997): 131–4.
Hollinger, Veronica. 'Cybernetic Deconstructions: Cyberpunk and Postmodernism'. *Mosaic: A Journal for the Interdisciplinary Study of Literature* 23.2 (1990): 29–44.
Horowitz, Irving Louis. 'New Technology and the Changing System of Author-Publisher Relations'. *New Literary History: A Journal of Theory and Interpretation* 20 (1989): 505–9.
Hubbard, Ruth. 'Gender and Genitals: Constructs of Sex and Gender'. *Social Text* 46–7 (1996): 157–66.
Hutcheon, Linda. *The Politics of Postmodernism.* New Accents. London: Routledge, 1989.
Huxley, Aldous. *Literature and Science.* London: Chatto and Windus, 1963.
Huxley, T.H. *Collected Essays.* Vol. 3. London: Macmillan, 1905.
Jacobus, Mary, Evelyn Fox Keller and Sally Shuttleworth, eds. *Body / Politics: Women and the Discourses of Science.* New York: Routledge, 1990.
Jakobson, Roman. *Main Trends in the Science of Language.* 1973. New York: Harper Torchbooks, 1974.
Janin, Hunt. 'The Post-Information Society'. *Virginia Quarterly Review: A National Journal of Literature and Discussion* 70 (1994): 38–50.
Jones, Steve. 'Hyper-punk: Cyberpunk and Information Technology'. *Journal of Popular Culture* 18.2 (1994): 81–92.

Jones, Steve. *The Language of the Genes: Biology, History and the Evolutionary Future*. London: Flamingo-HarperCollins, 1994.

Jordanova, L.J., ed. *Languages of Nature: Critical Essays on Science and Literature*. London: Free Association Books, 1986.

Keller, Evelyn Fox. *Reflections on Gender and Science*. New Haven: Yale University Press, 1985.

Kermode, Frank. *The Genesis of Secrecy: On the Interpretation of Narrative*. Cambridge, MA: Harvard University Press, 1979.

Kipperman, Mark. 'The Rhetorical Case Against a Theory of Literature and Science'. *Philosophy and Literature* 10 (1986): 76–83.

Kovel, Joel. 'Dispatches from the Science Wars'. *Social Text* 46–7 (1996): 167–76

Kuberski, Philip. *Chaosmos: Literature, Science, and Theory*. SUNY Series, The Margins of Literature. State University of New York Press, 1994.

Kuhn, Thomas S. *The Structure of Scientific Revolutions*. 2nd edn. International Encyclopedia of Unified Science 2.2. 1962. University of Chicago Press, 1970.

Landow, George, ed. *Hyper / Text / Theory*. Baltimore: Johns Hopkins University Press, 1994.

Lanham, Richard A. 'The Electronic Word: Literary Study and the Digital Revolution'. *New Literary History: A Journal of Theory and Interpretation* 20 (1989): 265–90.

Laplace, Pierre Simon. *A Philosophical Essay on Probabilities*. Trans. Frederick Wilson Truscott and Frederick Lincoln Emory. 6th edn. 1819. New York: Dover, 1951.

Lears, Jackson. 'Reality Matters'. *Social Text* 50 (1997): 143–6.

Leavis, F.R. *The Great Tradition*. 1948. London: Chatto and Windus, 1962.

Leavis, F.R. and Michael Yudkin. *Two Cultures? The Significance of C.P. Snow with an Essay on Sir Charles Snow's Rede Lectures*. London: Chatto and Windus, 1962.

Lem, Stanislaw. *The Cyberiad: Fables for the Cybernetic Age*. Trans. Michael Kandel. 1967. London: Secker and Warburg, 1975.

Lemon, Lee T. and Marion J. Reis, trans. *Russian Formalist Criticism: Four Essays*. Regents Critics Series. Lincoln, USA: University of Nebraska Press, 1965.

Levidow, Les. 'Science Skirmishes and Science-Policy Research'. *Social Text* 46–7 (1996): 199–206.

Levine, George, ed. *One Culture: Essays in Science and Literature*. University of Wisconsin Press, 1987.

Realism and Representation: Essays on the Problem of Realism in Relation to Science, Literature, and Culture. University of Wisconsin Press, 1987.

'What is Science Studies for and Who Cares?' *Social Text* 46–7 (1996): 113–28.

Levine, George and David Leverenz, eds. *Mindful Pleasures: Essays on Thomas Pynchon*. Boston: Little, 1976.

Levins, Richard. 'Ten Propositions on Science and Antiscience'. *Social Text* 46–7 (1996):101–12.

Lindee, M. Susan. 'Wars of Out-Describing'. *Social Text* 50 (1997): 139–42.

Lyotard, Jean François. *The Postmodern Condition: A Report on Knowledge*. Trans. Geoff Bennington and Brian Massumi. Theory and History of Literature 10. 1979. Manchester University Press, 1986.

Madsen, Mark and Deborah L. Madsen. 'Structuring Postmodern Science'. *Science and Culture* 56 (1990): 467–72.

Martin, Emily. 'Meeting Polemics with Ironics'. *Social Text* 46–7 (1996): 43–60.

Mazlish, Bruce. *The Fourth Discontinuity: The Co-Evolution of Humans and Machines*. New Haven: Yale University Press, 1993.

McCaffery, Larry, ed. *Storming the Reality Studio: A Casebook of Cyberpunk and Postmodern Science Fiction*. Durham: Duke University Press, 1991.

McHale, Brian. 'Elements of a Poetics of Cyberpunk'. *Critique: Studies in Contemporary Fiction* 33.3 (1992): 149–75.

'Modernist Reading, Post-Modern Text: The Case of *Gravity's Rainbow*'. *Poetics Today* 1 (1979): 85–110.

Postmodernist Fiction. New York: Methuen, 1987.

McRae, Murdo William. *The Literature of Science: Perspectives on Popular Science Writing*. Athens: University of Georgia Press, 1993.

Mead, David G. 'Technological Transfiguration in William Gibson's Sprawl Novels: *Neuromancer*, *Count Zero*, and *Mona Lisa Overdrive*'. *Extrapolation* 32 (1991): 350–60.

Meynell, Hugo. 'Northrop Frye's Idea of a Science of Criticism'. *British Journal of Aesthetics* 21 (1981): 118–29.

Miller, Toby. 'Actually Existing Journal-ism'. *Social Text* 50 (1997): 147–8.

Murphy, Nancey. 'Scientific Realism and Postmodern Philosophy'. *British Journal for the Philosophy of Science* 41 (1990): 291–303.

Nadeau, Robert. 'Readings from the New Book of Nature: Physics and Pynchon's *Gravity's Rainbow*'. *Studies in the Novel* 11 (1979): 454–71.

Nash, Christopher, ed. *Narrative in Culture: The Uses of Storytelling in the Sciences, Philosophy, and Literature*. London: Routledge, 1990.

Nelkin, Dorothy. 'The Science Wars: Responses to a Marriage Failed'. *Social Text* 46–7 (1996): 93–100.

Newman, Robert D. *Understanding Thomas Pynchon*. Understanding Contemporary American Literature. Columbia: South Carolina University Press, 1986.

Nichols, Bill. 'The Work of Culture in the Age of Cybernetic Systems'. *Screen* 29.1 (1988): 22–46.

Nicholson, Linda J., ed. *Feminism / Postmodernism*. New York: Routledge, 1990.

Oldroyd, D.R. *Darwinian Impacts: An Introduction to the Darwinian Revolution*. Milton Keynes: Open University Press, 1980.

Olsen, Lance. 'Deconstructing the Enemy of Color: The Fantastic in *Gravity's Rainbow*'. *Studies in the Novel* 18 (1986): 74–86.

Ozier, Lance W. 'Antipointsman / Antimexico: Some Mathematical Imagery in *Gravity's Rainbow*'. *Critique: Studies in Modern Fiction* 16.2 (1974): 73–90.

'The Calculus of Transformation: More Mathematical Imagery in *Gravity's Rainbow*'. *Twentieth-Century Literature* 21 (1975): 193–210.

Palmeri, Frank. 'Neither Literally nor as Metaphor: Pynchon's *The Crying of Lot 49* and the Structure of Scientific Revolutions'. *English Literary History* 54 (1987): 979–99.

Parusnikova, Zuzana. 'Is a Postmodern Philosophy of Science Possible?' *Studies in History and Philosophy of Science* 23 (1992): 21–37.

Paulson, William R. *The Noise of Culture: Literary Texts in a World of Information*. Ithaca: Cornell University Press, 1988.

'Computers, Minds, and Texts: Preliminary Reflections'. *New Literary History: A Journal of Theory and Interpretation* 20 (1989): 291–303.

Peterfreund, Stuart. *Literature and Science: Theory and Practice*. Boston: Northeastern University Press, 1990.

Pinker, Stephen. *The Language Instinct: The New Science of Language and Mind*. 1994. London: Penguin, 1995.

How the Mind Works. 1997. London: Penguin, 1998.

Popper, Karl. *Unended Quest: An Intellectual Autobiography*. Rev. edn. 1974. London: Fontana, 1986.

Porush, David. 'Cybernetic Fiction and Postmodern Science'. *New Literary History: A Journal of Theory and Interpretation* 20 (1989): 373–96.

'Eudoxical Discourse: A Post-Postmodern Model for the Relations Between Science and Literature'. *Modern Language Studies* 20.4 (1989): 373–96.

The Soft Machine: Cybernetic Fiction. New York: Methuen, 1985.

Prigogine, Ilya and Isabelle Stengers. *Order Out of Chaos: Man's New Dialogue with Nature.* 1984. London: Flamingo, 1985.

Pynchon, Thomas, *The Crying of Lot 49.* 1966. London: Picador, 1979.

Gravity's Rainbow. 1973. London: Picador, 1975.

Mason and Dixon. 1997. London: Vintage, 1998.

Slow Learner: Early Stories. 1984. London: Cape, 1985.

Vineland. 1990. London: Minerva, 1991.

Richards, I.A. *Poetries and Sciences: A Reissue of 'Science and Poetry' (1926, 1935) with Commentary.* 1926. London: Routledge, 1970.

Practical Criticism: A Study of Literary Judgment. 1929. London: Routledge, 1964.

Principles of Literary Criticism. 1924. London: Routledge, 1989.

Rindos, David. 'The Genetics of Cultural Anthropology: Toward a Genetic Model for the Origin of the Capacity for Culture'. *Journal of Anthropological Archaeology* 5 (1986): 1–38.

Rose, Hilary. 'My Enemy's Enemy is – Only Perhaps – My Friend'. *Social Text* 46–7 (1996): 61–80.

Ross, Andrew. 'A Few Good Species'. *Social Text* 46–7 (1996): 207–16.

Introduction. *Social Text* 46–7 (1996): 1–13.

'Reflections on the Sokal Affair'. *Social Text* 50 (1997):149–52.

Rouse, Joseph. 'The Politics of Postmodern Philosophy of Science'. *Science* 58 (1991): 607–27.

Ruelle, David. *Chance and Chaos.* 1991. London: Penguin, 1993.

Rylance, Rick, ed. *Debating Texts: A Reader in Twentieth-Century Literary Theory and Method.* Milton Keynes: Open University Press, 1987.

Sacks, Oliver. *The Man Who Mistook His Wife for a Hat.* 1985. London: Picador, 1986.

Sanford, Anthony J. *Cognition and Cognitive Psychology.* Weidenfeld Psychology Series. London: Weidenfeld, 1985.

Scholnick, Robert J., ed. *American Literature and Science.* University of Kentucky Press, 1992.

Selden, Raman and Peter J. Widdowson. *A Reader's Guide to Contemporary Literary Theory.* New York: Harvester Wheatsheaf, 1993.

Serres, Michel. *Hermes: Literature, Science, Philosophy.* Eds. Josué V. Harari and David F. Bell. Trans. various. 1982. Baltimore: Johns Hopkins University Press, 1983.

Shelley, Mary. *Frankenstein: Or, The Modern Prometheus.* 1818. London: Penguin, 1985.

Shuttleworth, Sally. *George Eliot and Nineteenth-Century Science: The Make-Believe of a Beginning.* Cambridge University Press, 1984.

Sim, Stuart, ed. *The Icon Critical Dictionary of Postmodernism.* Cambridge: Icon, 1998.

Sinclair, Upton. *The Autobiography of Upton Sinclair.* 1962. London: W.H. Allen, 1963.

Slade, Joseph W. and Judith Yaross Lee, eds. *Beyond the Two Cultures: Essays on Science, Technology, and Literature.* Ames: Iowa State University Press, 1990.

Slusser, George and Tom Shippey, eds. *Fiction 2000: Cyberpunk and the Future of Narrative.* Athens: University of Georgia Press, 1992.

Snow, C.P. *The Two Cultures and the Scientific Revolution.* Cambridge University Press, 1959.

Sokal, Alan D. 'Transgressing the Boundaries: Toward a Transformative Hermeneutics of Quantum Gravity'. *Social Text* 46–7 (1996): 217–52.

Sokal, Alan and Jean Bricmont. *Intellectual Impostures: Postmodern Philosophers' Abuse of Science.* 1997. London: Profile, 1998.

Steinberg, Leo. 'Art and Science: Do They Need to be Yoked?' *Daedalus* 115.3 (1986): 1–16.

Stewart, Ian. *Does God Play Dice? The Mathematics of Chance and Chaos.* 1989. London: Penguin, 1990.

Stockwell, Peter. 'Bad Language: Towards a Poetics of Ineptitude'. *UCE Papers in Language and Literature* 1 (1994): 47–52.

Stonum, Gary Lee. 'Cybernetic Explanation as a Theory of Reading'. *New Literary History: A Journal of Theory and Interpretation* 20 (1989): 397–410.

Strehle, Susan. *Fiction in the Quantum Universe*. Chapel Hill: North Carolina University Press, 1992.

Toulmin, Stephen. *The Return to Cosmology: Postmodern Science and the Theology of Nature*. Berkeley: University of California Press, 1982.

Traweek, Sharon. 'Unity, Dyads, Triads, Quads, and Complexity: Cultural Choreographies of Science'. *Social Text* 46–7 (1996): 129–40.

Vonnegut, Kurt. *Breakfast of Champions*. London: Jonathan Cape, 1973.

   Cat's Cradle. 1963. London: Gollancz, 1974.

   Deadeye Dick. 1982. London: Cape, 1983.

   Galapagos. 1985. London: Grafton-Collins, 1987.

   Jailbird. London: Cape, 1979.

   Mother Night. 1966. St Albans: Panther, 1973.

   Player Piano. New York: Delacorte, 1952.

   The Sirens of Titan. 1959. London: VGSF-Gollancz, 1989.

   Slaughterhouse-Five: Or, The Children's Crusade: A Duty-Dance with Death. 1969. London: Vintage, 1989.

Waugh, Patricia, ed. *Postmodernism: A Reader*. New York: Routledge, 1992.

Weisenburger, Steven. *A 'Gravity's Rainbow' Companion: Sources and Contexts for Pynchon's Novel*. Athens: University of Georgia Press, 1988.

White, Eric. 'The End of Metanarratives in Evolutionary Biology'. *Modern Language Quareterly* 51 (1990): 63–81.

Wiener, Norbert. *The Human Use of Human Beings: Cybernetics and Society*. 2nd edn. 1950. London: Eyre and Spottiswoode, 1954.

Winner, Langdon. 'The Gloves Come Off: Shattered Alliances in Science and Technology Studies'. *Social Text* 46–7 (1996): 81–92.

Wolpert, Lewis. *The Unnatural Nature of Science*. London: Faber, 1992.

Yorke, James and Tien-Yien Li. 'Period Three Implies Chaos'. *American Mathematical Monthly* 82 (1975): 985–92.

Young, Robert. *Untying the Text: A Post-Structuralist Reader*. Boston: Routledge, 1981.

Ziegfield, Richard. 'Interactive Fiction: A New Genre?' *New Literary History: A Journal of Theory and Interpretation* 20 (1989): 341–72.

Index